# The
# NIGHT STALKER
# COMPANION
## A 25th Anniversary Tribute

Darren McGavin in his Carl Kolchak "uniform" of seersucker suit and "bird feeder" straw hat, holds some of the the tools of his reporter's trade, a tape recorder and microphone.

# The
# NIGHT STALKER
# COMPANION

## A 25th Anniversary Tribute

## By Mark Dawidziak

POMEGRANATE PRESS, LTD.
Beverly Hills          London

This is a Pomegranate Press, Ltd. book:

# The
# NIGHT STALKER
# COMPANION
## A 25th Anniversary Tribute

Copyright © 1997 by Mark Dawidziak.

Photographs used in this book are courtesy of ABC Productions, Dan Curtis Productions,
Francy Productions, Universal City Studios, WWOR-TV, CBS, Foto Fantasies,
Jeff Rice, Jack Grinnage, Carol Ann Susi, *Cinefantastique*, the Sci-Fi Channel
Jim's TV Collectibles, Image Publishing, the Academy of Television Arts and Sciences
and private archives. Author's photograph by Sara Showman.

Library of Congress Catalog Card Number: 97-067156
Tradepaper edition ISBN: 0938817-44-2

First Printing 1997
10 9 8 7 6 5 4 3 2 1

For Pomegranate Press, Ltd.

Publisher: Kathryn Leigh Scott
Creative Director/Book Design: Ben R. Martin
Cover Design: Cheryl Carrington
Editor: Jim Pierson
Typography Consultant: Leroy Chen
Ventura consultant: Wayne Kaplan

Printed and bound in the United States of America
by
McNaughton & Gunn, Inc.
Saline, Michigan

POMEGRANATE PRESS, LTD.
Post Office Box 17217
Beverly Hills, CA 90209-3217

# Dedication

This one is for Michael, the good twin,
who shared a childhood of *Famous Monsters*,
*Dark Shadows* and Universal horror.

# Selected Quotes

*"Don't look now, baby, but Kolchak's coming back in style."*
**— Carl Kolchak (Darren McGavin)**
***The Night Stalker* (1972)**

*"The unexpected always happens."*
**— English proverb**

*"I have learned not to think little of anyone's belief, no matter how strange it be. I have tried to keep an open mind. . . "*
**— Dr. Abraham Van Helsing**
***Dracula* (1897) by Bram Stoker**

*"When an honest writer discovers an imposition, it his simple duty to strip it bare and hurl it down from its place of honor, no matter who suffers by it; any other course would render him unworthy of the public confidence."*
**— Mark Twain**
***A Tramp Abroad* (1880)**

*"He's kind of a folk hero who's battling the forces of evil that we can't pin down ourselves and deal with. That's what Kolchak told us at the end of every show: 'It's true. Don't you understand? It's true.' "*
**— Darren McGavin (1991)**

*"Kolchak himself is a life-affirming creature of great activity."*
**— Stuart M. Kaminsky (1991)**
**Mystery writer and film historian**

*"So, when you have finished this bizarre account, judge for yourself its believability, and then try to tell yourself, wherever you may be, it couldn't happen here."*
**— Carl Kolchak (Darren McGavin)**
***The Night Stalker* (1972)**

# Table of Contents

Prologue with Acknowledgments . . . . . . . . . . . . . . . . . ix

Introduction . . . . . . . . . . . . . . . . . . . . . . . . 13

**PART I:** *The Night Stalker* . . . . . . . . . . . . . . . . 19

    Day of the *Night Stalker* . . . . . . . . . . . . . . 19

    The Four-Legged Monster . . . . . . . . . . . . . . 23

    Jeff Rice: Cold Facts About Kolchak . . . . . . . . . 23

    Richard Matheson: He is Legend . . . . . . . . . . 30

    Dan Curtis: From Soap to Stalker . . . . . . . . . . 33

    Darren McGavin: A Star is Cast . . . . . . . . . . . 43

    *The Night Stalker* . . . . . . . . . . . . . . . . . 48

    The Hook . . . . . . . . . . . . . . . . . . . . . 66

    Precedent and Progeny . . . . . . . . . . . . . . . 68

    After the Night . . . . . . . . . . . . . . . . . . . 70

**PART II:** *The Night Strangler* . . . . . . . . . . . . . . 73

    *The Night Strangler* . . . . . . . . . . . . . . . . 73

    The Complete *Night Strangler* . . . . . . . . . . . 87

    Kolchak in Print . . . . . . . . . . . . . . . . . . 88

    What Happened to the Third Movie? . . . . . . . . . 89

    The Further Adventures of Dan Curtis . . . . . . . . 90

**PART III:** *Kolchak: The Night Stalker* . . . . . . . . . . 97

    From Sequel to Series . . . . . . . . . . . . . . . 97

    Producer Out, Producer In . . . . . . . . . . . . . 103

    The Gang of Four . . . . . . . . . . . . . . . . . 111

    Whistling in the Dark . . . . . . . . . . . . . . . 118

    *Kolchak: The Night Stalker* . . . . . . . . . . . . 121

    1.) "The Ripper" . . . . . . . . . . . . . . . . . . 121

    2.) "The Zombie" . . . . . . . . . . . . . . . . . 126

3.) "U.F.O." ("They Have Been, They Are, They Will Be . . .") . . . . . . 128

4.) "The Vampire" . . . . . . . . . . . . . . . . . . . . . . . . . . . . 133

5.) "The Werewolf" . . . . . . . . . . . . . . . . . . . . . . . . . . . 135

6.) "Fire Fall" ("The Doppleganger") . . . . . . . . . . . . . . . . . . 137

7.) "The Devil's Platform" . . . . . . . . . . . . . . . . . . . . . . . 139

8.) "Bad Medicine" ("The Diablero") . . . . . . . . . . . . . . . . . . 144

9.) "The Spanish Moss Murders" . . . . . . . . . . . . . . . . . . . . 146

10.) "The Energy Eater" ("Matchemonedo") . . . . . . . . . . . . . . 148

11.) "Horror in the Heights" ("The Rakshasa") . . . . . . . . . . . . 150

12.) "Mr. R.I.N.G." . . . . . . . . . . . . . . . . . . . . . . . . . . . 152

13.) "Primal Scream" ("The Humanoids") . . . . . . . . . . . . . . . 156

14.) "The Trevi Collection" . . . . . . . . . . . . . . . . . . . . . . . 158

15.) "Chopper" . . . . . . . . . . . . . . . . . . . . . . . . . . . . . . 160

16.) "Demon in Lace" . . . . . . . . . . . . . . . . . . . . . . . . . . 163

17.) "Legacy of Terror" ("Lord of the Smoking Mirror") . . . . . . . 165

18.) "The Knightly Murders" . . . . . . . . . . . . . . . . . . . . . . 167

19.) "The Youth Killer" . . . . . . . . . . . . . . . . . . . . . . . . . 169

20.) "The Sentry" . . . . . . . . . . . . . . . . . . . . . . . . . . . . 170

The Kolchak Collapse . . . . . . . . . . . . . . . . . . . . . . . . . 172

Unproduced Kolchak . . . . . . . . . . . . . . . . . . . . . . . . . . 174

Sizing the Series . . . . . . . . . . . . . . . . . . . . . . . . . . . . 176

**PART IV: After ABC** . . . . . . . . . . . . . . . . . . . . . . . . . . 183

Late Night Stalker . . . . . . . . . . . . . . . . . . . . . . . . . . . 183

Cable Carl . . . . . . . . . . . . . . . . . . . . . . . . . . . . . . . 184

From Columbia House to Your House . . . . . . . . . . . . . . . . . 185

Carl By the Book . . . . . . . . . . . . . . . . . . . . . . . . . . . . 186

Comic Book Kolchak . . . . . . . . . . . . . . . . . . . . . . . . . . 187

Regarding Rice . . . . . . . . . . . . . . . . . . . . . . . . . . . . . 190

From Martian Blues to *Murphy Brown* . . . . . . . . . . . . . . . 191

Another Call for Carl . . . . . . . . . . . . . . . . . . . . . . . . . . 191

R.I.P. . . . . . . . . . . . . . . . . . . . . . . . . . . . . . . . . . . . 196

Bibliography . . . . . . . . . . . . . . . . . . . . . . . . . . . . . . . 197

Index . . . . . . . . . . . . . . . . . . . . . . . . . . . . . . . . . . 200

# Prologue with Acknowledgments

What you hold in your hands might be accurately described as the second edition of a book published in late 1991 as *Night Stalking: A 20th Anniversary Kolchak Companion*. Or, when you consider the completely new design and the pages of fresh material, perhaps it would be better described as a *new* edition of *Night Stalking*. How new? Well, there are enough updates and changes to warrant a new title: *The Night Stalker Companion: A 25th Anniversary Tribute*.

A great deal has happened on the Kolchak front during the last five years, which is one reason I'm grateful to Pomegranate Press and publisher Kathryn Leigh Scott for the chance to revisit and rework the territory. I'm also grateful because, well, there were a few small problems with *Night Stalking*. This edition gives me the opportunity to fix the goofs and oversights. For example, *The Night Stalker Companion* puts producer Cy Chermak on the record, as well as series regulars Jack Grinnage and Carol Ann Susi. They were sorely missed in the earlier version of this look at Carl Kolchak's career. And let us once and for all clear up any questions about Francy Productions, the company that produced the *Kolchak: The Night Stalker* series in association with Universal City Studios. It has been incorrectly assigned the wrong ownership in several standard reference books. The company belongs to the Chermaks. Francy is a combination of their first names (Francine and Cy). Got that?

Those were some of the small problems. But there was a BIG problem with *Night Stalking*. It wasn't available in bookstores. It quickly went out of print, and hardly a week goes by that someone doesn't ask – by phone, e-mail or conventional mail – where a copy might be purchased. I've even seen it listed as "rare and collectible" in catalogues specializing in horror and science-fiction items. I would have gladly forgone the honor of being rare and collectible in exchange for decent distribution and modest sales. Second chances should always be cherished. So, again, perhaps the thanks should start with Pomegranate Press –for deciding to be Carl's friend.

I always suspected that Carl Kolchak had more friends than his movies and ABC series indicated. During the researching and writing of this book, that suspicion was more than justified by a steady outpouring of cooperation, encouragement and enthusiasm.

Just as there would have been no *Night Stalker* movie without Darren McGavin, Kolchak creator Jeff Rice, producer Dan Curtis and screenplay author Richard Matheson, there would have been no *Night Stalker Companion* without the memories and information supplied by these four men behind "the" man. They were the invaluable contributors. Darren McGavin and his wife, Kathie Browne, remained splendidly gracious as their home was invaded by a coffee-guzzling writer on the trail of a fellow named Kolchak. Dan Curtis displayed remarkable good humor, through several interviews, as our prying researcher insisted on going over every title on his resumé. Richard Matheson made my decade by announcing that, yes, he had read and enjoyed my *Columbo* book (I have it on tape, so he can't take it back). And Jeff Rice. . . well, what can be said of a response that adds up to about sixty typewritten pages? After a few telephone calls, Jeff decided that he wished to answer all questions in writing. The bulk of his response was the forty-seven page *The Kolchak Story* (1984) and a nine-page letter with replies to each of my specific questions. In return for this wonderfully detailed account, he asked for nothing more than proper recognition of these documents as his copyrighted works quoted with his permission. This is acknowledged here and on the copyright page. For those who might be fearing that this suggests a rather formal exchange, fear not. Since the first edition of this book, Jeff has remained a faithful and lively correspondent. When Jeff suggested that I write the first original Kolchak novel in twenty years (the 1994 book that became *Grave Secrets*), he not only bestowed on me a great honor, he made me a happy part of Carl's history (one of those new developments addressed in this new edition).

For joyously summoning recollections and providing bits of insight concerning the *Night Stalker* movie, my deep gratitude goes to director John Llewellyn Moxey, associate producer Robert Singer (later the executive producer on such series as *Lois & Clark*), composer Robert Cobert, former ABC Productions President Brandon Stoddard and ABC publicist Dan Doran.

For their memories of working on the *Kolchak: The Night Stalker* series, I am indebted to producer Cy Chermak, story editor David Chase, regulars Jack Grinnage and Carol Ann Susi, episode writers Michael Kozoll (later an Emmy winner for *Hill Street Blues*) and Robert Zemeckis (later an Oscar winner for *Forrest Gump*), Universal Pictures Vice President Harry Tatelman and guests stars Lara Parker, William Daniels and Tom Skerritt.

I also appreciate the views and remembrances of *X-Files* creator Chris Carter, *Dark Shadows* writer Sam Hall, television music expert Jon Burlingame (author of *TV's Biggest Hits*), Barry Schulman (the Sci-Fi Channel vice president for programming), director Joe Dante and, of course, Kathie Browne. For the generous loans of material and valuable pushes in wise directions, my sincere thanks to Tom Rogers (owner of Foto Fantasies in East Meadow, New York), Karen Reynolds (director of media relations at the Sci-Fi Channel), *Dark Shadows* maven and all-around good guy Jim Pierson, Jim Benson (owner of Jim's TV Collectibles in San Diego), author and researcher Scott Skelton, Gretchen Lindensmith (product coordinator for the Columbia House Video Library), *Cinefantastique* magazine editor and publisher Frederick S. Clarke, collector extraordinaire David Billman (the Forrest J Ackerman of Akron), the gang at *Scarlet Street* and Keith Simpson, the ultimate Darren McGavin enthusiast. And I'd like to recognize the belief and support expressed by Edward Gross, who suggested and published *Night Stalking* with good intentions (and no business acumen).

For his friendship, scholarship and efforts to keep Kolchak cooking, a tip of the straw hat goes to Mark Schultz, editor of the excellent newsletter, ". . .*it couldn't happen here.*" For thoughts on his friend Richard Matheson, for acres of great writing and for inscribing my copy of *Psycho,* I cherish the memory of the late Robert Bloch.

For their reflections on *Dark Shadows,* my thanks to the already mentioned Curtis, Scott, Parker, Cobert and Hall, as well as Jonathan Frid, David Selby, John Karlen and Jerry Lacy.

I'm also grateful to a stellar panel of experts for a vast array of opinions about the Kolchak character and the *Night Stalker* series: mystery writer and film scholar Stuart M. Kaminsky, director of Florida State University's Motion Picture, Television and Recording Arts Conservatory; television historian Ric Meyers, author of *TV*

*Detectives* and *Murder on the Air*; David Bianculli, TV critic at the *New York Daily News* and author of *Teleliteracy*; John Carman, TV critic at the *San Francisco Chronicle*; Tom Feran, TV critic at the *Cleveland Plain Dealer*; and R.D. Heldenfels, TV critic at the *Akron Beacon Journal*.

And, finally, there is Sara, who smiles wisely every time I scream despair and head back to the manuscript, renewed by her patience, understanding, confidence and love. Every writer should have one.

# Introduction

*"I take great relish in savoring each separate horror. I roll them over on my tongue."*
**Lord Byron (Gavin Gordon)**
*The Bride of Frankenstein* **(1935)**

Sunday, July 11, 1993: Huddled over a cup of coffee and a reporter's notebook, I sat tired and bleary-eyed in the main ballroom of the Universal City Hilton Hotel. Days and days of non-stop interviews, screenings and press conferences can leave you in this zombie-like state. But that's business as usual when the nation's television critics assemble every summer for the press tour, a three-week event where the networks, PBS, cable services and syndicators showcase their wares for the upcoming fall season. After a while, your blitzed senses hit overload. Every producer sounds the same. Every spiel sounds familiar. The shows start to blend together. You lose track of time. You lose brain cells.

Outside, it was a typically hot and smoggy summer day in the San Fernando Valley. Those scribes brave enough to stroll into the oppressive heat would have noticed that the hotel, perched high on a hill, overlooked Universal, the studio where ABC's *Kolchak: The Night Stalker* series was shot in 1974 and 1975. Inside the excessively air-conditioned ballroom, an executive producer I'd never seen before was touting the merits of his new Fox series — something called *The X-Files*. He was promising plenty of chills and scares. Tanned and curly-haired, Chris Carter looked like he should be writing about surfing instead of monsters (indeed, I later learned that Carter had written for a surfing magazine). After responding to a few routine questions, the young executive producer said something that made my weary eyes snap wide open: "There was a show on when I was kid called *The Night Stalker*."Huh? What was that? Did he say *Night Stalker?*

"And it was a very, very scary show," Carter continued, "and I loved that show. And I had an opportunity to create a show for Fox. And they said, 'What do you want to do?' And I said, you know, *The Night Stalker* was this fantastic show and I was scared out of my pants. I said there's nothing scary on television anymore. Let's do a scary show. If you remember *The Night Stalker. . . "*

Did I remember *The Night Stalker?* I'd written an entire non-fiction book about Carl Kolchak, the intrepid reporter played by Darren McGavin in two hit TV movies and twenty series episodes. I was at that very moment working on a novel about the character, with the blessing and assistance of Kolchak creator Jeff Rice. Now here was a producer proudly admitting that his new series was inspired by Kolchak. And it wouldn't be the last time Carter would voice such sentiments. In almost every interview he has given since that smoggy Sunday, the creator of *The X-Files* has gone out of his way to mention that Kolchak was the jumping-off point for his hit series.

I would need to pursue the matter with this Carter fellow. I got my chance in January 1994. I caught up with the executive producer at a working party for press and Fox stars. The scene was fittingly surreal. The network had rented out a hangar at Burbank Airport for the *X-Files*-themed event. The vast structure was filled with journalists, actors, producers, publicists and a thick blanket of fog maintained by dry-ice machines. "I don't remember specific episodes very well," Carter said of *Kolchak: The Night Stalker*. "I just remember particular moments being very scary. There was nothing like it on television at the time. I don't think there's been anything like it since. There were moments that were as scary as anything that's been done for television."

A few days later, at 4:31 a.m., all of Los Angeles got a scary moment when the Northridge earthquake shook up the area. Standing on the lawn of a Pasadena hotel with other guests shaken, rattled and rolled out of bed, I couldn't help thinking that, if the quake had hit while I was talking to Carter, everyone would have believed it was just another party stunt cooked up by the Fox publicity department. The tragic toll of that jolt started to sink in when friends, like *Kolchak: The Night Stalker* producer Cy Chermak, described the damage to their homes and the disruption to their lives.

Still, even with an earthquake providing the exclamation point to this meeting with Carter, I was grateful for the opportunity to compare *Night Stalker* notes with the creator of *The X-Files*. There have been other chances since that January chat – chances to discuss how a character named Kolchak inspired a producer to launch a series that became a pop-culture phenomenon. And chances for me to respond by explaining how that same character had inspired a career in journalism.

Here is that explanation as I've given it to Chris Carter, Darren McGavin, Jeff Rice, Dan Curtis, Cy Chermak and others with Kolchakian connections: In September 1974, I was starting my work towards a journalism degree at George Washington University. Journalism schools were doing standing-room-only business in those heady days. *All the President's Men* had been published that year, so I was surrounded by headline-crazy college freshmen who dreamed of being Woodward and/or Bernstein. Who could blame them? What a life! They gave you Pulitzer Prizes and million-dollar book contracts for meeting sources in underground parking garages and pulling down world leaders. It was, of course, a generation asleep. They would be shook – rudely – into awakening by the realities of having to start unceremoniously at the bottom ("Is that coffee ready yet?"), tracking down endless bits of less-than-glamorous information ("Better check those county sewage laws one more time"), and looking up the correct spelling of Caribbean at least once a week.

The "Woodstein" dream, however, passed me by. I dreamed of becoming Carl Kolchak, a hero perfectly embodied by Darren McGavin in those two hit TV movies, *The Night Stalker* (1972) and *The Night Strangler* (1973). No, wise guy, I didn't expect to find vampires lurking in the halls of Washington, D.C. — at least not the blood-sucking variety. But what did I know of Woodward and Bernstein? Heck, if they ever did the movie, they'd probably get Robert Redford and Dustin Hoffman to play the parts. As naive as I was, folks, I knew that much. And I knew that nobody was confusing me with Robert Redford, not with my ancient-fashion suits, scruffy looks and European surname.

Ah, but with his ancient suit, rumpled looks and European surname, Carl Kolchak was a role model I might grow into. Who needed Woodstein? Kolchak was every sloppy inch the hero determined to uncover the truth, yet he was the type of hero to whom I could relate. While certainly resourceful, he was prone to mistakes (lots of mistakes). While obviously dedicated, he was eager for a share of the glory that goes with a front-page byline. While capable of great courage, he at times ran in fear.

While skeptical about everything around him and inside him, he was optimistic about tomorrow.

Perhaps it was a childhood twisted by Universal horror films, *Famous Monsters of Filmland* magazine and daily doses of *Dark Shadows*. Maybe it was my delight in a lowbred hero with a wit sharp enough to puncture pompous windbags (heightened, no doubt, by an early Marxian conversion of the Groucho variety). Whatever the reason, something inside that would-be journalist of 1974 responded to Carl Kolchak. Something about Carl's personality fit me like a cheap suit. Lucky me.

When the realities of the profession crashed in on so many of those Woodstein dreamers, they packed up their bruised ambitions and pursued other callings. But in the midst of fantasy and fiction, I found a healthier, more realistic role model. Sure, the Deep Throats that Carl Kolchak encountered in late-night meetings usually were jugular-minded vampires, not White House sources. No matter how fantastic his adventures may have seemed, though, Carl had no illusions to sell. He knew journalism was about long hours, tedious work, thankless service and roads that lead to more dead ends than Pulitzer Prizes.

Long before Fox, Mulder and *The X-Files* came along, Carl was telling us that "the truth is out there." But Carl also told us that you had to push and push and push to get anywhere near the truth, and, even if you found it, your reward might be a swift kick in the teeth. These were insights that mentally prepared me for working on a newspaper (if anything can).

Yet there was more for those willing to listen. Okay, since I knew the Woodstein dream would never fit me, I wouldn't fit in with the rest of the freshman class of 1974. So what? Carl was showing me that the happiest writers are those who pursue their own enthusiasms, no matter how eccentric or unfashionable they may seem. By the way, this is guidance that usually doesn't make it into journalism textbooks. Still, without these secrets to a long writing life, many reporters burn out, cop out or drop out.

So, thank you, Carl Kolchak, for taking time out from rescuing an ungrateful world from vampires and swamp monsters to rescue a grateful me from the miserable and monotonous path into journalism.

To my great delight, I have discovered that these feelings are shared by other journalists. Crossing a newsroom several years ago, I chanced upon a familiar scene at an editor's desk. I saw one of the newspaper's finest reporters waving his arms in a manner that suggested a condition somewhere between outrage and apoplexy. As I neared the seemingly calm editor's desk, I heard our burly star newshound bellowing words that started a lightbulb flickering in a dusty attic of my memory.

"This," the indignant reporter shouted as he waved a late edition under the editor's nose, "is a newspaper. We are a newspaper! We are supposed to print the *news!*"

The words weren't exactly right. If the delivery had not been letter perfect, the lightbulb may never have reached the illumination stage. But I realized he was borrowing Carl Kolchak's fiery tirade to editor Tony Vincenzo in *The Night Stalker.* I got it and couldn't resist saying so.

"You're doing Kolchak," I mumbled at the furious fellow's back. He wheeled around, and I half-expected a blast of invective for pushing my know-it-all nose where it wasn't wanted. Instead, the reporter's scowling face was instantly transformed into a mask of glee. He resembled nothing more than an actor absolutely tickled by a rave review.

"You're right," he said, all smiles. "You got it. You're the first one who got it. I love that speech. I've never forgotten it. I've used it several times with editors. I've always thought that Kolchak was the closest television ever came to capturing a real reporter."

Mind you, this was well after the enlightened days of *Lou Grant*. A few weeks into the writing of this book, I was engaged in casual conversation with another columnist employed as a newspaper's television critic: Tom Feran of the *Cleveland Plain Dealer*. When I told him of the project at hand, Tom said, "You're kidding? I loved that character. Did I ever tell you that when I was in college I dreamed of being Carl Kolchak? Everybody around me was into the Woodward-and-Bernstein craze, and I thought Carl Kolchak was what a real reporter was all about."

Now this was getting a little too weird for me. Tom and I are about the same age, and I was ready to accuse him of sneaking into my den and reading an early draft of this introduction. But Tom meant he literally dreamed of being Carl Kolchak. Get this: "I dream not only in black-and-white *and* color, but sometimes with plots and music and titles," he said. "And, when I was in college, I had a dream called *The Vampire Mummy*. I know that's what it was called because I saw the title appear in dripping words. The vampire mummy lived in the Boston subway, dressed like Dracula and had his face wrapped in bandages. He would take his victims' skins and graft it onto his own for cosmetic reasons. And I remember going into a dark subway station to search for him. I didn't pass a mirror, so I can't tell you if I had on a striped summer suit and pork-pie hat. I thought it was hilarious when I woke up, but it was quite scary when it was happening. I think that indicates the extent of my identification with Mr. Kolchak. And I know I'm not alone, because at a press dinner with the stars of NBC's *Around the World in 80 Days* miniseries, a bunch of TV critics rushed over to Darren McGavin's table to talk *Night Stalker* with him."

Convinced? So, as you might imagine, a study of Carl Kolchak's career is a labor of love for me. It is my hope that this affection, along with the character's contagious sense of fun, will glide through these pages like a vampire bat through the night air.

A word of explanation about the subtitle: We're all a little anniversary happy these days, and the *25th Anniversary* is defined by the night that most of America met Carl Kolchak — January 11, 1972. That, of course, is the date that *The Night Stalker* shattered all ratings records for TV movies. But Carl Kolchak first found life in the typewriter of Jeff Rice, who finished his novel, *The Kolchak Papers*, on October 31, 1970, "just at midnight." From Jeff's typewriter, the character jumps to television. From that tremendous January evening, he jumps to a sequel movie, *The Night Strangler*. From the sequel to cult (and occult) hero?

Well, not quite. There was another stop. My college career wasn't the only thing that started in September of 1974. On Friday the 13th of that month, Kolchak began a one-season ABC run in a series version of *The Night Stalker*. Although there would be no more prime-time Kolchak capers after 1975, his following has demonstrated a durability that defies logic.

From a ratings standpoint, after all, the *Night Stalker* series was a flop. There were only twenty episodes, hardly enough to build a following on years of repeats (compare that paltry number with the original *Star Trek*, with about eighty episodes, or Rod Serling's *The Twilight Zone*, with 156 episodes). Defying programming logic (if such a thing actually exists), *Kolchak: The Night Stalker* developed generations of new followers with showings on the *CBS Late Night* schedule, in syndication and on cable's Sci-Fi Channel. The Columbia House Video Library's Collector's Edition of the series has been a runaway success. There are plans for a line of Kolchak comic books. There is talk of a big-screen Kolchak movie. There has been, as already mentioned, a new Kolchak novel. There are Kolchak sites on the World Wide Web. And a couple of outstanding Kolchak newsletters have been launched in the last year. In any event, if you want an anniversary, you've got one — the 25th or silver (or, in Kolchak's case, perhaps the silver bullet) anniversary. But the territory we'll be covering does not start with a signpost up ahead that reads January 11, 1972, nor does it end with a tombstone of cancellation in 1975. We refuse to let *The Night Stalker* go quietly into that dark night.

Why does Kolchak continue to fire our imaginations more than twenty years after his last known encounter of the supernatural kind? Mystery writer and film historian Stuart M. Kaminsky has one possible answer that sounds extremely probable: "He dressed like a slob, offended almost everyone, had little sensitivity, but maintained a sense of purpose which anyone might well admire. He was a hero whose sense of professionalism always got the better of his quite reasonable fear. Carl was, in a number of episodes, the saviour of the world and this saviour was not a swashbuckling hero, a brilliant scientist, a great leader of men. He was the Harry Truman of heroes, the guy who did his job and accepted responsibility when he had to do so. He was not brilliant. He was not strong. But did Carl have integrity. Maybe that's what appealed to me and those like me who loved the series."

That certainly speaks for me today and that eighteen-year-old me of 1974. Darren McGavin, who should know better than anyone, elaborates on the Kolchak appeal by harkening back to the original source material. "Jeff Rice wrote this wonderful book because he couldn't write about the Las Vegas of the mob and official corruption," the actor explains. "That's the key. If you take the secrets that go on in the world in which we live, we are surrounded by mysteries that we don't know how to combat or deal with. Kolchak is the seeker of truth who will break that veil of secrecy. That's the initial springboard of the character, and that's what I always wanted to play. All the network saw were those cockamamie monsters. There are more bloodsuckers in Beverly Hills than you can ever put on television. Who knows what's going on in the White House or big business or the halls of Congress or the oil companies? Kolchak really wants to get in there and expose all of the true monsters that are affecting our lives. He's a kind of a folk hero who's battling the forces of evil that we can't pin down ourselves and deal with. That's what Kolchak told us at the end of every show. 'It's true. Don't you understand? It's true.' "

Not a bad role model for an aspiring writer, huh? McGavin is articulating a point proven again and again by Rod Serling in his *Twilight Zone* anthology series (CBS, 1959-64): Network executives, advertisers and viewers often will accept social criticism when it's dressed in the colorful robes of fantasy. The same themes that made the networks quiver when addressed in contemporary dramas – the very same – Serling explored freely in *Twilight Zone* episodes.

In *The Night Stalker*, the monsters became the metaphors. Yet the Kolchak magic works on three levels – hero, horror and humor.

If horror was the tool for making social points, it also was a fabulously eerie hook with which to snare our interest. Edgar Allan Poe mapped out Kolchak's travel plans in the poem "Dream-Land":

*"By a route obscure and lonely,*
*Haunted by ill angels only,"*

Yep, that's the detour Kolchak always managed to find, all right. Try these high points from Mr. Poe's travel brochure:

*"By the dismal tarns and pools*
*Where dwell the Ghouls, –*
*By each spot the most unholy–*
*In each nook most melancholy, –*
*There the traveller meets, aghast,*
*Sheeted Memories of the Past…"*

Sound familiar? Lead on, Carl. I was ready to follow.

Then there was the humor. In the middle of the heroics and the horror. Kolchak's audacious sense of humor tied the bizarre package together. You got the feeling that Kolchak was going to live a good long life because, despite all of the setbacks, he had the ability to laugh at himself and the world around him.

Some people connected with the *Kolchak* movies and series episodes have suggested that the mixture of humor and social consciousness made *The Night Stalker* a TV entity way ahead of its time. From a pop-culture standpoint, I suppose I must agree. From a personal standpoint, I know this isn't so. Kolchak arrived right on time for me.

Mark Dawidziak
Cuyahoga Falls

## Part I

# The Night Stalker

### or, "Stalking the Wild Reporter"
### or, "Wild Rice Grows at ABC"

*"There are mysteries which man can only guess at,*
*which age by age they solve in part."*
**– Dr. Abraham Van Helsing**
***Dracula* (1897) by Bram Stoker**

*". . . and then – then all is mystery and terror."*
*– "Berenice"*
**by Edgar Allan Poe**

# Day of the Night Stalker

Cloudy skies did nothing to ease the Tuesday travail of New Yorkers in their second week of work or school after the New Year's holiday break. Yes, January 11, 1972, was a rainy Tuesday in New York City, but the weather wasn't completely unkind to commuters dashing for the Long Island Railroad or braving one of the congested bridges connecting Manhattan with an outer-world that on occasion does know the silence of sleep. It was an unseasonably warm day. The temperature strayed between forty-five and fifty-three degrees – positively balmy for the Big Apple in January.

Meanwhile, over on the West Coast, some gloomy clouds also were hanging over the office of the perennially third-place American Broadcasting Company. There were mixed feelings about a little vampire thriller that ABC had scheduled to air at 8:30 p.m. Oh, the slick on-air promotions had been very effective, and *The Night Stalker* would air between two of the network's most popular shows: *The Mod Squad*, which had finished eleventh among all series aired during the 1970-71 season, and *Marcus Welby, M.D.*, which, despite ABC trailing behind NBC and CBS in overall viewers, had been the previous season's highest-rated series. And the NBC competition looked pretty weak (the 8:30 news special *Suffer the Little Children*, reporter-

**19**

producer Robert Northshield's look at violence in Northern Ireland, and James Garner's *Nichols*, the offbeat 9:30-10:30 Western that, despite favorable critical reaction, was having a difficult time finding an audience). The CBS opposition promised to be a bit stiffer. *Hawaii Five-O*, the 8:30-9:30 police drama starring Jack Lord, had been a top-ten series the previous season. William Conrad's 9:30-10:30 *Cannon* was one of the several successful character-cop programs launched during the fall (the colorful crop of cops that included Peter Falk's *Columbo* and the late James Franciscus as the blind *Longstreet*).

Yet it wasn't the strong CBS Tuesday lineup that caused those clouds of doubt at ABC. Some of the network brass types just weren't comfortable with this *Night Stalker* thing. One of the few accomplishments ABC had to cheer about was its development of the TV movie (then called a movie of the week). Much of the credit belonged to a young entertainment division vice president named Barry Diller, who would later become the chairman and chief executive officer of Paramount Pictures. He would leave Paramount to start fourth-network Fox Broadcasting. After leaving Fox, he would emerge as the executive in charge of the company that operates the Home Shopping Network.

"Even though we were the third-place network," says Brandon Stoddard, who joined ABC in 1970 as the vice president in charge of daytime programming, "it was a very exciting place to be at that time. There was an incredible enthusiasm from young executives like Barry Diller and (future Disney chairman) Michael Eisner. It was great. You had a feeling of possibilities."

Stoddard, who would later become ABC's vice president in charge of motion pictures and president of the entire entertainment division, credits Diller with establishing the network's leadership in the TV movie field. "He understood the format's possibilities," notes Stoddard, who, in the early '90s, after about twenty years with the network, took charge of ABC Productions (the entity that absorbed ABC Circle Films, which produced *The Night Stalker*).

In 1968, Diller had recommended an ambitious commitment to the then-little-used movie of the week. He suggested that ABC produce ninety-minute TV movies on a scale capable of supporting a weekly series. Roy Huggins, a writer-producer whose credits include *Maverick* and *The Rockford Files*, had taken the idea to CBS and NBC before pitching it to ABC. Diller and fellow programming executives Martin Starger and Leonard Goldberg jumped on the concept and pitched it to network founder Leonard H. Goldenson and the ABC board. Huggins wanted to produce a full season's package of twenty-six TV movies. ABC, arguing that the job was too big for one man, offered him eight. He refused, so Diller took the package to Universal (owned by entertainment giant MCA). Lew Wasserman, chairman of MCA, insisted on $400,000 for each film. Diller tried to bargain. Wasserman wouldn't budge. Diller told Goldenson that he could produce the movies for $350,000 if the project stayed at the network. In his autobiography, Goldenson describes this decision as "vitally important" because it "jump-started ABC's television network."

By January 11, 1972, the decision had paid enormous financial and creative dividends. Not only was ABC poised to become a legitimate network contender in the '70s, the reputation for quality was growing. Indeed, during the 1971-72 season, the TV movie truly came of age, with ABC leading the way. One wonderful drama did the trick. *Brian's Song* starred James Caan as Brian Piccolo, the Chicago Bears running back who relied on a sense of humor and his friendship with teammate Gale Sayers (played by Billy Dee Williams) to battle the cancer that would end his career and claim his life. There was hardly a dry eye left in America. *Brian's Song* packed in a stadium of rave reviews and set a ratings record for TV movies.

So ABC was riding the wave of praise from *Brian's Song*. With Emmys and another round of glory sure to come their way in a few months, network executives were slightly uncomfortable with the presence of a horror story full of violence and murdered Las Vegas showgirls. To make matters worse, the morning's newspapers carried stories certain to intensify the violence-on-TV debate. The U.S. Surgeon General's Scientific Advisory Committee on TV and Social Behavior had concluded that violence in television programs does not have adverse effects on the majority of the nation's youth, but it might influence small groups of youngsters predisposed to aggressive behavior. That "but" was a conjunction of concern, all right. And with *The Night Stalker* airing that night... well, maybe it would pass without much notice.

For those not interested in the Surgeon General's report, there were headlines about a different kind of Las Vegas horror story. Reclusive billionaire Howard Hughes had told reporters that Clifford Irving's as-told-to "autobiography" was a fake, and Irving was doing his best to keep the literary fraud going. For those not interested in the Surgeon General or Howard Hughes, the international news told of the death of Chen Yi, China's foreign minister. Party Chairman Mao Tse-Tung led the country in mourning, even though Chen had been purged by his orders during the Cultural Revolution. For those not interested in the Surgeon General, Howard Hughes or Mao, several movies offered escape routes on January 11, 1972. Clint Eastwood's *Dirty Harry* continued to be a strong box-office presence. If Clint wasn't your style, you could have caught Sean Connery's sixth outing as super spy James Bond, *Diamonds Are Forever*. In fact, the movie theaters were full of leading men to suit every taste: Dustin Hoffman in director Sam Peckinpah's *Straw Dogs*, Warren Beatty in *$*, Paul Newman in *Sometimes a Great Notion*. Or you could have seen the reissues of Charlie Chaplin's *Modern Times* (1936) or Disney's *Lady and the Tramp* (1955). Hot tickets on Broadway that night included Cliff Gorman in *Lenny* and Peter Falk in Neil Simon's *The Prisoner of Second Avenue*. The scope of the musicals was staggering: *Hair, Follies, Fiddler on the Roof* (with Jan Peerce as Tevye), *Applause*, the revival of *No, No Nanette* and the controversial *Oh, Calcutta*.

After you got past the headlines and the movie listings, maybe you would have checked out the TV listings. Hmm, Dana Wynter was guest-starring in the first half of a two-part *Hawaii Five-O*. Tab Hunter was the guest star on *Cannon*. And someone named Margot Kidder (about six years away from her Lois Lane stint opposite Christopher Reeve in *Superman*) was listed as the guest star on *Nichols*. The *New York Times* blurb for *The Night Stalker* described the TV movie in terms that must have pleased those concerned ABC executives — "Newsman fights censorship, from his editor and the police, trying to prove Las Vegas is being terrorized by a vampire." Gee, we're talking a fight against censorship here. Real First Amendment stuff. It must have some class.

Not enough for the *Times*, of course. Television critic John J. O'Connor devoted his January 11th space to a review of a political program that New York City educational station WNET (Channel 13) had aired the previous night. On January 13, he reviewed *Suffer the Little Children,* the NBC News special that had aired opposite *The Night Stalker*.

Night owls looking for a late movie on January 11 could try *The Forty-Eight Hour Mile,* a 1970 TV movie that spliced together two episodes of the NBC detective series *The Outsider.* New York station WOR (Channel 9) had it scheduled for 11:15 p.m. Its star? Why, it was that newsman fighting censorship in Las Vegas — Darren McGavin. This was the day of *The Night Stalker*. And when it was over, *Brian's Song* no longer would be the highest-rated TV movie of all time.

Jeff Rice

Dan Curtis

Richard Matheson

Darren McGavin

# The Four-Legged Monster

*"I wants to make your flesh creep."*
*– The Pickwick Papers* **(1836-37)**
**By Charles Dickens**

*"Listen to them. Children of the night. What music they make."*
**– Count Dracula (Bela Lugosi)**
*Dracula* **(1931)**

A straight line is rarely the way that leads you into television history. The route is usually a bit more complicated. There are twists and turns involving writers, agents, producers, directors, actors, studios and networks. In the case of *The Night Stalker*, when you stand back and look at the overall terrain, you see that four paths had to come together at ABC. The four paths belonged to:

**1.) Jeff Rice,** the writer who created Carl Kolchak and wrote a novel with the novel idea of a vampire on the loose in Las Vegas.

**2.) Richard Matheson,** the veteran fantasy author who adapted Rice's book.

**3.) Dan Curtis,** the producer who assembled the team capable of turning Rice's book into a stylish TV movie.

**4.) Darren McGavin,** the actor who gave Kolchak a voice, a hat and a seersucker suit.

Think of *The Night Stalker* as a finely carved four-legged table of delights. Knock out one of the legs, the table collapses. Before you start analyzing the craftsmanship of this table, consider the foundation on which it was built. And that consideration begins with Jeff Rice.

## Jeff Rice

### Cold Facts About Kolchak

Was there a real Carl Kolchak? Well, he is based in part on a reporter-editor Jeff Rice met in Las Vegas. The other part Rice got from himself.

"Kolchak was born out of a part of my own life and so, I think, I must begin with my own birth," Rice relates in his forty-seven page *The Kolchak Story* (1984).

Jeff Rice was born on February 22, 1944, in Providence, Rhode Island. His early childhood was spent in Beverly Hills. In 1955, he became a resident of Las Vegas. Since 1969, he has divided his time between Las Vegas and Los Angeles.

That's the skeleton of the story. Rice will put the flesh and blood on for you. From an early age, he seemed "to take a great delight in reading scary stories and going to see scary movies. I was about thirteen or fourteen years old in the period 1957-58 when Universal released to TV stations all over the country a package of its old horror films which ran as *Shock Theatre* or under similar titles.

"I fed on those Friday night double-bill horror flicks like a vampire on a soft and downy neck and, when not engaged in anything as dull and compulsory as school, indulged in the two potential career pursuits that interested me then, and now; acting and writing."

At the age of eight, he landed his first major role in a play and "was badly bitten by the acting bug." At the age of eleven, he wrote his first short story, "and it was a wonderful feeling to create characters and make them do what I wanted them to do."

The youngster became fascinated with the silent films of horror specialist Lon Chaney and the British comedies of Alec Guinness. In his daydreams, he envisioned himself as an actor known for his mastery of makeup and dialects – a mixture of Chaney and Guinness.

"When you're not athletic at all," Rice says, "short, shy, and somewhat hesitant with girls; you turn to whatever gives you pleasure and to what you're good at. I found I was good at writing, good at theatrical makeup, and good at acting. So I stuck with those things, while reading voraciously – always did and probably always will – and, little by little, polished my skills."

During a three-year span (1961-64), Rice pursued three different majors at three different colleges: journalism at the University of Oregon, drama at the University of Southern California and English at the University of Nevada at Las Vegas. "Ironically," Rice remembers, "after managing to flunk out of a college English course – not because I couldn't cut the work but, because the teacher and I agreed to disagree – I wound up getting a job as a reporter on the *Las Vegas SUN*."

His *SUN* career began in 1966 after turns as a men's shop shoe salesman and a versatile member (actor, makeup artist, instructor, advertising director and dialogue coach) of the Gallery Theatre in Las Vegas.

"I'd been a copyboy (at the *SUN*) back in '63 and had met an itinerant reporter named Alan Jarlson, who bounced from newspapers to radio, and back to newspapers, and to TV, and so forth," Rice says in *The Kolchak Story*. "For a while, he was my editor at the *SUN*, though only briefly, and in time, served as a partial prototype for the character of Carl Kolchak. Many of the things Kolchak says have come out of my own thoughts and feelings. Many of them came from what I was taught and told by Jarlson. Many of Kolchak's habits, his rages at his editor, came from factual incidents in Jarlson's career. Throwing a heavy object through Tony Vincenzo's window in *The Night Strangler* came from one such incident, except that when Jarlson did it, it was a typewriter he threw, and he didn't stop at the window; he went to work on the wood paneling as well. He was a pistol... and a helluva reporter."

Rice remained with the *SUN* for two years, and, by his account, was fired fourteen times by the prototype for Kolchak's long-suffering editor, Tony Vincenzo. He left the *SUN* in 1968 "because even Kolchak couldn't live on what I was being paid." Before moving into public-relations work, however, Rice was named the state's outstanding journalist by the Nevada State Press Association. He worked as a public relations director of the United Fund of Clark County and director of advertising and promotion for the Thunderbird Hotel. At each stop, the young writer was gathering intimate knowledge of the Las Vegas behind the bright lights — knowledge that he would put to use in *The Night Stalker*.

Throughout the middle and late '60s, he also continued to pile up acting credits in Las Vegas (with the Gallery, Theatre Guild and Clark County Theatre Association) and Phoenix, Arizona (with the Portal Theatre and Circle Star Theatre).

At the end of the decade, Rice accepted a copy director's position with an advertising agency in Los Angeles. When not "grinding out copy for political speeches" or "extolling the virtues of a newly-devised noodle that was nineteen percent protein," he was pursuing opportunities as an actor and a writer. It was in late 1969 and the

Jeff Rice, circa 1992, when he led an anti-drug, anti-gang watch-patrol group in Hollywood.

A recent photograph of author Jeff Rice, creator of intrepid investigative reporter Carl Kolchak.

early part of 1970 that he compiled detailed notes for a horror novel that would draw on the intimate knowledge of newspaper reporting, politics and Las Vegas.

This is how Rice describes the writing process: "Aside from knowing, in my gut, that things would not end at all well for Kolchak, I had no idea, after the first two chapters or so, what was going to happen. I swear I just sat there, working in a form of stream-of-consciousness, seeing the story unfold in script-like 'shots' in my mind; dream-reading it as if one of my teen-years heroes like Richard Matheson had written it, and then my bleary eyes would snap open and I'd type out what I'd just 'read' or 'viewed' inside my skull."

The novel that Rice would call *The Kolchak Papers* was a conscious attempt to blend the traditional vampire legend with the boisterous style of plays and movies about American newspaper reporters. To boil the concept down to terms that even a network executive could understand, it was *"Dracula* meets *The Front Page."*

Both traditions were well established when Rice was pounding away through two drafts of *The Kolchak Papers* in 1970. Vampire legends appear in almost every culture on the globe. Literature's first significant vampire has its origins in the same Geneva brainstorm that gave us the Frankenstein monster. On a June night in 1816, in a villa along the shores of Lake Geneva, Lord Byron made his famous challenge: "We will each write a ghost story." The ghostly gauntlet was thrown down to Mary Shelley, Percy Bysshe Shelley and Byron's personal physician, John Polidori.

This, of course, was the night that set Mary Shelley on the road to *Frankenstein.* Byron, though, started work on a vampire story. When he abandoned it, the twenty-year-old Polidori took over the story and published it as "The Vampyre" in April 1819. It was followed a year later by a somber vampire of sorts, Irish clergyman Robert Maturin's *Malmoth the Wanderer.*

In 1847, Thomas Preskett Prest published his gothic horror novel, *Varney the Vampire or The Feast of Blood,* quite a best-selling potboiler for its Victorian day. Another Irishman, Joseph Sheridan Le Fanu, took the next step into the world of the undead with "Carmilla," which was published in his best-known collection of short stories, *In a Glass Darkly* (1872).

All of these literary vampire excursions set the stage for still another Irishman to write the most famous horror novel of all time. For *Dracula* (1897), Bram Stoker not only researched the vampire legends and literature, he investigated the bloody career of one Vlad Tepes, a ruthless Wallachia ruler known as Vlad the Impaler. He also was known as Dracula (meaning "son of the dragon" or "son of the devil"). It was Vlad the Impaler (1431-76) who provided Stoker with an ideal historical model for his vampire.

Throughout the next century, Count Dracula invaded Broadway, films and television, in the bodies of such actors as Max Schreck (in director F.W. Murnau's classic silent version, *Nosferatu*), Bela Lugosi, John Carradine, Francis Lederer, Christopher Lee, Jack Palance, Louis Jourdan, Klaus Kinski, Frank Langella, Michael Nouri and Gary Oldman. Rice's story opened the crypt doors for a veritable vampire renaissance in the 1970s. The decade saw two acclaimed television versions of *Dracula* (with Palance and Jourdan) and two landmark vampire novels: Stephen King's *'Salem's Lot* (1975) and Anne Rice's *Interview With the Vampire* (1976). In the '80s, America went batty for vampires on the big screen: *The Hunger* (1983), *Fright Night* (1985), *Once Bitten* (1985), *The Lost Boys* (1987), *To Die For* (1989). And this bloodlust continued in the '90s with director Francis Ford Coppola's stab at *Bram Stoker's Dracula* (1992), *Innocent Blood* (1992), *Buffy the Vampire Slayer* (1992), the film version of *Interview With the Vampire* (1994), *Cronos* (1994), Mel Brooks' *Dracula: Dead and Loving It* (1995), *From Dusk Till Dawn* (1995), *Vampire in Brooklyn* (1995) and *Bordello of Blood* (1996).

But if *The Kolchak Papers* has one foot planted in this rich tradition, the other is in the seemingly incongruous world of Hollywood's ink-stained wretches of the press. If Count Dracula is the literary ancestor of Rice's vampire, Rumanian nobleman Janos Skorzeny, then Kolchak belongs to a Hollywood lineage that boasts Hildy Johnson (Pat O'Brien) in *The Front Page* (1931), Peter Warne (Clark Gable) in *It Happened One Night* (1934) and Wally Cook (Fredric March) in *Nothing Sacred* (1937). In each of these films, a wisecracking veteran reporter, like Kolchak, has a stormy relationship with an easily agitated editor (like Tony Vincenzo). The combination of blood and printer's ink proved a magic formula for Rice.

"*The Kolchak Papers* wouldn't be the first novel in the genre to deal with an explosive editor-reporter relationship," he explains. "That had been going on in books, on stage, and in films since the late 1920s, certainly since (Ben) Hecht and (Charles) MacArthur had established a benchmark with *The Front Page*. And, surely, horror stories had been with us almost since the dawn of mankind. . . But my first novel would probably be the first to combine — at least successfully as time subsequently proved — both the newspaper and horror genres. That wasn't my main consideration when I started the actual drafting. All I wanted to do was create a 'good read' of the type I thought *I* would find entertaining; something for people to use to kill time in airports, on planes, or in hotels when stuck overnight in a strange town. Of course, I also felt I could use the book as a vehicle to say a few serious things about my town; to use it as an intrinsic part of the story rather than as a mere background setting; and to make a few pithy comments about the misuse of power, the latter being an underlying theme both in the novel and in my own emotional makeup."

It's entirely possible that Rice's magic mixture would have worked in another city. It's doubtful that it would have worked as well. The corruption so much a part of "official" Las Vegas makes Kolchak's fight for truth all the more quixotic, and there's something fiendishly appropriate about a vampire preying on a town known as Sin City. What better feeding ground for a vampire than a place that comes alive at night? It's right on his feeding schedule.

No matter what innovations and permutations other talents brought to *The Night Stalker* during the five years after *The Kolchak Papers* was completed, these are the basic ingredients that make the premise work. Darren McGavin recognizes this when he advises those seeking to understand Carl Kolchak to start with "Jeff Rice's wonderful book." Film historian and mystery writer Stuart M. Kaminsky recognizes this in precise and straightforward terms: "Most of the credit for the accomplishments of the series belong to Jeff Rice, whose original novel and characters were brought to life in both the films and the series."

Rice finished *The Kolchak Papers* on October 31, 1970 – about midnight. "Perhaps I was moved by a subconscious desire to conclude things at that propitious hour," he would later speculate. Whatever the reason, Halloween became the literary and actual birthday of Karel Michail Kolchak (nicknamed Carl and born, according to his creator, in New York City to Janos and Fanny Kolchak).

Less than a month after finishing *The Kolchak Papers*, "through a friend of a friend," Rice was introduced to the agent who would represent *The Kolchak Papers*. Related in great detail in the copyrighted *The Kolchak Story*, Rice's account of what happened during the next few months is hardly shocking by Tinseltown standards. It has often been said that writers are the doormats of Hollywood, and, according to the dates and figures cited in *The Kolchak Story*, Rice ended up with more than his share of muddy footprints on his back.

This is Rice's recollection of the next eight months:

Shortly after Thanksgiving 1970, the agent told Rice that he believed *The Kolchak Papers* was a viable commercial property. The agency primarily handled television and film scripts, so an interested movie producer might be found before a book publisher. But, despite such enthusiasm, the agency did not agree to officially represent Rice at this point.

Rice was hoping that agent would quickly work his way through a four-step process:

1.) Sign an agent-client agreement.

2.) Secure the best possible deal for screen rights.

3.) Arrange for book publication.

4.) Make a deal for Rice to adapt his novel or, at the very least, co-write the screenplay.

"As the situation was," Rice recounts in *The Kolchak Story*, "he had my manuscript, uncopyrighted and unprotected, and he also had, among his more notable clients, a writer who'd been one of my favorites for a decade: Richard Matheson. And he started almost at once to secure a deal which would be favorable, primarily, to Matheson.

"As early as December 7, he sent a copy of *The Kolchak Papers* to Allen Epstein, who was then in charge of production for ABC-TV's *Movie of the Week*. I didn't know this, nor would I for years to come. He was trying to set up deal for Matheson to adapt my novel into a screenplay. As he admitted, under oath, years later: 'I was attempting to sell Mr. Matheson to ABC. . .' Well, I knew none of this. And a whole month went by and I heard nothing of substance, nothing encouraging. He hadn't committed himself or his partners, on paper, to officially representing me and my work. But he was out there, somewhere, with my unprotected manuscript."

It was time to get some protection. Worried and unfamiliar with the Hollywood system, Rice asked the Copyright Office what he had to do to register his novel. "Basically," he explained, "all I had to do was see that the book was available for sale — I didn't even have to actually sell a single copy — and that would constitute publication and thus make it possible to register it for copyright. So, I had a sizable number of copies printed up and, almost at once, sold quite a few to friends and others around Las Vegas. Then I applied for my copyright certificate with January 1, 1971, as the publication date."

A word to nervous writers out there: Changes and clarifications in copyright law have made life a little simpler (though no less dangerous) for authors. Any work, published or unpublished, can be registered for a fee with the Register of Copyrights in Washington, D.C. Although registering a work with the Copyright Office is wise, it is not necessary. The law recognizes the author as the sole and only copyright holder (unless the writing is done on an agreed work-for-hire basis).

On January 12, 1971, Rice was sent a fully signed and executed agent-client agreement. Rice says he found out years later that, on the same day, Matheson was hired by contract to adapt *The Kolchak Papers*. It is Rice's contention that this was more than a double deal involving two writers. This, he says, sniffed of double-dealing.

"That's an important date because it was only then, after he'd secured Matheson's deal, that he and his partners signed and dated their agreement to represent me," Rice explains in *The Kolchak Story*. "Because, confident he'd obtained the deal he wanted for Matheson, and thus could not fail to secure a sale of the screen rights to my novel, my new agent was now willing to make his representation official.

"A very strange situation, indeed, because ABC had committed itself to pay Mr. Matheson $20,000 to adapt a property ABC did not own. They would, years later, deny this, though the documents put the lie to this position."

It was on March 11 that Rice was told about ABC's plans to turn *The Kolchak Papers* into a TV movie. The next day, the agent informed Rice that Richard Matheson was adapting the screenplay.

The agent said "he'd described the plotline to Matheson and that Matheson had flipped over it, asked to take it home, had done so, read it, and now wanted to do the teleplay," Rice recalls. "I was knocked out by this. Matheson! Doing an adaptation of *my* work. Maybe I'd get a chance to work with him. One of the things he failed to tell me was that Matheson was *his* client and another was that he'd already set up Matheson's adaptation deal two months earlier."

There were some attractive points to the deal. Rice would be paid a fee as the movie's location consultant. And the screen rights were for only one film. No sequels or series could be made without Rice's permission. Rice might have been, to use his words, "still living in a world of innocence," but this item and his copyright maneuver would salvage his legal and literary claims to Kolchak during the coming years. They would guarantee that Rice would live to tell the tale.

It's important to note that Rice does not in any way blame Matheson for what he views as shady Hollywood dealings. In fact, he places much of the blame on his own ignorance and innocence — "Boy, was I an innocent abroad in Tinseltown." He readily admits to being naive about the business of networks, studios and agents. He believes that people were less-than-aboveboard with him at several turns, but, then, candor and kindness were never traits to be easily detected in the shark-eat-shark world of La-La Land. If you're going to swim in these waters, it's best to first get some lessons. And, yes, there are some harsh lessons in all this for writers who are reluctant to study contracts, scrutinize figures, challenge companies, document everything and push for answers. Those lessons amount to: study contracts, scrutinize figures, challenge companies, document everything and push for answers. *You* have to be the one to look after the welfare of your literary offspring. It's *your* responsibility. Anything less is irresponsible parenting. That's a tough assignment for most writers, who are timid and uncomfortable around legal documents and ledger sheets. Rice learned the hard way that innocence must give way to skepticism. That's life in any number of big cities. So, as that *Kolchak* descendant, *The X-Files*, warns us time and again, "Trust no one." In 1997, Rice could give Fox Mulder lessons in paranoia.

On March 12, 1971, however, Rice was just delirious with joy over the prospect of *The Kolchak Papers* being made into a TV movie.

ABC assigned a producer, Everett Chambers, to the Kolchak project. Rice, still ready to keep his acting career alive, asked for a chance to audition for the role of Los Angeles Police Department pathologist Dr. Mohandas Mokurji (a nod to Hollywood's "coroner to the stars," Thomas T. Noguchi, the Los Angeles County Chief Medical Examiner whose cases included Marilyn Monroe, Sharon Tate, Janis Joplin, Robert F. Kennedy, William Holden and John Belushi). Chambers seemed pleased with Rice's reading and makeup shots for the East Indian pathologist. He was assured that the role was his.

"Now," Rice says, "I was convinced that my careers as an actor and writer were really starting to gather steam. I'd done a lot of stage work, on and off, through the years, and even a few walk-ons in some films. But now, I was to play a sizable role in a film made from my first novel."

Chambers, though, withdrew from the project to produce first-season episodes of a series starring his friend Peter Falk. Chambers was also with *Columbo* during the acclaimed mystery's fourth, fifth and sixth seasons.

Yet when Chambers was still in charge, Rice left Los Angeles for some location scouting in Las Vegas, confident that he'd soon be playing Mokurji.

## Richard Matheson

### *He Is Legend*

Richard Matheson is the second of the four crucial artistic links that take Kolchak to the night of January 11, 1972, and the writer came to the project with a list of fantasy and television credits that stretched from Los Angeles to Pluto.

Born in Allendale, New Jersey, on February 20, 1926, Richard Burton Matheson grew up in Brooklyn. After combat duty in Germany during World War II, he majored in journalism at the University of Missouri. In the summer of 1950, Matheson sold his first short story, "Born of Man and Woman," to *The Magazine of Fantasy and Science Fiction.*

"I grew up reading the classic fairy tales and all the fantasy I could get my hands on," he recalls. "Later, in my teen years, I read Arthur Machen and Ambrose Bierce. I always liked fantasy. I was never into science fiction. I never read science fiction. I didn't even know what science fiction was until I sold my first story and they told me it was science fiction. And I was never really drawn to horror. I never read Lovecraft. I was never drawn to that dark stuff. How I got into it, I don't know. I think it was just that when I started writing, there was this huge batch of magazines beginning. They wanted horror and science fiction, so I started doing them."

In 1956, Matheson packed up his growing reputation and moved to Los Angeles, where he quickly became part of a circle of writers whose specialties were horror and fantasy. Charles Beaumont, Ray Bradbury and William F. Nolan became three of his closest friends. With Bradbury as their elder statesman, these writers defined the fantasy territory that Rod Serling would call *The Twilight Zone.* It seemed only natural that Matheson and Beaumont would be the first two writers recruited by Serling for his classic fantasy anthology.

During the series' five CBS seasons, Matheson would write fourteen episodes, including such *Twilight Zone* favorites as "The Invaders," with Agnes Moorehead as a woman whose lonely farmhouse is invaded by little creatures from another planet, and "Nightmare at 20,000 Feet," starring William Shatner as a terrified flier who can't convince anyone that there is a gremlin on the plane's wing. Reworked for *Twilight Zone: The Movie,* with John Lithgow replacing Shatner as the nervous passenger, this story has become so much a part of pop-culture mythology that Lithgow could spoof it in an airplane scene on his hit NBC comedy, *Third Rock From the Sun.* Two more Matheson gems, "Disappearing Act" (retitled "And When the Sky Opened") and "Third From the Sun," were adapted by Serling for the "land of both shadow and substance."

Other *Twilight Zone* episodes written by Matheson include "A World of Difference," starring Howard Duff as a businessman with an identity crisis; "A World of His Own," with Keenan Wynn (later a guest star in two episodes of *Kolchak: The Night Stalker*) as a writer who can talk characters into flesh-and-blood existence; "Nick of Time," with Shatner as a superstitious newlywed obsessed with a fortune-telling machine; "Little Girl Lost," about parents searching for their daughter, who has slipped into another dimension; "Steel," starring Lee Marvin as the manager of a robot boxer; and "Night Call," with Gladys Cooper as an elderly woman getting a *long* long distance telephone call.

"Other writers were eventually brought in," Matheson says, "but there was a time, in the early going, when Rod, Charles Beaumont and I were writing almost all of the episodes. And Rod, more than anybody, was really working himself to death. It was a busy, wonderful time."

Very busy. During his *Twilight Zone* tenure, Matheson teamed up with actor Vincent Price and director-producer Roger Corman for a series of films loosely based on Edgar Allan Poe short stories: *Fall of the House of Usher* (1960), *The Pit and the Pendulum* (1961), *Tales of Terror* (1962) and *The Raven* (1963). In this same stretch, he wrote two other screenplays for Price, *Master of the World* (1961) and *The Comedy of Terrors* (a 1964 romp that also starred Boris Karloff, Peter Lorre and Basil Rathbone).

After *The Twilight Zone*, Matheson, like his close friend Robert Bloch, wrote one of the earliest episodes of *Star Trek*. A showcase for Shatner, who had starred in two of the writer's *Zone* stories, "The Enemy Within" told of a transporter malfunction that split Captain Kirk into two beings — one good, one evil. Airing October 6, 1966, the fifth *Star Trek* episode was Matheson's only excursion on the starship Enterprise.

Having used these television gigs to visit "a wondrous land whose boundaries are that of imagination" and "the final frontier," Matheson established himself as a master of the TV movie. During a three-year span, his name appeared on three of the most acclaimed TV movies of all time — *Duel* (1971), which put director Steven Spielberg on the Hollywood map, *The Night Stalker* (1972), which we'll get to in a moment, and *The Morning After* (1974), a shattering study of alcoholism starring Dick Van Dyke.

"I've had more satisfaction by far from the television film," Matheson says. "I'd rather write features because you don't have to worry about commercials and they pay a heck of a lot more. But I've just had more creative satisfaction from television films."

Other television credits include a miniseries version of pal Ray Bradbury's *The Martian Chronicles* and *The Dreamer of Oz*, a 1990 TV based on the life of L. Frank Baum.

Even if Matheson had never written a film or television script, of course, he'd still be considered a legend in the fantasy field. Matheson, Bradbury, Bloch, Jack Finney and a few others redirected fantasy and horror fiction throughout the '50s, blasting the way for such later best-selling authors as Stephen King, Peter Straub, Clive Barker, Dean R. Koontz and Robert R. McCammon. King has often acknowledged his debt to Matheson. During a 1992 interview, Bloch told me, "There is little that can be said about the mechanics of the business (writing). But I'd say that Richard Matheson is a wonderful role model. . . I'd tell anyone wanting to be a writer to read Richard Matheson."

The Matheson short stories have been published in six collections: *Born of Man and Woman* (1954, later reprinted as *Third From the Sun*), *The Shores of Space* (1957), *Alone By Night* (1961), *Shock!* (1961), *Shock! II* (1964) and *Shock! III* (1966). He is also the author of more than twelve novels, several of which have been turned into films. The most famous of these are: *I Am Legend* (1954), made first as *The Last Man on Earth* (1964), with Vincent Price, then as *The Omega Man* (1971), with Charlton Heston; *The Shrinking Man* (1956), filmed by director Jack Arnold as *The Incredible Shrinking Man* (1957), starring Grant Williams; *Hell House* (1971) as *The Legend of Hell House* (1973); and *Bid Time Return* (1975) as *Somewhere in Time* (1980), starring Christopher Reeve and Jane Seymour. Other noteworthy Matheson novels are *The Beardless Warriors, A Stir of Echoes, Ride the Nightmare* and *What Dreams May Come*. His 1984 World Fantasy Lifetime Achievement Award was entirely inevitable.

You can imagine that such a writer might be hard to impress. But when Richard Matheson read Jeff Rice's novel, he was very impressed.

"It was quite a complete novel," Matheson said. "Don't make any mistake about that. The story was all there, the structure was there, and that's what got everybody excited. It was sort of a cinema verite vampire story. It seemed so realistic. You're reading this story, and it sounds like something that really happened. That's what makes it so remarkable, and that feel did come from the book. If you watch the movie and read the book, you see that all the basic story steps are in the novel."

But Matheson did see the need to make a few alterations. In *The Kolchak Papers* (later revised and printed in 1973 by Pocket Books as *The Night Stalker*), Carl — given name Karel — Kolchak says that he grew up hearing vampire legends from his Rumanian grandfather, Anton, a cabinetmaker with an endless supply of folk tales. Curiously enough, somewhere along the line, Darren McGavin decided that Kolchak was a Polish name and made references to this switched heritage in interviews and episodes of the series. Anton, of course, could have been the grandfather on his mother's side, making Carl half-Polish, half-Rumanian, yet Rice rules this out as a possibility. According to Carl's creator, the paternal grandfather is Anton Mihail Kolchak (nicknamed Mike). Genealogical debates aside, Matheson was bothered by Kolchak's predisposition to legends and superstitions.

"Kolchak was a big, heavy Rumanian who already believes in vampires, or comes to accept the vampire very fast, which I didn't think was going to work at all," Matheson explains. "If he starts out like that, where do you have to go? Jeff Rice made him a smart-ass reporter, so I made him more of a smart-ass reporter who finally has to believe it. The other major change I made was to pick up on the *Front Page* humor in the book and emphasize it even more. The realistic approach and the smart-alecky sense of humor are what give the story an edge, so I decided to play it more like *The Front Page*."

Rice's disappointment over not getting the chance to adapt his novel did not in any way diminish his appreciation of Matheson's screenplay.

"Well, basically, I wrote my novel because I had some things I wanted to say about Las Vegas and I also wanted to write a vampire story in a modern setting," Rice responds when asked about the differences between his book and Matheson's script. "Matheson, on the other hand, was writing on assignment, with no particularly personal point of view, and working with someone else's concept fully fleshed out as a novel rather than working with a synopsis-form 'story,' or springboard, or (as is so popular today) a 'high concept' consisting of one sentence.

"Matheson was writing to fill a time slot, so things had to be tightened a bit; many of my more pithy observations on Las Vegas and the whole milieu had to be eliminated or toned down; and few characters, like FBI Agent Bernie Fain and Lieutenant Jenks of the Clark County Sheriff's Office, combined [as they were into the film's FBI Agent Bernie Jenks].

"Still, he managed to keep a good deal of the flavor of my approach and much of the style of my own work intact, and in so doing got in a few shots at the 'Don't let the public know, it's bad for business' attitude of the authorities that was so much a part of Las Vegas at that time. . . In keeping with the story I had written, he also contributed some excellent dialogue almost wholly original with him."

So Matheson was very pleased with Rice's novel, although he had a few nits to pick, and Rice was very pleased with Matheson's screenplay, although he, too, picked a nit here and there. "I think Matheson did a fine job and, in the main, realized at least seventy-five percent of my novel," Rice concludes. "I have no complaint in regard to his scripting at all."

With Matheson working on the adaptation, ABC's next step was to choose a producer. Looking over the network ranks in 1971, the selection must have seemed obvious.

Dan Curtis had made his mark as the producer and creator of ABC's supernatural soap opera, *Dark Shadows*, the daytime serial that turned vampire Barnabas Collins into a matinee idol. But Matheson, who already was at work adapting Rice's novel, was far from pleased when told that Curtis would be producing.

"I didn't know that Curtis was going to do it," Matheson states. "I had an antipathy towards Curtis from the beginning because when my war novel, *The Beardless Warriors*, came out, someone made a blind bid of $10,000 for the movie rights, which I turned down in a rage. It was ridiculously low. Then I found out it was Curtis. So when I first met him at ABC, I was very cold to him. I didn't realize at the time that I was risking my life. He had such a temper that he could have leaped across the room and torn my throat out. And he might have, if he hadn't respected my work so much. That was my main in with him, although we did share a bizarre sense of humor. He just respected my work so much, he decided he wouldn't kill me."

## Dan Curtis

### From Soap to Stalker

*The Night Stalker* was a vampire drama that aired in prime time, where it belonged. Vampires, after all, aren't supposed to like sunshine, yet, for five years (1966-71), Barnabas Collins and company chilled viewers with their daytime supernatural soap opera, *Dark Shadows*. This rather incredible experiment put Dan Curtis on the map as a producer and a master of the macabre, but there was little in his past to suggest such a creepy turn of careers.

Born on August 12, 1928, in Bridgeport, Connecticut, Curtis got his start in show business as a sales executive with NBC and MCA. By 1966, he had set up Dan Curtis Productions and was best known as the producer of *The CBS Golf Classic*. At the age of thirty-seven, Curtis hadn't put one foot in the horror field. Horror wasn't even part of the original *Dark Shadows* mix.

Unless you count the ratings, there was nothing particularly horrific about *Dark Shadows* during the first ten months of its afternoon existence. The series was heading nowhere except for cancellation. Curtis had sold ABC on his idea for a gothic soap opera, but viewers weren't flocking to the fictional town of Collinsport, Maine. The serial began on June 27, 1966, with Victoria Winters (Alexandra Moltke) arriving at Collinwood mansion to assume her duties as governess to young David Collins (David Henesy). By far the biggest name in the cast was Joan Bennett, a studio-system star whose leading men had included Spencer Tracy (*Father of the Bride*), Humphrey Bogart (*We're No Angels*), Bing Crosby (*Mississippi*), Edward G. Robinson (*The Woman in the Window*), Cary Grant (*Big Brown Eyes*), Ronald Colman (*Bulldog Drummond)* and Douglas Fairbanks Jr. *(Green Hell)*. Not even this splash of Hollywood glamour was helping *Dark Shadows*, which was languishing under the long, dark shadows of cancellation.

Curtis credits his children with hitting on the idea of spiking his gothic brew with some supernatural flavoring. "There was nothing supernatural in it," he says. "When it was going down the tubes, my kids said to make it scary. I said, 'Why not? I've got nothing to lose.' So I put a ghost on, and when the ghost appeared, the ratings jumped. And that's when I started experimenting."

In April 1967, Willie Loomis (John Karlen) opened the chained coffin of a 175-year-old vampire named Barnabas Collins (played by Shakespearean actor Jonathan Frid).

"Barnabas was brought in because I wanted to see exactly how much I could get away with, never intending that he would be anything more than a vampire that I would drive a stake into," Curtis recalls. "I wanted to see how far I could go on the show into the supernatural, and I figured there was nothing more bizarre than a vampire."

Barnabas was out of his coffin, and *Dark Shadows* was on its way to becoming a cult hit and a pop-culture phenomenon.

"Who knew?" its creator and executive producer muses. "I brought the vampire in and it suddenly became this gigantic hit. Then I thought, 'Now what am I going to do?' I couldn't kill him off, so that's when I turned him into the reluctant vampire. It really caught the imagination of the audience. *Dark Shadows* came from my mind as the way I remembered classic horror films that were around when I was a kid, even though they weren't that way. That was my memory of them. It was that same haunting quality we were after."

And the viewers responded. The merchandising explosion included *Dark Shadows* bubblegum cards, comic books, board games and posters. There were Viewmaster reels, a syndicated comic strip for newspapers, a hit soundtrack album and a series of thirty-two paperback novels. At the age of forty-four, Frid was receiving about 6,000 fan letters a week.

"The irony is that I'm not a horror fan," says Frid, who had studied at London's Royal Academy of Dramatic Arts and earned a master's in directing from the Yale School of Drama. "I remember seeing Bela Lugosi in *Dracula* when I was very young, but I graduated very quickly to Cary Grant pictures and had no more interest in horror."

Frid decided it would be best to approach an unrealistic role in a realistic manner. "I know I had a good approach to the character," he says. "I tried to make him a perfectly sensible person. I never played a vampire. I played him as man with a hell of a conflict. But I never could perfect what I wanted to do, and that stiffness just fed Barnabas because he was so uptight."

Bennett was a star. Frid and Grayson Hall, who played Dr. Julia Hoffman, were established stage performers. And Thayer David, who played Professor Stokes, was in demand as a character actor (his fantasy credits included the 1959 version of Jules Verne's *Journey to the Center of the Earth*). But most of the soap's regulars were young performers getting their first taste of television.

"I looked at *Dark Shadows* as the first rung of a giant ladder," says Lara Parker, the future *Kolchak* guest star who played Angélique as a witch and a vampire on the ABC soap opera. "Now I look back on it as the most fun I ever had in this business. It was my first professional job. There were beautiful costumes and terrific plots. There was always a group of fans recognizing you at the skating rink, in the subway, at a ballgame. My acting seems terrible to me today. I cringe. There are some good moments, though. But we were learning. As the show went on, I got better."

For Kathryn Leigh Scott, who played Maggie Evans in the first episode and continued with the series until September 1970, *Dark Shadows* was "a baptism by fire."

"For a lot of us, it represented our first work," she says. "I was nineteen years old, it was my first job. . . I was so young that I didn't know enough to feel the pressure."

It helped, Scott says, that the cast was "a close group. We'd meet for drinks after the show. Thayer David called us a repertory company, and that's exactly what we were. We all enjoyed working with each other."

"You had to be a good team player," John Karlen says. "I think that notion of being a good player helped me on *Cagney & Lacey*" (where he won an Emmy for his portrayal of Harvey Lacey).

With the success of Barnabas as a character, Curtis opened the supernatural gates with a vengeance. He and producer Robert Costello introduced a warlock (Humbert Allen Astredo as Nicholas Blair), a man-made monster (Robert Rodan), witches, werevolves and ghosts. Lightning struck again for Curtis when he cast David Selby as the silent spirit of Quentin Collins. Decked out in his muttonchop sideburns, Selby (later in the prime-time soaps *Flamingo Road* and *Falcon Crest*) played poor Quentin as a ghost, a zombie, a werewolf and in a *Picture of Dorian Gray* phase.

Dan Curtis

Jonathan Frid as Barnabas Collins, the "reluctant vampire", in *Dark Shadows.*

"I hadn't been in New York too long before the offer to do *Dark Shadows* came along," Selby remembers. "That was the first television I'd ever done, and the character didn't even speak for a while. That built up a sort of mystique about him. The character had a lot going for it. I was lucky to hit a show with longevity and popularity."

Helping the spooky proceedings along were the eerie compositions of musical director Bob Cobert. His "Quentin's Theme" remains one of the biggest selling singles to come out of daytime television. "I had done one horror show before — *Way Out* (CBS, 1961) for David Susskind," Cobert says. *"Dark Shadows* was very easy to do. Dan had a good ear and he's very direct. You always know where you stand with Dan." It was the beginning of a long association between Curtis and Cobert, an association that would encompass *The Night Stalker.*

**Musical director and composer Bob Cobert and producer Dan Curtis.**

The writing team was headed by Art Wallace, Gordon Russell and Sam Hall. "Dan can come off strong and tough," Hall says, "but I think he's a complete romantic at heart. he's certainly a very exciting man to work with."

While the show was taped, the cameras very rarely stopped rolling.

"That's why it had a spontaneous feel to it," Parker notes. "Sometimes we had to tape without even a dress rehearsal. It had an edge to it. It was easy to deal with the fear because we believed it would go out once and never be seen again. I can remember actually stopping only two times in five years."

Taping soaps "in those days was akin to being live because it was difficult and expensive to edit," says Jerry Lacy, who played lawyer Tony Peterson and two different Reverend Trasks. "So you only stopped for a real disaster. That's why so many goofs got on the air."

"I have a lot of good memories," Selby says of taping *Dark Shadows* episodes. "You talk about learning on your feet. You taped an episode once through, and if you made a mistake, you just kept going."

"It was live on tape was what the hell it was," Curtis says. "There was no turning back. You taped for a half-hour and all the music and all the commercials were in. You talk about excitement. You talk about getting your heart going early in the morning."

Despite the goofs, *Dark Shadows* has attracted such fans as Tim Burton, Bruce Springsteen, Stephen King, Joe Dante, Whoopi Goldberg, Madonna and Quentin Tarantino.

As *Dark Shadows* ran out of steam, Curtis and the writers were reworking everything from *Rebecca* and *Wuthering Heights* to *Dr. Jekyll and Mr. Hyde*. "I wanted to say good-bye to it so bad I couldn't see straight," Curtis reflects. "We got around to the last year and I was completely tapped out ideawise. And we ended up with some dreadful stories during that last year. It was like being in jail. At the end, I was barely associating with it. I just couldn't deal with it anymore. I was so glad when they finally put me out of my misery and got me the hell out of there. I couldn't have gone on any longer."

It all came to an end after 1,225 episodes on April 2, 1971. Some of the regulars moved into prime time: Karlen, Selby, Kate Jackson (*Charlie's Angels*, *Scarecrow and Mrs. King*) and Roger Davis (*Alias Smith & Jones*). Others stayed in daytime (Louis Edmonds who portrayed Roger Collins, spent many years on *All My Children*). Others starred on Broadway: Jerry Lacy as Humphrey Bogart in Woody Allen's *Play It Again, Sam*, Donna McKechnie in *A Chorus Line*.

Before *Dark Shadows* finished its ABC run, however, Curtis solidified his standing as a merchant of menace with three horror projects.

The first of these was *The Strange Case of Dr. Jekyll and Mr. Hyde* (1968). Many problems and delays plagued this television version of Robert Louis Stevenson's much-filmed classic. Rod Serling was supposed to write the adaptation and Jason Robards was first announced as the star. Agreements fell apart. Serling and Robards dropped out. London shooting schedules were scrapped. Using music composed, conducted and arranged by Cobert (later re-recorded for *Dark Shadows*), Curtis forged ahead as producer of this ambitious project. Although recovering from a broken left shoulder, Jack Palance delivered a towering performance — sympathetic as the English Jekyll and diabolical as the evil Hyde. Charles Jarrett directed. Ian McLellan Hunter wrote the script. Dick Smith provided the fifteen makeup transformations. Curtis started production in New York, but a technicians strike forced him to abandon already-constructed sets and move the drama to Toronto. Despite the troubles, the dramatization emerged to ecstatic reviews. "It was incredibly gratifying," Curtis recalls. "The reviews on that thing were absolutely incredible." Many still consider it the finest of the many adaptations of the disturbing Stevenson tale (no small compliment since Palance is in competition with such actors as John Barrymore, Fredric March, Spencer Tracy, Christopher Lee, Anthony Andrews, Michael Caine and John Malkovich). Curtis also assembled a strong supporting cast: Billie Whitelaw, Denholm Elliott, Leo Genn and Oscar Homolka. Shot on videotape, this translation was not repeated as often as it deserved, so many horror fans aren't aware of its existence. Fortunately, like much of the Dan Curtis Collection, it's available through MPI Home Video.

Two years after *The Strange Case of Dr. Jekyll and Mr. Hyde,* Curtis made his debut as a director with *House of Dark Shadows* (1970), a fine big-screen version of his ABC soap opera. Filmed in Tarrytown, New York, while the daytime serial continued taping in the city, the movie featured most of the series' major stars repeating their TV roles: Jonathan Frid, Kathryn Leigh Scott, Grayson Hall, Joan Bennett, John Karlen, Roger Davis, Thayer David, Louis Edmonds, Nancy Barrett, Don Briscoe and David Henesy. Written by Sam Hall and Gordon Russell, the MGM release incorporated many of the basic plot elements from the soap (although

Producer Dan Curtis on the Paramount Studios backlot.

significant differences included the turning of Barrett's character into a vampire). "I looked at the feature film we made and thought it held up amazingly well," Curtis says. "It wasn't done like the soap. It was done like a very classy piece of film. It was the same premise, except we killed everybody, which you couldn't do on the show."

With the ABC serial about to end its days, Curtis directed and produced a second *Dark Shadows* feature film, *Night of Dark Shadows*. This 1971 release — without Frid and Bennett — was not so warmly received. In his *TV Movies* book, Leonard Maltin clobbers the movie (which suffered heavily from excessive editing mandated by the studio) with his lowest possible rating. The lackluster outing focuses on David Selby's Quentin character. Lara Parker and Kate Jackson co-star. Hall, Karlen and Barrett are back from the first film, but as different characters.

Still, the Curtis reputation had been established, and the next five years would be packed with triumphs in the horror field – including *The Night Stalker*.

"People don't realize that it's far more difficult to do a horror picture well than a straight drama," Curtis says. "That's why most supernatural pictures stink. It attracts a lot of people who have no talent and don't know what the hell they're doing. Now, I'm telling you from experience. I know that the supernatural pictures I made were really good because I knew what the hell I was doing. It was very, very difficult. Anybody can make a gory, slasher type of horror. That's easy, and it's not really horror. Those things are abominations as far as I'm concerned.

"*Dark Shadows* was never a gory, slasher type of horror. Anybody can make a horror movie if you don't have to end it or make it clever. It's an enormously tough thing to do right, and that's why you see really terrible things all the time. I got into the field because I love it. This sprang from a deep childhood fascination with the genre."

*Dark Shadows* went off the air on April 2, 1971. A few weeks later, Curtis, who was in upstate New York shooting *Night of Dark Shadows,* was chosen to replace Everett Chambers as the producer of *The Kolchak Papers*. The call came from Barry Diller of ABC.

"I almost didn't do it," Curtis says. "You know what I did? I told him I was a great big movie director now, so I wasn't interested in doing television. Can you believe it? But Barry says to just sit tight. He wants to send me the story. That did it. . . What a great story – so traditional yet so modern. And it had a sense of humor. It was a great premise waiting to be made into a great movie."

Another reason also convinced Curtis to sign on as producer. "Barry told me he had Dick Matheson working on the script," he says. "I thought Matheson was a bloody genius. I always wanted to work with him. So how could you not be sold by the combination of Jeff Rice's story and a screenplay by Dick Matheson?"

Although an ABC Circle Film, *The Kolchak Papers* was about to become a Dan Curtis Production. That meant key members of the team would be "Curtis" people. Cobert was asked to compose the score and *Night of Dark Shadows* veteran Robert Singer was brought in as an assistant to the producer. Curtis would have liked the director's chair, but, when he took over production, John Llewellyn Moxey already had been given the assignment. Fortunately for all, Moxey was a sweet-tempered Englishman who believed in running a happy set. And Curtis was not about to undermine Moxey's authority. "I guess they thought about me because of *Dark Shadows*," says the producer. "I guess that made sense. But they were lucky that the project ended up in the hands of people who understood the horror field. And that's not easy to find. And I don't mean just me. Remember, we had Matheson and Moxey working on that."

The only piece of the puzzle missing was an actor to play Carl Kolchak.

# Darren McGavin

## *A Star Is Cast*

On August 11, 1971, Jeff Rice came face to face with Carl Kolchak at the Universal Studios commissary. Exactly five months before *The Night Stalker* hit the air (and about two weeks before filming started in Las Vegas), Kolchak's creator was getting his first peek at the actor chosen to be the flesh and blood embodiment of the rumpled reporter.

As lunch progressed, Rice discussed a few central story elements with Darren McGavin and his wife of less than two years, Kathie Browne. At McGavin's request, Rice supplied a copy of the novel so the actor "could pick out some fine points for his characterization."

Carrying twenty-five years packed with Broadway, film and television credits, McGavin was forty-nine years old, but looked younger.

"I particularly admired the work he did as private detective David Ross in the two telefilms and the series, *The Outsider*, as he came to personify the hard-bitten, somewhat Chandleresque type who, far from being physically invincible, took more than his share of lumps as he persisted in a dogged pursuit of the truth," Rice says of the sentiment he took into the commissary meeting. "His being given the role of Kolchak was an inspired bit of casting."

It is a sentiment that has been echoed by fans for twenty-five years.

Born May 7, 1922, in Spokane, Washington, Darren McGavin attended high school near San Francisco before entering the College of the Pacific. Attracted to theater productions, he decided to become a scenic designer. That career choice went by the wayside when he auditioned for a small role in *A Song to Remember*, director Charles Vidor's 1945 film biography of Chopin (played by Cornel Wilde). McGavin won the part and a new profession. The inauspicious debut was followed by another half-dozen small roles in movies, including *Fear* (1946), director Alfred Zeisler's low-budget remake of *Crime and Punishment*. Rather than stay on what Fred Allen might have called a "treadmill to oblivion," McGavin decided it was time to learn the fundamentals of his chosen profession. Heading for New York City, he enrolled in Sanford Meisner's Neighborhood Playhouse, then studied his craft at Lee Strasberg's Actors' Studio. Working with two of the most respected acting teachers in America poised McGavin to make his mark during the Golden Age of live television drama. During the early '50s, he appeared in more than a hundred live dramas produced in Manhattan. Starting in 1952, McGavin's name appeared on most of the leading anthology series: *Studio One, Philco Playhouse, The U.S. Steel Hour, Kraft Theater, Robert Montgomery Presents, Armstrong Circle Theatre, Suspense, Goodyear Playhouse, Tales of Tomorrow* and *The Alcoa Hour.* An eighteen-month tour with the national company of Arthur Miller's *Death of a Salesman* was followed by such Broadway plays as *My Three Angels* (with Walter Slezak and Jerome Cowan), *The Rainmaker* (with Geraldine Page), *The Innkeeper* (again with Page) and *The Lovers.*

Armed with training, experience and impressive credits, McGavin renewed his assault on the movie industry in the mid-'50s. There were bigger roles and steady work: director David Lean's *Summertime* (1955), director Otto Preminger's *The Court-Martial of Billy Mitchell* (1955), Preminger's *The Man With the Golden Arm* (1955), *The Delicate Delinquent* (playing straight man to Jerry Lewis in 1957), *Beau James* (the 1957 film biography with Bob Hope as New York Mayor Jimmy Walker), *The Case Against Brooklyn* (1958), Disney's *Summer Magic* (1963), *Bullet for a Badman* (1964), *The Great Sioux Massacre* (1965) and *Mrs. Polifax — Spy* (1970).

But it was television that continued to throw the steadiest work at McGavin. Over the fifteen-year span that preceded his commissary meeting with Rice, the actor was a featured guest star in episodes of *Gunsmoke, Death Valley Days, Alfred Hitchcock Presents, Route 66, The Defenders, Dr. Kildare, Rawhide, The Virginian, Ben Casey, The Rogues, Felony Squad, Cimarron Strip, The Name of the Game, The Man from U.N.C.L.E., Mission: Impossible, Mannix, Bracken's World, Matt Lincoln* and *Love, American Style.* He also had starred in four series: *Crime Photographer* (a live 1951-52 CBS newspaper drama based on George Harmon Coxe's novels about Casey of *The Morning Express*), *Mickey Spillane's Mike Hammer* (1957-59, seventy-eight episodes for syndication), *Riverboat* (NBC, 1959-61) and *The Outsider* (NBC, 1968-69).

"I really learned the business doing *Mickey Spillane*," McGavin says. "Do you know why? We were doing half-hour shows in two days — seventy-eight shows in two years. It was a pressure I enjoyed."

In the late '60s, McGavin jumped into the TV movie form with *The Challengers* (1969), a drama about Grand Prix racing drivers. The offers kept coming. He would star in more than fifteen TV movies during the next ten years. There were three in 1970 — *The Challenge, Berlin Affair* and, most significantly, the Emmy-winning *Tribes.* McGavin received rave reviews for his portrayal of a tough Marine drill instructor faced with a nonconformist recruit (Jan-Michael Vincent).

"I was the king of the TV movies," McGavin announces with a grand sweep of his right hand. "*TV Guide* wrote an article about me being the king of the TV movies, at which point I didn't work for a year. If you get recognition and acclamation like that, everybody says, 'Well, I'm not going to hire the sonafabitch for this.' "

But that was the mid-'70s. Getting TV movies wasn't a problem for the actor in 1971. In fact, when he agreed to meet with Rice, McGavin had just finished work on *The Death of Me Yet*, a fine TV movie that would air October 26, 1971. The director was John Llewellyn Moxey.

So, it would be an exercise in something far beyond understatement to say that McGavin was no newcomer to television. The instincts sharpened by about twenty years in the medium kicked into high gear when he first heard about a project called *The Kolchak Papers.*

"My representatives called to say that ABC had purchased the rights to a book called *The Kolchak Papers*." McGavin recalls. "They were into a kind of first draft of a script by Richard Matheson, and they called the agency to ask them if I'd be interested in doing it. My representative read it and called me."

Far from enthusiastic about the project, the agency felt obliged to run the offer past McGavin.

"Listen," the actor's representative told him by telephone, "there's this crazy story about a reporter and some kind of monster in Las Vegas. You don't want to do this."

"Well," McGavin replied, "send it over."

McGavin, like Matheson and Curtis before him, was intrigued by the story. He showed it to his wife. "You're right," Kathie Browne told him. "It's terrific."

That's all McGavin needed to hear. He was back on the phone with his representative: "I think it's wonderful. It's terrific. It's suspenseful and very scary. I'm very interested. Yes, I want to do it. What are the particulars involved? Who's going to produce it?"

"The guy who does *Dark Shadows* in New York," he was told.

"What's that?" McGavin asked.

"You know, it's a soap opera."

"I don't watch soap operas," McGavin said.

"Well, he's coming out to Los Angeles next week, so perhaps you can meet with him and see if it will work out."

Producer Kathie Browne on the set of her film "Zero to Sixty"
starring her husband, Darren McGavin.

The meeting was arranged. This was the crucial moment. ABC knew that McGavin was the ideal actor to play Kolchak. And the network knew that Dan Curtis was the ideal producer for *The Kolchak Papers*. But would they hit it off?

This is how McGavin remembers the meeting: "Dan Curtis was a very eager fellow who wanted to do a good job. I liked his energy and his enthusiasm for the project. It was tough not to be impressed by his energy."

"The minute I saw him," Curtis says, "I knew he was the only actor to play Carl Kolchak. Darren McGavin was a big reason that *The Night Stalker* worked so well. Nobody can deny that. And nobody should have been surprised by that. He was one of the most underrated actors in show business."

And it didn't hurt McGavin's enthusiasm level when he learned that the director would be that "lovely English fellow," John Llewellyn Moxey.

Yet, despite his confidence in Curtis, Moxey, Rice and Matheson, McGavin was going to take a firm hand in the shaping of Carl Kolchak. He would start with the wardrobe.

"In the first draft of the script," McGavin explains, "Kolchak was wearing Bermuda shorts, socks and brown shoes, a Hawaiian shirt and a golf cap. Apparently, somebody thought that was the uniform for a newspaperman in Las Vegas. But there was a line in there about him wanting to get back to New York, so I got this image of a New York newspaperman who had been fired in the summer of 1962 when he was wearing a seersucker suit, his straw hat, button-down Brooks Brothers shirt and reporter's tie, and he hasn't bought any clothes since. Well, I knew that was the summer uniform of reporters in New York of that time, so that's how the wardrobe came about. I added the white tennis shoes, and that was Kolchak. It might have been totally at odds with what everybody else was wearing in Las Vegas, but he hasn't bought any clothes since then. You need goals for character, and Kolchak's goal is to get back to the big time. He always wanted to get back to New York and work on the *Daily News*."

Although chosen for motivational reasons, Kolchak's suit, hat and sneakers became a rumpled trademark every bit as distinctive and quirky as Columbo's raincoat. Like Peter Falk's equally wrinkled (and persistent) hero, Kolchak rarely was "out of uniform."

While working on Kolchak's wardrobe, McGavin also was assembling a basic character sketch of the Las Vegas reporter: "Never married. He graduated from college, went to work for a newspaper and eventually landed on the police beat. He's got a big mouth that always gets him into trouble. He clamors to get his stories printed."

Nothing in that description contradicts the biographical material provided by Rice in his books. According to Rice, Karel Kolchak was born in 1922 (the same year as McGavin). During World War II, he saw two years of combat ("most of it behind a typewriter") in Europe. He left the service with a trick knee that kept him out of the Korean War. In 1948, he graduated near the bottom of his class with a bachelor's degree in journalism from Columbia University. His first job was as copy boy at the *Boston Globe*. He loves beer, spaghetti and Scotch. In 1970, he had spent seven of his forty-seven years at the *Las Vegas Daily News*.

Still, there are significant differences between McGavin's Kolchak and Rice's Kolchak. In Rice's book, Kolchak is a paunchy, foul-mouthed slob who drinks too much. Kolchak himself says he resembles a "boozy ex-prizefighter." McGavin's Kolchak is just as aggressive but less crude and, perhaps due to network sanitation practices, never profane. Rice's Kolchak took adult-education courses, and it's difficult to imagine McGavin's Kolchak sitting in a college classroom. Rice's Kolchak smokes cigars, a practice apparently never cultivated by McGavin's Kolchak. Rice's

Kolchak wears chinos and a bush jacket, and, well, we know what McGavin's Kolchak wears.

It is, of course, entirely natural for an actor to make a character his own. Whatever the differences, Rice had no complaints.

"Basically, he was perfect," Rice says of McGavin's portrayal. "He didn't have the face of the Kolchak I imagined, but he so quickly merged himself with the character, bringing his own personality to Kolchak's similar one, that he very quickly *became* Kolchak.

"To create Kolchak for the novel, I'd started with what I imagined I'd look like ten-to-twenty years older and having no beard, only a mustache, and being McGavin's size; having lived a somewhat disappointing, frustrating life of hard-drinking and constant fighting with editors. So I made Kolchak look like me, though, perhaps, a bit taller. But just watching McGavin work. . . was seeing my creation come to life, in the flesh.

"In point of fact, when it looked like a film would actually be made of my novel, I called his agent and alerted him to the fact that it was being scripted and the role would be perfect for McGavin. The rest, they say, is history."

Rice goes right to the heart of the characterization when he talks about the merging process and McGavin "bringing his own personality to Kolchak's similar one." Cigars, alcoholic intake and bush jackets are the merest trifles compared to the greater character traits that McGavin and Rice see in Carl Kolchak. Since the actor and the character merged so quickly and effortlessly, the obvious conclusion is that Darren McGavin and Carl Kolchak are very close to being the same person. It's a conclusion that McGavin does not dismiss.

"Well, when you're working that fast in television." he says, "you have to draw on yourself. You use who you are to a greater extent than you would in a play or a film."

Kathie Browne McGavin, the one person who should know, has a stronger and far more direct response. "He's very, very close to Kolchak," she says. "The people who really love *The Night Stalker* love Kolchak because he never gives up. He's fighting, always fighting. You can take the monsters and take them to be anything you want — the government, big business, corrupt officials. Their hero comes at the end, beaten up but ready to go on fighting another day. I think Darren has a lot of that in his own personality."

"Think about someone else in that part," Matheson says. "Go ahead. Try to think of someone else from that time playing Carl Kolchak. I'm not saying it couldn't have happened. I'm just saying we were enormously lucky to get Darren McGavin."

Rice's story. Matheson's script. Curtis in charge of the production team. And McGavin's portrayal of Carl Kolchak. The stage was set for the night of January 11, 1972.

*"The 'Red Death' had long devastated the country. No pestilence had ever been so fatal, so hideous. Blood was its Avatar and its seal. . . And now was acknowledged the presence of the Red Death. He had come like a thief in the night. And one by one dropped the revellers. . . "*

**— "The Masque of the Red Death"**
**By Edgar Allan Poe**

# The Night Stalker

## Original airdate: January 11, 1972

Teleplay by Richard Matheson
Based on the novel by Jeff Rice

Produced by Dan Curtis
Directed by John Llewellyn Moxey
Music by Robert Cobert
Director of photography: Michael Hugo
Art director: Trevor Williams

Film editor: Desmond Marquette, a.c.e.
Assistant editor: Mike Crumplar
Sound effects: Metromedia Producers Corp.
Production manager: Neil T. Maffeo
Assistant director: Christopher H. Seitz
Assistant to the producer: Robert Singer

Chrysler vehicles provided by Chrysler Corp.
Filmed on location in Las Vegas and at Samuel Goldwyn Studios
Copyright © 1971 by the American Broadcasting Companies, Inc.

## CAST

Carl Kolchak......................................Darren McGavin
Gail Foster.................................................Carol Lynley
Tony Vincenzo......................................Simon Oakland
Bernie Jenks..........................................Ralph Meeker
Sheriff Warren Butcher.........................Claude Akins
Police Chief Edward Masterson.......Charles McGraw
District Attorney Thomas Paine... ..........Kent Smith
Janos Skorzeny......................................Barry Atwater
Medical Examiner Robert Mokurji.......Larry Linville
Dr. John O'Brien................................Jordan Rhodes
Mickey Crawford...............................Elisha Cook, Jr.
Fred Hurley...........................................Stanley Adams

**SYNOPSIS:** *A cassette is popped into a tape recorder. The voice that emanates from the machine belongs to reporter Carl Kolchak. While the tape runs, Kolchak gets a beer out of an ancient and almost-empty refrigerator, stretches out on the bed in his sparsely decorated apartment and follows the words with the manuscript in his lap: "Chapter One. This is the story behind one of the greatest manhunts in history. Maybe you read about it, or rather what they let you read about it, probably in some minor item buried somewhere in a back page. However, what happened in that city between May 16 and May 28 of this year was so incredible that to this day the facts have been suppressed in a massive effort to save certain political careers from disaster and law enforcement officials from embarrassment. This will be the last time I will ever discuss these events with anyone, so, when you have finished this bizarre account, judge for yourself its believability, and then try to tell yourself, wherever you may be, it couldn't happen here."*

The story Kolchak has to tell us starts on May 16. At 2:30 in the morning, Cheryl Ann Hughes, a twenty-three-year-old swing-shift change girl at the Gold Dust Saloon, was waiting on a Las Vegas corner for a ride that already was twenty-five minutes late. Mad and disgusted, she decided to walk the eight blocks to her house. She didn't make it. Later that morning, her body was found by sanitation workers. The corpse had been stuffed into a garbage can.

To the shock of the medical examiner, Robert Mokurji, the body has been drained of blood. Called back early from his first vacation in two and a half years, *Las Vegas Daily News* reporter Carl Kolchak is assigned the story that he describes as "a two-day-old, third-rate murder." The man calling him back is his "lovable managing editor," Tony Vincenzo. Kolchak is not amused.

"Rumor has it," the veteran reporter tells us, "that the day Anthony Albert Vincenzo was born, his father left town. The story may be apocryphal, but I believe it. The only point I wonder about is why his mother didn't leave, too."

That about sums up Carl Kolchak's relationship with his editor, Tony Vincenzo.

Kolchak's first stop is his most reliable spy at County General Hospital, Dr. John O'Brien — "at least he used to be reliable." The reporter wants to know why it says "officially undetermined" under the cause of death for Cheryl Hughes. The only thing O'Brien can tell him is that the dead woman "lost a lot of blood."

The second stop for Kolchak is the Gold Dust Saloon, where he talks to Gail Foster, "one of Cheryl Hughes' fellow workers and a rather close friend of mine." Gail tells Carl that Cheryl had a brown belt in karate.

"In any town the size of Las Vegas," Kolchak says, "the murder of one young woman hardly causes a ripple. But then the ripples started. Thursday, May 20, 7:02 a.m."

A second body is found, but this one is surrounded by sand with no footprints anywhere near it. The victim would have to have been thrown at least fifteen feet.

"Is that physically possible?" Kolchak asks.

"If it happened, it's possible," says Sheriff Warren Butcher, who has no great affection for reporters in general and Kolchak in particular.

Bonnie Reynolds — twenty-seven, divorced, cocktail waitress — is the second victim. She lost a great deal of blood, but there's no blood at the scene.

"Cheryl Hughes lost a lot of blood, too," Kolchak says.

"You read that in the newspaper, did you?" Butcher asks, knowing that this is a detail being kept quiet.

"No, I didn't read that in the newspapers," Kolchak tells him.

Back at the *Daily News*, Kolchak pushes to get details about blood loss in the paper. Vincenzo refuses to run the story without confirmation from the police or the coroner. He also tells Kolchak to stop bugging the police. They don't need "any help from amateur bloodhounds like you," Vincenzo adds.

On Friday, May 21, a third body is found. Carol Hanochek, swing-shift cocktail waitress at the Bird of Paradise Show Lounge, died in her apartment — suddenly, quietly and without disturbing her sleeping roommate only a few feet away. "Something of a pattern was starting to form," Kolchak says, "and it was ugly. It was then that people stopped talking."

Desperate for leads, Kolchak turns to his friend, FBI agent Bernie Jenks. He asks Bernie to check the insane asylums across the country to see if they recently released "a nut who thinks he's Count Dracula."

"Do you believe in vampires, little boy?" Bernie replies jokingly. But he agrees to think about it and tells Kolchak about a special report being given by the pathology experts. Before Mokurji and his team present their findings, however, Kolchak gets a call from O'Brien. Parkway Hospital has just been knocked over. The robber didn't take cash, drugs or equipment. The only thing stolen was blood.

To head off the growing hysteria, District Attorney Thomas Paine has called the meeting at Clark County Courthouse so Mokurji can submit his special report. Present at the briefing are Butcher, Paine, Jenks, Police Chief Edward Masterson and members of the fourth estate, including one Carl Kolchak.

Mokurji drops a bombshell. Each victim died of shock due to a massive and extremely quick loss of blood. And, oh, yes, each of the victims had been bitten on the throat. No, not by a dog or any other type of animal. That was confirmed by a substance found in the throat wounds — saliva, human saliva.

Kolchak wonders if the murderer could be a lunatic who thinks he's a vampire. Paine and Butcher reject the notion as ludicrous. Mokurji, though, tells them that he wouldn't "be too inclined to reject Mr. Kolchak's theory out of hand, if I were you. It is, at best, highly speculative, but not altogether unwarranted." Paine's response is to impose a news blackout on the details of the murders.

Kolchak's response is to suggest a *Daily News* story with the following headline: "Vampire Killer in Las Vegas?" Vincenzo tells him "no vampire stories."

As the investigation heats up, so does Kolchak's relationship with Gail Foster.

A fourth victim, showgirl Mary Brandon, is found dead, but this time the killer was seen. The police artist's drawing is circulated to the newspapers when a fifth woman, Shelley Forbes, disappears. Vincenzo is reluctant to feed the growing panic. Kolchak is furious at his reluctance, which the reporter views as irresponsible.

"This nut thinks he is a vampire," Kolchak shouts at Vincenzo. "He has killed four, maybe five women. He has drained every drop of blood from every one of them. Now that is *news*, Vincenzo, *news*! And we are a newspaper. We are supposed to print *news*, not suppress it!"

Finally, there is a break in the case. A likely suspect purchased an automobile from a used-car dealer named Fred Hurley. About the same time, Gail asks Carl what he knows about vampires. "They wear dinner suits and talk with marbles in their mouth," he answers. Still, Kolchak is intrigued when she gives him a book with a chapter on vampirism. The newshound smells a story. He's more convinced than ever that Las Vegas is being terrorized by a psychotic killer who actually believes he's a vampire.

Even this theory seems mild when Kolchak sees the suspect rob a hospital's blood bank. Several times surrounded, the tall, snarling suspect easily tosses aside burly orderlies and police officers. Shot at point-blank range, he outruns a police car.

At another briefing, Bernie Jenks identifies the murderer. He is Janos Skorzeny. He was born in Rumania — in 1899. It's another bombshell. How can a man older than seventy outrun a police car and bounce around teams of men as if they were rag dolls?

The next shocking turn of events convinces Kolchak that Skorzeny is a real vampire. Surrounded by police and chased to a back-yard pool, Skorzeny is riddled with bullets, beaten and half-drowned, yet, each time, he gets up and fights back. He eventually escapes.

Paine, Butcher and Masterson now have no choice except to consider the persistent Kolchak's suggestions. Each officer is to be armed with a cross, a wooden stake and a mallet. In exchange for the help, Kolchak wants exclusive rights to the story of Skorzeny's capture.

That night, Kolchak's street spy, Mickey Crawford, tells the reporter that he has found Skorzeny's house. Unwilling to wait for the police, Kolchak enters the house by himself. In the refrigerator, he finds bottles of stolen blood. In an upstairs

Las Vegas reporter Carl Kolchak (Darren McGavin) questions Gail Foster (Carol Lynley) about a murdered co-worker in *The Night Stalker.*

bedroom, he finds the missing fifth victim. Skorzeny has kept her barely alive as a human blood bank.

Kolchak is discovered by Skorzeny, and the reporter does his best to hold off the enraged vampire. Even when Bernie Jenks joins the struggle, it is obvious that they can't subdue the monster — until rays of sunshine streak through curtains and boards. Caught in the sunshine, Skorzeny is helpless. Kolchak ends the manhunt by driving a wooden stake through the vampire's heart.

Knowing that he has covered the story of his life (and almost of his death), Kolchak is convinced that he has his ticket back to the big time. But an unusually subdued Tony Vincenzo tells his exuberant employee that Paine wants to see him. Before Kolchak leaves, Vincenzo pays the ultimate compliment: "You're one hell of a reporter."

What's waiting for Kolchak is a committee of cover-up — Paine, Masterson, Butcher and a reluctant Bernie Jenks. They can't let that preposterous vampire story get out. It would be bad for the town's image and bad for their careers. If Kolchak prints the real story, they'll charge him with first-degree murder. Several witnesses saw him pound a wooden stake through the heart of a suspect wanted only for questioning. His only choice is to gather up what's left of his career and leave town.

Kolchak warns us that any attempt to verify his story will be difficult. The bodies of the victims and that of Janos Skorzeny were cremated.

Official records are missing, altered or unavailable. And Gail Foster, told to leave town, has disappeared.

"So think about it," Kolchak asks us, "and try to tell yourself, wherever you may be, in the quiet of your home, in the safety of your bed, try to tell yourself, it couldn't happen here."

**PRODUCTION HISTORY:** When Everett Chambers became the producer assigned to ABC's *The Kolchak Papers*, it seemed that the first major role to be cast would be the pathologist, Mohandas Mokurji. "I'd written the role," Rice explains, "in the hopes that if a film was ever made from my book, I'd be able to play the part. I am, after all, also an actor. I'd obtained an audition to read for the role. Chambers evidently liked my reading, my interpretation of the part, and the photos I'd supplied him showing, in makeup, how I proposed to alter my appearance to play an East Indian. He said I had the part."

While Matheson continued to work on the screenplay, Rice left Los Angeles for a round of location scouting in Las Vegas. Taking his consultant's role very seriously, Rice made detailed maps so the production crew could get around town easily and efficiently.

"I took a considerable number of photos of pertinent locations," he says, "including an excellent, rather English-looking, half-timbered house which could serve as a visually interesting place for the vampire to hole up; especially as it was located on a tree-lined street and if a camera did a slow pan, from the house, around one side, it would pick up a huge, revolving neon sign, seemingly out of nowhere, which advertised three different casinos and suddenly revealed the quiet neighborhood to be set in the heart of Las Vegas. Great visual incongruity.

"The house I'd described in the book was a simple, cheap, modern cinderblock affair, roughly near the University, but still set off in the desert, and I found one perfect for the film if the art director should decide to stick closer to the book."

Actually, neither house was the original model for Skorzeny's lair. For his book, Rice chose one of the most nondescript houses he could find. Located on an undeveloped street at the edge of the desert, the house was the type of dwelling where just about anyone, including a vampire, might live. In fact, one of Rice's best friends lived there. After the book was completed, Rice asked the friend if the house

Carl Kolchak (Darren McGavin) with hammer in hand, searches for the vampire (and a wooden stake) to put an end to the murderous rampage.

Director John Llewellyn Moxey, that "lovely English fellow."

could be used in the event of a movie version. The friend, who had a copy of *The Kolchak Papers*, agreed, even though, in the book, the house is burned down to destroy any trace of evidence. About two months after Rice finished *The Kolchak Papers*, the friend called him with one of those stories that makes you check over your shoulder to see if Rod Serling is talking about you. Life had imitated art. The house had burned down. About the only thing left was his copy of *The Kolchak Papers*, which wasn't even singed. Then, shortly before ABC's crew arrived in Las Vegas, the other nondescript house Rice had chose also burned to the ground.

But blissfully unaware of the blaze ahead, Rice blazed back to Los Angeles. He turned over his notes, maps and photographs to art director Trevor Williams and production manager Neil T. Maffeo.

Rice's next meeting was with the director assigned to *The Kolchak Papers*, John Llewellyn Moxey, who was wrapping up work on *A Taste of Evil,* a TV movie with Barbara Stanwyck, Barbara Parkins and Roddy McDowall.

Born in 1920 in Hurlingham, England, John Llewellyn Moxey was no novice when it came to horror or to TV movies. There were several spookers among the films he directed in England: *The City of the Dead* (1960, American title: *Horror Hotel*), *Foxhole in Cairo* (1960), *Death Trap* (1962), *The £20,000 Kiss* (1962), *Richochet* (1963), *Downfall* (1964), *The Face of a Stranger* (1964), *Strangler's Web* (1965) and *Circus of Fear* (1967, American title: *Psycho-Circus*). He'd also directed the "Who's Who?" episode of *The Avengers*. In the late '60s, the director moved to America and found that TV movies offered the steadiest work. Before Rice and Kolchak came along, Moxey had directed such TV movies as *Escape* (1970), *San Francisco International Airport* (1970), *The House That Would Not Die* (1970, with a script by Henry Farrell, author *Whatever Happened to Baby Jane?*) and *The Last Child* (1971).

"Actually, I was going to work with Dan [Curtis] on something else," Moxey recalls. "One day, this story was there and we were all excited about it. I read the Jeff Rice book on the beach, and I was pleased. I read Richard Matheson's screenplay, and I was more pleased. I always thought it was going to be a very special piece. The fun of it was the mixing of the humor and the horror. There was lot of that in Jeff Rice's book. That was very much a part of the original concept. Everybody understood that and elaborated on it — Richard Matheson's script, Darren's portrayal, the driving force of Dan Curtis as producer, my direction. There was a great deal of evolution, but we often referred back to the book."

Curtis and McGavin agree. "Whenever we had a question," Curtis said, "we would go back to the book. We'd find something from the book and put it back in."

To McGavin, Moxey was that "lovely English fellow." It's an assessment that meets with almost universal agreement.

"Moxey was an Englishman who'd started making dramatized documentaries for the RAF right after World War II," Rice says, "working first as an assistant director, and then as an actor so he could learn to see things from the actor's point of view. He was a very gentle, very courteous man — seemingly unflappable on the set or on location, with a genuine appreciation of writers and a positive affection for actors, unlike many, more egotistical members of his profession.

"To him, 'actors' were 'lovely people,' and trying to take the point of view of writers as well, he told me, 'They're the ones who are dramatizing what would be your own words if you were the old storyteller who went from village to village and sat under a tree and gathered the people around him and told a story."

"To me," Moxey told Rice, "my actors are the *most* important people. . . so are my crew, but my actors are the ones who get out there and *do* it."

Moxey and Rice discussed the novel in great detail. "He agreed with most of my suggestions," Rice says, "and, if memory serves me, congratulated me on having won the role of Mokurji."

Meanwhile, Matheson was at work on the screenplay. Some of the differences between Rice's book and Matheson's script were the result of necessary tightening. The adaptation, after all, was being done at a time when the networks still made ninety-minute TV movies (that's seventy-three minutes, minus the commercials). Other differences between novel and screenplay were changes demanded by ABC's standards and practices office (or, if you will, censors). Still other differences must be chalked up to casting. Tony Vincenzo, for instance, is described in the book as "a small, dried-out" man. Simon Oakland, the actor cast as Tony, was tall and stocky, but, like McGavin, he made the part his own.

Matheson jettisoned the character of managing editor Llewellyn Cairncross, publisher Jacob E. Herman "the Heinous," reporter Meyer Moss, tough-as-nails labor columnist Janie Carlson, Kolchak's Hemingway-like buddy Pete Harper and elderly college humanities teacher Kirsten Helms. Traces of Llewellyn, Kirsten and Janie would show up in reworked characters for the Kolchak sequel movie, *The Night Strangler*.

The prototype for Gail Foster, Carol Lynley's character, is Sam, a Las Vegas prostitute who is Kolchak's friend — not his "rather close friend." The network was nervous about a hooker as the leading lady (how times would change!), so her occupation, her relationship with Kolchak and even her name were changed.

The standards and practices people weren't finished. Some of the more graphic scenes in the book had to be toned down. Skorzeny's rather nasty closet disintegration (a combination of sun and holy water) was eliminated as too strong for television. The vampire's forehead gash in the pool scene oozes a clear fluid, not blood (Kolchak makes a quick mention of this in one of the briefing scenes, but the supporting closeups are gone). For some reason, the clear fluid offended the censor more than blood. Shots of the victims' throat wounds were edited out (ironic, since Carl complains to Gail that the newspaper has airbrushed out the throat wounds in pictures of Skorzeny's victims). And no mention could be made of the vampire's foul breath. "Someone at the network thought it was 'disgusting,'" Rice explains.

In the book, several witnesses, including used-car salesman Fred Hurley, mention the vampire's bad breath. Skorzeny is "just about knocking me over with his breath," Hurley says. "I ain't never smelled anythin' so bad in my life." Although Stoker made a similar issue of Count Dracula's need of breath mints, standards and practices opted for something closer to a breath of fresh air.

When Rice returned from his Las Vegas scouting trip, he learned that Dan Curtis had replaced Chambers as producer. Still confident of being cast as Mokurji, Rice breezed through a reading with casting director Hoyt Bowers. With Curtis in control, however, Rice was asked to give a reading at the Goldwyn Studios, where most of the interiors for the movie would be filmed. This time he read for Moxey, Curtis, Bowers and the assistant to the producer, Robert Singer. Moxey judged the audition "quite acceptable," yet Curtis, while open to most of Rice's suggestions, decided on another actor.

"Since all I needed to play the role I'd virtually written for myself was to comb my hair in a slightly different manner, wear a latex nose, rimless glasses, and some dark makeup," Rice comments, "you can imagine my surprise when Curtis chose Larry Linville, tall, pale, and as WASPish a guy as one could hope to meet, to play my East Indian pathologist. The character's first name was changed from Mohandas to Robert, the last name was Americanized in pronunciation, and he was given the call to report to work only the night before his scenes were to be shot."

Rice sees a certain irony in the fact that, just months after his scalpel-and-surgical-mask scenes in *The Night Stalker*, Linville was cast as surgeon Frank Burns on the acclaimed series version of *M*A*S*H* (which CBS premiered September 17, 1972).

But Rice did not let his disappointment color his enthusiasm for the project. On Monday, August 23, with the cast and crew assembled in Las Vegas, Rice drove McGavin, in costume, to the filming site on the Las Vegas strip. Arriving at the Tropicana Hotel, author and actor saw Moxey, dressed in white tennis shorts and smoking a Dublin pipe, surrounded by assistant director Christopher Seitz, director of photography Michael Hugo, cameraman Ralph Gerling and other members of the company.

Seitz shouted, "Action!" It was about three p.m. when filming started on Scene 232 — Kolchak driving away from Las Vegas (one of the last in the screenplay). Rice talked with Curtis as McGavin drove Kolchak's 1968 blue Camaro convertible through the desired paces. The title of the TV movie already had been changed twice. Unhappy with *The Kolchak Papers*,

ABC had switched to *The Kolchak Tapes*. Then, with the theatrical film *The Anderson Tapes* in production, the network wanted to avoid any confusion, so the title was switched back to *The Kolchak Papers*. It would be changed at least twice more. The network considered *Fee Fi Fo Fum, I Smell the Blood* before finally deciding on *The Night Stalker*.

The title was at least original, even if it did have a familiar ring. Well, after all, Hollywood always has preferred night to day — literally. In the 1989 edition of *TV Movies*, Leonard Maltin lists about 140 films beginning with the words night or nightmare: *Night Passage, Night Shift, Night at the Opera, Night in Casablanca, The Night the Lights Went Out in Georgia, The Night They Raided Minsky's, Night and Day, Night After Night, Night Unto Night, Night Creature, Night Creatures, Night Cries, Night Crossing, Night Tide, Night Games, Night Gallery, Night Song, Night Editor, Nightmare Alley, Nightmare on Elm Street, Night Moves, Night Monster, 'Night Mother, Night Caller, Night Nurse, Night Call Nurses, Night School, Night Train, Night of the Lepus, Night of the Demons, Night of the Generals, Night of the Living Dead, Night Shadows, Night of Dark Shadows* (and where have we heard that one before?), *The Night of the Iguana, The Night of the Hunter, Night of Terror, The Night That Panicked America, Night Watch, A Night to Remember, Night Has Eyes, Night Has a Thousand Eyes*. But, in 1971, there had been no *Night Stalker*. The closest title to it was *The Night Walker*, director William Castle's 1964 horror flick with Barbara Stanwyck and Robert Taylor (scripted by Matheson's good friend, Robert Bloch). And accept no substitutes: In 1987, *The Night Stalker* was used as the title of a feature film starring Charles Napier (the police officer turned into a butterfly by Hannibal "the Cannibal" Lecter in *The Silence of the Lambs*) as a Los Angeles cop tracking a serial killer (no, not Hannibal). In 1989, NBC aired *Manhunt: Search for the Night Stalker*, a fact-based TV movie about the 1985 serial killer who terrorized Los Angeles.

On Wednesday, August 25, Rice was watching Moxey film a scene at the Sahara Hotel's pool. Kolchak was talking with his friend, FBI agent Bernie Jenks. Like McGavin, Meeker had Broadway and live-television experience. Like McGavin, Meeker had once played Mike Hammer (in the 1955 film version of *Kiss Me Deadly*).

As the scene progressed, Rice realized that he was standing next to a tall, professorial fellow who kept puffing on a pipe while eyeing the curvaceous extras walking by. "Ah, lovely, just lovely," the fellow murmured to Rice. "I'd really like sink my fangs into her. . . and her. . . and her!"

This was Barry Atwater, who, without the dark suit, blood-red contact lenses and black wig, looked nothing like vampire Janos Skorzeny.

Although hardly a household name, Atwater had been active in television for more than a decade. His credits included a classic first-season episode of *The Twilight Zone*, Rod Serling's "The Monsters Are Due On Maple Street" (which starred Claude Akins, who was playing Sheriff Warren Butcher in *The Night Stalker*). Atwater also had played the Vulcan philosopher Surak in "The Savage Curtain," a 1969 episode of *Star Trek*. And he had already made three of his four *Mission: Impossible* appearances: "Elena" in 1966, "The Play" in 1968 and "Gitano" in 1970. His film credits included Serling's *The Rack* (1956), director Lewis Milestone's *Pork Chop Hill* (1959) and *Sweet Bird of Youth* (1967).

That afternoon, while Moxey filmed a scene with Kolchak and Gail (Carol Lynley) in the Thunderbird Hotel's casino, Rice noticed a tall, bearded man talking to ABC executive Allen Epstein. Months later, he learned that this tall man was Richard Matheson.

"My wife and I were on vacation with our kids," Matheson explains, "and we stopped in Las Vegas while they were shooting the movie. I was talking to Darren McGavin and his wife, and I noticed several colored pages in his script. Now that usually means changes, so I thought, 'Oh, oh, they've changed everything in the script.' So I left in a rage. I didn't want to know what they did to it. But when I finally saw the film, I realized they hadn't changed that much. They added a scene or two, but, fundamentally, it was exactly the same and I was utterly delighted."

Matheson's trepidations aside, *The Night Stalker* was, by all accounts a very happy set.

"Moxey was a terrific director who had a wonderful sense of enjoyment," McGavin points out, "which you hope to get in a director. He encouraged people. And Dan [Curtis] and I became very close during production. We shot for about a week in Las Vegas and then finished the picture over at the Sam Goldwyn Studios because it was an in-house production and ABC didn't have any studios or anything. And Barry was so wonderful. He never complained."

Dan Doran, the ABC publicist assigned to *The Night Stalker*, was present for almost the entire shoot, and he confirms McGavin's statements.

"Barry Atwater was a very nice man," Doran says. "He had to get into that makeup every day. We all worried about him because those awful red contact lenses were terribly uncomfortable. But he thought it was great.

He thought the whole project was great fun. He was willing to try anything. While we were in Las Vegas, Dan Curtis was just amazed at how gamblers only saw gambling and nothing else around them. So we asked Barry if he would walk through the Sahara's casino in full makeup to see if anyone paid attention to him. He didn't even hesitate. We did this for about forty minutes and nobody batted an eye. That's the kind of fun we had. It was a very nice cast of warm people. Darren McGavin is the best type of actor to work with — he's a pro. Almost twenty years later, I still fondly remember working on *The Night Stalker*, and I can't say that about too many productions."

Rice, too, recalls a happy and cooperative company: "I was allowed to contribute as a writer. At one point, when the company was on location in Las Vegas, Curtis asked me to punch up some scenes in regard to the police and, while they were shooting in the Thunderbird Hotel's casino, I was in my old PR office at that hotel just typing away like mad. I don't recall what, if anything, was done with what I wrote. Today, I don't even remember, specifically, what it was that I wrote."

Robert Singer, the production assistant who would become executive producer of such NBC series as *Midnight Caller* and *Reasonable Doubts,* enthuses, "For me, *The Night Stalker* was a terrific experience. I got to go to Las Vegas. It was a happy shoot. And about halfway through the filming, I think everybody sort of got the sense that something terrific was going on. It was a new slant on the vampire story. But the book was just terrific. That was where the new slant came from."

"It was one of the better experiences of my career," Moxey announces. "Everybody just sort of came together in a very happy working team. I believed from the start that we had something very special on our hands. I don't know how much that view

Barry Atwater steps out of the shadows as vampire Janos Skorzeny.

was shared by others. I do know we enjoyed making the movie. It was fun — outrageous fun, great joy, a happy collaboration."

If intent on having a good time, Moxey also was intrigued by the challenges presented by Rice's story and Matheson's script.

"People always tell me, 'You know, your work is very stylish,'" the director says. "I never really know what they're talking about. I never can really define it. It's an instinct. You have to be conductor at the head of an orchestra. The piece you're about to perform has a certain style, and you set out to try to capture that. With *The Night Stalker*, the style was a mix of '40s newspaper drama and a gothic vampire story. As you say, it's *The Front Page* blended with Bram Stoker. That was the challenge of *The Night Stalker*. Can you mix those two very different styles and make it work? Can you present straight horror with lots of humor? Darren played a big part in finding the humor in it while Dan was a driving force in getting the script and casting right. Dan's casting ideas were excellent. He was a good producer to work with, always open to discussion. It's nice to have a producer you can talk to, and Dan contributed greatly. It was a very happy set. Most of my sets are."

And Moxey, too, marveled at the good humor and quiet professionalism maintained by Barry Atwater.

"We gave Barry those contact lenses," he comments, "and they were such a problem because his eyes got very tender after wearing them any length of time. After a while, he didn't need the lenses to make his eyes look red. We had a doctor on the set to help him with that. He was a remarkable man. Here was this talented actor playing this silent vampire. But he was a nice man willing to do his part as a team player. And that's the secret, really. We worked together as a team. Dan was the prime mover and Darren was the star player. Darren is an actor of immense talent. He brought a spark to that part. He's a very funny man. He has a wry sense of humor, and that's what made the part work. Everybody remembers Darren, but there also was this splendid ensemble of great actors. Everybody enjoyed making it. It was a very tightly knit cast."

The only tense moment for Moxey occurred while filming Skorzeny's escape from the hospital. Stunt coordinator Dick Ziker, as usual, was doubling for Atwater.

"When we did that shot outside the hospital," Moxey recalls, "a motorcycle was supposed to come sliding to a halt in front of the camera. Well, it got away from the driver and started skidding toward me. I thought that was it. I thought, 'This is going to come right through and slice us in two.' Luckily, it hit a pipe that was sticking up and stopped just short of us. You know, with all the stunts in that film, that was the only thing that came close to going wrong."

Although he'd been around a few movie sets, Rice was rather bewildered by the breakneck pace of a TV movie. "I found it a bit hard," he says, "watching the individual scenes being shot, picturing in my mind how all this confusion of bits and pieces would ever be assembled into a cohesive motion picture. It all seemed so haphazard."

The film's veteran sound mixer, Harold Lewis, laughed away his concerns. "This is all very routine," he told the writer. "Don't worry. It's going very well. You only have to worry when the egos get out of hand, and Mr. Moxey doesn't let that sort of thing happen."

After a week of location shooting, it was time to leave Las Vegas. "Everybody was terribly kind when we filmed in Las Vegas," Moxey reflects. "It was a good deal of fun shooting there. The joke was putting the vampire in Las Vegas. I mean, Las Vegas is a town full of vampires."

On Monday, August 30, the filming of interior scenes began at the Goldwyn Studios. Mokurji's autopsy was to be filmed that morning.

"Then Larry Linville arrived on the set," Rice says. "Poor Larry. He'd only been given the script the night before, while at a party, and he was nursing a hellish hangover. He looked more fit to be the subject of an autopsy than to be the pathologist performing it."

After Rice introduced himself, Linville was called to the set. "I think I'll die now," the actor told Kolchak's creator. "Just be gentle with my body. You'll need a piano case for my head."

Linville, another pro with stage training, got through it, all right. The resulting scene was one of the most innovative and memorable in the movie.

A little later, Rice met the actor cast as Carl  Kolchak's long-suffering editor, Anthony Vincenzo. Born in New York City in 1922, Simon Oakland was one of Hollywood's busiest character actors. Like McGavin, he had Broadway experience. Like Akins and Atwater, he had appeared in episodes of *The Twilight Zone* ("The Rip Van Winkle Caper" and "The Thirty-Fathom Grave"). Like Meeker, he had appeared in several major films (*The Brothers Karamazov, The Sand Pebbles, Bullitt, On a Clear Day You Can See Forever*). Perhaps Oakland's most famous movie roles were the police lieutenant in director Robert Wise's Oscar-winning version of *West Side Story* (1961) and the psychiatrist who explains what went wrong with Norman Bates at the end of Alfred Hitchcock's *Psycho* (1960). A gentle man and a former professional violinist, Oakland often was cast as a tough guy. But his ability to play both villainous and sympathetic roles kept him working as a guest star in almost every major television drama of the '60s: in Westerns (*Gunsmoke, Bonanza, Wagon Train, Rawhide, Maverick, The Virginian, The Big Valley*), medical programs (*Ben Casey, The Nurses, Medical Center*), courtroom shows (*Perry Mason, The Defenders, Trials of O'Brien, Judd for the Defense*), cop shows (*The Untouchables, Felony Squad, Hawaii Five-O, The FBI, Ironside, The Mod* Squad). He'd even done his share of situation comedies (*Get Smart, My Favorite Martian, Captain Nice* and *Car 54, Where Are You?*). Whether cast as a mob boss or a cowboy, however, this World War II veteran was a serious actor who prepared for each part with the greatest of care. Rice was about to discover just how carefully.

The writer, who based Kolchak partly on himself, approached Oakland, who seemed to be running lines on the set. The actor, however, was making up speeches on the spot. They were Tony Vincenzo speeches. Simon Oakland was crawling into Tony Vincenzo's skin. He was turning *into* Tony Vincenzo, working with the tools of an editor — grease pencils, glossy photographs, raw copy. Pacing through the make-believe newsroom, Oakland bumped into a fascinated Rice. He fixed the writer with a stare, then exploded, "Mr. Rice, I don't ask a helluva lot from you. Show up on time. Do your work. And get it right. But where the hell do you get off going out on your own on stories that weren't assigned to you? I don't like reporters who make end runs around me or go over my head to the boss. You work for *me* and the sooner you get that into your head the sooner we'll get along."

For a second, Rice was back in the newsroom of the *Las Vegas SUN*, facing the model for Tony Vincenzo, editor Vince Anselmo. Rice actually was about to yell back, then he started laughing.

"Yeah," the smiling Oakland observed. "I think that's got it." The good-natured actor was more than willing to explain: "Well, I get up to Vegas every now and then. I asked around about you and your boss. This. . . what you just saw. . . well, it's just part of the way I work."

Still reeling from his close encounter of the Vincenzo kind, Rice watched McGavin and Oakland waltz through what would be the second scene between Carl and Tony. Kolchak has turned in his first story on the murders. "Quit bugging the P.D.," Tony tells Carl, "if something turns up, they'll let us know. Meanwhile, use your head and lay off."

At this, point, Tony goes back in his office and slams the door. But the scene wasn't finished. McGavin leaned his head against a partition and started banging it in frustration. Rice was astonished. It was a habit he'd picked up after many shouting matches with Vince Anselmo. "Where did you get that piece of business?" Rice inquired.

"Oh, we talked to your old boss in Vegas," McGavin told him. "He had a *lot* to say about you. We asked a few questions and learned a lot about the way you used to operate. Gotcha!"

"Art imitating life?" Rice wondered almost fifteen years later.

"Perhaps. But here, on this soundstage, art was doing it exceedingly well."

"Si and I improvised all the time," McGavin says. "We had fun. He was a wonderful actor to work with, very smart and very nice."

Rounding out the *Night Stalker* cast were film veterans Carol Lynley (*The Cardinal, Harlow, Bunny Lake is Missing*), Kent Smith (*Cat People, The Spiral Staircase, The Fountainhead*), Charles McGraw (*The Bridges at Toko-Ri, The Defiant Ones, In Cold Blood*) and Elisha Cook, Jr. (best known as Wilmer in director John Huston's *The Maltese Falcon* and later Icepick in *Magnum, p.i.*). Cook's horror credits included *Voodoo Island* (1957, with Boris Karloff), director William Castle's *House on Haunted Hill* (1958, with Vincent Price) and *Rosemary's Baby.* He also played eccentric Samuel Cogley, the book-loving lawyer who defended Captain Kirk in the 1967 "Court Martial" episode of *Star Trek.*

Called in for a one-scene appearance as used-car salesman Fred Hurley was character actor Stanley Adams, whose television credits included episodes of *Alfred Hitchcock Presents* (the detective in "Pen Pal"), *The Twilight Zone* (Rollo to Buster Keaton's Woodrow in Matheson's "Once Upon a Time") and *Star Trek* (Cyrano Jones in "The Trouble With Tribbles").

"Believe me," Doran says, "I've worked on a lot of movies where people didn't get along or conditions were unpleasant. That wasn't the case on *The Night Stalker.* The budget was around $350,000, and, with Moxey at the helm, everything went very smoothly."

The last day of filming was Thursday, September 9. The final scene to be shot was the clash between Skorzeny and police officers around and in a back-yard swimming pool. The action sequence was filmed at the Columbia Ranch in Burbank. When Dick Ziker, Atwater's double, was dragged from the pool, the scene was stopped so Atwater could get in hands-and-knees position at the edge of the pool. Rice was troubled enough to speak up just as Moxey was about to resume shooting. Assistant director Christopher Seitz was furious over this breach of Hollywood etiquette, but the ever-courteous Moxey was willing to listen.

Well, Rice explained, Barry is absolutely neat and dry when he's supposed to be drenched and beaten.

The scene wouldn't match Ziker being dragged from the pool. "I'm afraid Mr. Rice has a very valid point, gentlemen," Moxey decreed. Three stuntmen dressed as police officers — Hal Needham, Eddie Hice and Ronnie Rondell — filled their helmets with pool water and drenched Barry Atwater. Dripping water and sarcasm, the actor bared his fangs at Rice and said, "Thanks, I needed that."

The scene continued to the moment when Skorzeny scrambles over the fence with police firing away at him. Cut. That was a wrap — at four-thirty a.m. Friday, September 10. For Rice, it was a melancholy moment.

"There was a brief wrap party, very informal," he recalls, "while various crew members began to put away the equipment, and, one by one, the cast and crew began to depart until only Moxey and I were left. The sun began to rise and we said our good-byes, a little sad to have to let it all go. For Moxey, it had been one more film in a succession of films, but for me, it had been a singular and thrilling experience."

A less thrilling experience was reading a letter sent from the agency about a month and a half later. Dated December 29, it stated: "For the record, this letter will constitute a release to you by us of our representation on your behalf of the unpublished manuscript of *The Kolchak Papers* in the publishing field. Therefore, effective immediately, you are free to seek publication of the material as you wish." With the movie finished and about to hit the air, Rice was being cut loose. It took him nine months to find another agent. In the summer of 1972, a New York agent agreed to represent a revised version of *The Kolchak Papers* ("sufficiently rewritten to require a separate copyright"). But, in the fall of 1971, blissfully unaware of the cold turn of events around the winter corner, Rice was trying to interest ABC in the concept of monthly Kolchak movies.

Meanwhile, Curtis was overseeing the post-production phase of *The Night Stalker.* His *Dark Shadows* composer, Bob Cobert, was given the music assignment. He decided a punchy, jazzy score was in order.

"It was spooky stuff," Cobert explains, "but it wasn't a *Dark Shadows* type of spooky. I mean, it was Las Vegas in 1971. That's the whole point. You need something that is spooky but contemporary. Sure, I'd done horror for Dan Curtis, but this was a different story so it needed a different feel. Dan said, 'What do you think?' And I immediately started humming the main theme. We'd worked together so much that he just trusted me to come up with something in the right style – something with an edge to it."

Desmond Marquette edited the film into a very, very brisk seventy-three minutes.

With a January 11 airdate, Doran was turned loose on the on-air promotion campaign.

"This was a campaign that you enjoyed because the movie was so much fun," Doran says. "Don't get me wrong. We didn't do anything out of the ordinary to promote it, but that's because we didn't think it would be anything more than a Tuesday movie of the week programmer. Remember, we'd just done *Brian's Song* in November, and that was special. Barry Diller was in charge of movies of the week, and he sent me a letter thanking me for the wonderful promotion campaign for *Brian's Song*. Well, let me put it this way: *Night Stalker* wasn't going to win any awards for public relations campaigns. But we didn't have to do anything special with *Night Stalker*. The subject — a vampire in Las Vegas — made for great on-air promos, which is what really sold it. Those spots were so darn intriguing, I think it had people talking."

They were not only talking, they were watching. An estimated audience of seventy-five million viewers turned to *The Night Stalker* at eight-thirty p.m. Tuesday, January 11. The A.C Nielsen Company said that Kolchak attracted 33.2 percent of all the country's television households. In TV terms, that's called a rating. And *The Night Stalker* snared a whopping fifty-four percent of the TV sets actually in use from eight-thirty to ten p.m. Tuesday. That's called a share. There's also a term for what ABC was experiencing — that's called shock.

"We were concerned," Doran remembers. "It had beaten *Brian's Song* as the highest-rated TV movie of all time, and we were all shocked. Everyone was stunned. Everyone. How can this be? Sure, we were also happy, but it made us wonder. I think that the answer was very basic. The movie just had a very basic appeal. You could sit down and have a good time with it."

"It didn't surprise me," Cobert admits. "It was a terrific picture. Look, you never know how the public is going to accept anything, but all the elements were in this. It was quality — fun and scary and different. The ratings were delightful, but they weren't surprising."

"I knew it would be successful," Moxey says, "but I never dreamed it would cause the sensation it did. *Brian's Song* came out about the same time and got all the praise, which it deserved. The two movies couldn't have been more different, but along we came with *The Night Stalker* and made a bigger splash. It was huge."

Rice describes a similar reaction: "I'd expected it to do well. I'd targeted my book at an audience of TV viewers, but I felt. . . it would get very respectable ratings, and then it would be quickly forgotten unless there was a swift follow-up. This is one reason I was so hot to come up with a sequel to launch a series. . . I don't really know for certain (why it was so successful). I try to consider the type of story I wrote, the film that resulted from it, and the era in which it 'burst' upon the tube. This was, after all, nearly twenty years ago. Perhaps its success depended partially on the fact that the public has always responded well to a good horror story that has enough suspense and thrills to succeed on its own merits without actually horrifying or revolting its audience. In this respect, and for its time, *The Night Stalker* was perfect TV fare.

"Perhaps it had something to do with a slowly-growing paranoia. We'd had years of a widening, increasingly unpopular war polarizing society; a growing and demonstrative anti-war movement; societal changes; the 'light at the end of the tunnel' that receded day by day. *The Pentagon*

Papers had just been made public and the public's growing awareness of the abuse of power and authority, and its growing distrust of all the reassurances handed to it by people in positions of authority and trust, must surely have been a factor.

"Perhaps there was a general yearning for someone who would verbally fly in the face of authority; call a spade a spade; and put his ass on the line for his belief in the public's right to know what is really going on. "These ruminations may be 'at best highly speculative, but not altogether unwarranted.' "

The only thing Rice didn't like about the TV movie was the score composed by Cobert. And, "to put it bluntly, I hated it," he says, "from beginning to end. Awful! Saturday morning cartoon music at its worst!"

He is, however, in the minority on that one. Far from sharing this harsh judgment, the other principals are very fond of Cobert's *Night Stalker* music. Several started humming it without provocation.

Indeed, Jon Burlingame, the leading expert on music composed for television and the author of *TV's Biggest Hits* (Schirmer Books, 1996), has nothing but praise for Cobert's *Night Stalker* score. "Bob Cobert did something very sophisticated with the *Night Stalker* music," Burlingame says. "It's a schizophrenic score in a very good and fitting sense. Given the assignment of a horror story set in modern Las Vegas, he combined the traditional horror approach — which is dark, ominous, gothic, minor key, extremely low sounds — with these strange, attractive, upbeat, surprising and irreverent jazz rifts. It's the dark coupled with the jazz; the light coupled with the extremely heavy. And it's that combination that is so right for this story and for Kolchak. The music is Kolchak. It not only encapsulates what the story is all about, it encapsulates the character of Carl Kolchak. It is *so* right. It's Carl because it is irreverent.

"And what I think is even more remarkable about Cobert's music for that film is that nobody else in this town would have done it that way. It's also a measure of the degree of respect Dan Curtis had for Bob Cobert. As you know, Bob Cobert was always Dan's number-one choice. It's a remarkable collaboration spanning more than thirty years, but I think *The Night Stalker* may be the best thing Cobert ever did for Curtis. And Dan had the wisdom to say, 'Bob, you know what you're doing, just do it. I'm not going to interfere.' Today, fifty people, including network executives, would be all over him, saying, 'Can't you change that third note in the fourth measure?' They'd wouldn't get what Cobert was trying to do. People who don't know anything about music would be saying, 'That doesn't work, what's that all about.' Well, heck, it works. It's inspired."

But back to the state of shock at ABC.

"There was no realization while we were doing it that this was going to turn into an event," McGavin points out. "I went from that project into something else a week and a half later. It was fun and it was wonderful and I loved the character, but we didn't think it would be anything beyond that."

The reviews (the few that were printed in advance of the airing) certainly didn't prepare anyone for the ratings frenzy. In a column that January 11 in the *Los Angeles Times*, critic Kevin Thomas called the TV movie "genuinely scary" and praised McGavin's "zesty performance as a hard-driving reporter of the old green-eyeshade school of journalism." Thomas described *The Night Stalker* as "a good example of the incredible credible." But there was nothing in this or any of the other reviews that suggested the film was what NBC would later call must-see TV.

As to what it was about *The Night Stalker* that caused such a ratings sensation, McGavin again returns to the original concept: "The first movie is so fresh and original. You start with the concept. I mean, who has a newspaperman chasing a vampire in Las Vegas? That's an interesting idea."

Some perspective may be in order here. Yes, *The Night Stalker* did make quite a stir in January of 1972. After all, about one out of every three people in the United States was watching Carl Kolchak track Janos Skorzeny. Still, Kolchak's 33.2 rating (percentage of all TV homes) and fifty-four share (percentage of sets actually in use) don't put *The Night Stalker* anywhere near Nielsen's fifty highest-rated programs in television history (a list, by the way, that includes more than fifteen Super Bowls and seven of the eight chapters of the 1977 miniseries *Roots*). Compare Kolchak's numbers with the *M\*A\*S\*H* finale, which remains the highest-rated program of all time. The series closer pulled a staggering 60.2 rating and a seventy-seven share. And, in the two decades since *The Night Stalker* aired, four TV movies have broken its rating record.

But, on the other hand, TV movies must be judged in a separate category. They are not the colossal rating draws of network television — certainly not in the same league with Super Bowls and miniseries and series finales. In fact, until *The Day After* exploded on the scene in November 1983, no TV movie was in the top-fifty list. So, even though he's no longer the TV movie champion, Kolchak's ratings remain quite impressive. His place in TV history is secure. Consider the following list of highest rated TV movies (broken down by rank, program, network, season and rating/share)supplied by Nielsen:

**1.)** *The Day After*, ABC 1983-84,46.0/62

**2.)** *Little Ladies of the Night*, ABC 1976-77, 36.9/53

**3.)** *The Burning Bed*, NBC 1984-85, 36.2/52

**4.)** *The Waltons' Thanksgiving Story*, CBS 1973-74, 33.5/51

**5.)** *The Night Stalker,* ABC, 1971-7233.2/54

**6.)** *A Case of Rape*, NBC 1973-74, 33.1/53

**7.)** *Return to Mayberry*, NBC 1985-86, 33.0/49

**8.)** *Dallas Cowboy Cheerleaders*, ABC 1978-79, 33.0/38

**9.)** *Brian's Song*, ABC 1971-72, 32.9/48

**10.)** *Women in Chains*, ABC 1971-72, 32.3/48

**11.)** *Magnum, p.i.*, CBS 1987-88, 32.0/48

**12.)** *Something About Amelia*, ABC 1983-84, 31.9/46

**13.)** *Heidi*, NBC 1968-69, 31.8/47

**14.)** *My Sweet Charlie*, NBC 1969-70, 31.7/48

**15.)** *The Feminist and the Fuzz*, ABC 1970-71, 31.6/46

\* (This list does not include such two-part network dramas as *Helter Skelter* and *Fatal Vision*. The networks call these miniseries. Nielsen defines the true miniseries as something three nights or longer. So, others call these two-part movies, especially since they usually are edited into one-night presentations for syndication. But David Bianculli of the *New York Daily News*, the television critics' resident expert on the miniseries form, maintains that two-parters are indeed miniseries. What seems clear is that the two-parter is neither fish nor fowl. It's a form stuck somewhere between the TV movie and the true miniseries. In any event, to be absolutely clear, this is a list of the highest-rated single-night TV movies. Okay?)

Yes, *The Night Stalker* still stands quite tall. No TV movie of the last ten years has come anywhere near matching its Nielsen performance. For instance, the highest-rated TV movie of the 1989-90 season was the *Twin Peaks* opener. It managed a paltry 21.7 rating (one out of five TV households compared to Kolchak's one out of three). The highest-rated TV movie of the 1988-89 season was *The Karen Carpenter Story*. It managed a 26.4 rating. And the highest-rated TV movie of the 1987-88 season was *The Ann Jillian Story*, which triumphed with a 23.8 rating. The increasing fragmentation of the television audience (split by cable choices, new networks and syndication) make it unlikely that a TV movie will ever attract more than fifty percent of the people watching television on a given night. Super Bowls still can post these heavyweight numbers. The Green Bay Packers' January 1997 victory in Super Bowl XXXI pulled about eighty-eight million viewers (thirteen million more than watched *The Night Stalker* in January 1972). Yet no TV movie of 1997 has pulled more than twenty-five million viewers (that's fifty million *less* than watched *The Night Stalker*).

Everybody has an explanation for Kolchak's success. All seem valid.

Yet, perhaps McGavin points us in the right direction when he says to look back at Jeff Rice's original novel. In an industry where everyone is scared of making the wrong decision, Rice delivered that rarest of all commodities — a natural. Matheson recognized it. ABC recognized it. Curtis recognized it.

McGavin recognized it. Moxey recognized it. And Doran, although he might not have fully realized it, certainly recognized that the combination of elements in *The Night Stalker* made it a natural. The individual reactions to the story are convincing and compelling. The building of reactions make what happened on January 11 seem entirely logical.

## The Hook

So, with a distance of almost twenty years for perspective, let us consider *The Night Stalker*. If you happen to rent a tape of the TV movie or chance upon it in syndication, you'll discover how amazingly fresh and vital it seems. Very few TV movies from the late '60s and early '70s hold up in the '90s. Don't take my word for it. Give 'em a try. Most of the message movies seem tame and dated (sometimes even unenlightened). Most of the mere entertainments seem merely silly. But, except for some of the clothes (and let's remember that fashion is a ridiculously moot point when we're talking about Carl Kolchak), *The Night Stalker* hardly has aged at all.

What worked then, works now. And nothing works better than what Richard Matheson described as a cinema verite approach to a vampire story. There's this immense hook that emerges from the opening of *The Night Stalker* — a hook that grabs our interest and refuses to let go of us for a second. The hook is called reality.

In a horror film, you usually worry about reality intruding on the fantasy. In *The Night Stalker*, we're told to plant our feet in reality — yes, in a world of slot machines, autopsies, FBI traces, official reports, deadlines, headlines and bylines. This isn't Transylvania and legends and castles and cobwebs and the "children of the night, what music they make." In Carl Kolchak's world, the children of the night are gamblers, prostitutes and mobsters. That's the reality, and fantasy is about to intrude on it.

There is, in this reversal of formula, an answer to a rather formidable question: How can you do a modern-day vampire story set in the United States? Make it as realistic as possible. Give it the trappings of a genuine police investigation. Open the story with a no-nonsense reporter telling us that it's not silly to believe in vampires. Decide for yourself. It's only the foolish among you who will not accept that possibility. The presence of Darren McGavin, an actor whose approach to his craft screams integrity, only makes the setup more realistic. Hey, this isn't Peter Cushing or Edward Van Sloan warning us that something is out there. This is rugged, shoot-from-the-hip, all-American Darren McGavin, for crying out loud. You'd better listen up.

When Kolchak/McGavin says "judge for yourself its believability, and then try to tell yourself, wherever you may be, it couldn't happen here," he's giving us the hard-boiled reporter's variation on the lines delivered by Dr. Van Helsing (Van Sloan) in Lugosi's *Dracula*: "The superstition of yesterday can become the scientific reality of today. . . The strength of the vampire is that people will not believe in him." Yet, with Kolchak, it's so much more than just what he's saying. It's how he says it with facts and figures.

Look, when the first victim, Cheryl Hughes, is attacked, all Kolchak has to tell us is that a woman was found dead. But he tells us her name. He tells us the day and time of the attack. He tells us what streets she followed. We know where she worked. We know she was twenty-three. We know she weighed 113 pounds. We know she had been waiting for a ride. We know the color of her hair (blonde) and the color of her eyes (light brown). That's a reporter at work — details and more details. Kolchak tells us who, when and where. He's pushing to find out why, how and what. Cheryl Hughes immediately becomes more than a victim. She's a person with a name and a job and light-brown eyes.

There are at least two more formula reversals in *The Night Stalker*, and these twists seem no less innovative after two decades. The obvious experiment is a vampire film in which the vampire is not the central character. Think about it. All the way back to *Nosferatu*, movies about vampires have a vampire as the main or at least dominant figure. We don't see much of Janos Skorzeny in *The Night Stalker*. He never speaks. We usually glimpse him in the shadows (setting an effective trend for the later series). Kolchak is the central and dominant figure of *The Night Stalker*, which means we've got a vampire story that's not the story of a vampire. It's the story of a reporter.

The third formula reversal involves the mixing of humor and horror, hardly a new concept in Hollywood. Comedians had been doing it for decades: Bud Abbott and Lou Costello in *Hold That Ghost* (1941), Bob Hope in *Ghost Breakers* (1940), the Bowery Boys in *Spooks Run Wild* (1941), Ole Olsen and Chic Johnson in *Ghost Catchers* (1944), Dean Martin and Jerry Lewis in *Scared Stiff* (1953). In the two decades after *The Night Stalker*, Mel Brooks unleashed *Young Frankenstein* (1974), George Hamilton played Dracula for laughs in *Love at First Bite* (1979), and a trio of paranormal investigators (Bill Murray, Dan Aykroyd and Harold Ramis) became known as the *Ghostbusters* (1984). Nobody blended humor and horror better than Abbott & Costello in their 1948 meeting with Frankenstein (and Dracula and the Wolf Man and the Invisible Man). What all of these films have in common is that they are comedies using horror as the background for the humor. *The Night Stalker*, however, is a horror film using humor as a constant element. This is more than the wicked little jokes director James Whale tossed into *The Bride of Frankenstein* (1935) so audiences would laugh with the film, not at it. Humor is an integral and ongoing part of *The Night Stalker*, not just punctuation. And it's not mocking or self-deprecating laughter. It's humor that arises from human relationships (mostly the love-hate tango between Kolchak and Vincenzo).

Splendidly paced, *The Night Stalker* is a stylish and innovative TV movie that manages to preserve the official-coverup-paranoia of Jeff Rice's book. From the cold opening with Kolchak—no titles, no music—setting up "the story behind one of the greatest manhunts in history," there is the feeling that we're watching television that's a little different, a little smarter. Everything that follows confirms this feeling.

The attack on Cheryl Hughes is indicative of both the film's excellent pacing and offbeat approach. The vampire and the camera close in on the unconscious victim. Our point of view is that of the vampire until the camera is covered by the blackness of his jacket — darkness. The camera pulls back as a sanitation worker discovers the body in a garbage can. He's looking down at the grisly discovery. In a flash, the camera is looking up. But this time, when faces come into view, they belong to the three masked pathologists, who are looking down. The autopsy is beginning. Our point of view is that of the corpse. The scalpels are slicing toward us. We hear Larry Linville say, "Peel back the. . ." Yecch! It's a gruesomely effective scene. More than that, though, it's stylish and terribly efficient: not a wasted second. We get the sequence one-two-three.

Who encountered Cheryl (first alive, then dead)? We see them in brisk order — vampire, sanitation worker, medical examiner. Now we get the credits, over the autopsy. Everybody let out a long sigh.

There are many other clever scenes. There is a terrific cast. But this movie, first scene to last, belongs to Darren McGavin. Without the vampire, Las Vegas and corruption, McGavin's Carl Kolchak still would be an incredibly interesting fellow. This is not your typical TV hero. In a supernatural adventure endowed with the logic of a reporter's cynical approach, Kolchak is at once the most virtuous and most cynical character in the story.

"Do you believe in vampires, little boy?" asks Bernie Jenks (Ralph Meeker) in an early scene. No, he doesn't. Kolchak can only be convinced by hard realities. If professional and heroic, Kolchak also has some darker shadings, and McGavin doesn't mind peeling back these less attractive corners.

"All these murders mean to you is a byline," yells Tony Vincenzo. Kolchak doesn't reply right away. Tony has hit a spot of partial truth.

Kolchak also doesn't deny the accusation. He simply brushes it away: "Well, what the hell difference does it make what it means to me?"

Yet there's more than a byline. Kolchak tells us that he's been fired often — twice in Washington, D.C., three times in New York, twice in Chicago, three times in Boston. "I'm becoming extinct in my own lifetime," he grumbles. Underneath the grumble, there is the desire to prove to Tony Vincenzo and Las Vegas and himself that he's not a "has-been big-city reporter."

And the hook takes a stronger hold of us because McGavin reached deep into a fictional character and found a reality.

## Precident and Progeny

Shortly before *The Night Stalker* was to begin filming, American International Pictures (AIP) informed ABC that a lawsuit was imminent. AIP owned the rights to *Progeny of the Adder*, a 1965 horror novel by Leslie H. Whitten (*The Alchemist*). With a film version of *Progeny of the Adder* in the planning stages, AIP was claiming that Jeff Rice had plagiarized Whitten's book for *The Night Stalker*.

Rice calmly insisted that he hadn't read Whitten's novel. AIP replied that, since the book had been out for five years, he had "implied access." Because someone wasn't with him for every minute of those five years, Rice asked, how could he prove that he hadn't purchased or read *Progeny of the Adder*? Finally, Rice pointed out that the characters in *The Night Stalker* were based on real people, and he'd "subpoena half of Las Vegas" to prove it. That was enough. AIP dropped the lawsuit.

But charges of literary theft tend to linger. When horror fans talk about *The Night Stalker*, it's not uncommon for someone to mention *Progeny of the Adder*. All right, it's time to put this one to rest. Yes, there are some remarkable similarities. But remarkable similarities are not uncommon in fantasy literature. David Gerrold was horrified to discover that his *Star Trek* episode "The Trouble With Tribbles" used a central gimmick remarkably similar to the one in Robert A. Heinlein's *The Rolling Stones*. Heinlein laughed off any similarities and suggested that both stories were similar to Ellis Parker Butler's "Pigs is Pigs." In his book about the episode, Gerrold concluded that it was entirely natural for the same idea to occur to two or more writers. It was what the different writers did with the idea — plot, characters, structure, pacing – that was important.

And since there is a common idea at the core of *The Night Stalker* and *Progeny of the Adder*, on the surface, they may seem similar. Each deals with a big-city police force searching for a vampire. Each has scenes where the cornered vampire levels a police team and escapes. Each book has a scene where a used-car salesman recalls the vampire's horribly bad breath.

So, there is a common idea – a vampire on the loose in a major American city. Yet, once you push past this, the two books are completely different in tone, mood and characters.

Start with Whitten's hero, veteran homicide detective Harry Picard. He is Kolchak's polar opposite. Picard, unlike Kolchak, is a workmanlike police detective just going about his job. He's as deliberate and colorless as Kolchak is unpredictable and flamboyant. Picard is an establishment hero working as part of an official police investigation. Kolchak is an anti-establishment hero – a discourteous dissenter who doesn't trust the official police investigation. Picard works in the system so *Progeny of the Adder* is an inside story. Kolchak is an outsider who has no faith in the system. Picard is part of the official circles. Kolchak sniffs around the edges of these circles. Picard is a team player. Kolchak is a loner. Picard is a workhorse. Kolchak is a maverick.

The two books also are completely different from a stylistic standpoint. *The Night Stalker*, or, if you prefer, *The Kolchak Papers*, hits the ground running and cruises along at a breathless clip. *Progeny of the Adder* is more deliberately paced as it follows the by-the-book police procedure. It has a far more low-key start and none of the *Front Page* sensibility that Rice brought to Kolchak's story.

In fact, there is very little humor in *Progeny of the Adder*, and what humor does exist is quite grim. While the tone of Rice's book suggests a collaboration between Bram Stoker and Ben Hecht, the police procedural approach of Whitten's book brings to mind Stoker and Jack Webb.

Then there's the setting. Las Vegas is such an overwhelming presence in Rice's book that it almost becomes another character. *Progeny of the Adder*, like Whitten's *The Alchemist* (1973), is set in Washington, D.C. Two different cities. Two different characters. Two different approaches. Two different books. Kolchak is as different from Picard as Las Vegas is from Washington.

Okay, there are the scenes with the used-car salesmen mentioning noxious breath. That might raise an eyebrow or two, but, remember, Stoker had Harker pass out when he got a good whiff of Count Dracula. If they had used cars in London when Dracula called to visit, he might have purchased one to cart things around. It's logical.

The two books have something else in common. Each is a fun read that works *on its own terms.*

## After the Night

*The Night Stalker* owned the ratings record for TV movies, but most everyone connected with the film knew the lady named Emmy would turn her back on a horror story. In late January, though, full-page ads were placed in *Variety* and *The Hollywood Reporter* to crow about the *Night Stalker* victory. The ad named Darren McGavin, Dan Curtis, Richard Matheson, Robert Cobert and several other players. No mention was made of Jeff Rice or his novel. Nor had he been mentioned in the credits listed by the *Los Angeles Times* with the January 11 review by Kevin Thomas (although the credit box listed twelve actors, as well as director of photography Mike Hugo, art director Trevor Williams and film editor Desmond Marquette). Neither the original ABC press release for *The Night Stalker* nor the one for a January 1974 rebroadcast (which was teamed on a Wednesday-night double-bill with *Scream of the Wolf*, a terror tale directed by Curtis and written by Matheson) mentions Rice's name.

"Later on," Rice says, "I discovered my name had been carefully deleted from *all* network press releases. As far as the trades and general press were concerned, I had become the invisible man."

Matheson could sympathize. That same season, *Duel* had put Steven Spielberg on the map as a director.

"A friend of mine put a huge one-page ad in *Variety* lamenting that everybody always was referring to it as Steven Spielberg's *Duel*," Matheson said. "He argued that surely there was enough room for Richard Matheson to have his name in there, too!"

Surely there was enough room for Jeff Rice to have his name in there, too. On January 31, 1972, Rice sent a letter to ABC's Allen Epstein. He proposed a sequel: "I would like to strongly suggest a sequel but this time to have Kolchak deal with a genuine mystery based on life rather than legend. I think there are enough unsolved crimes, from murder to political intrigue, that could serve as the basis for a fast, tight drama which would show Kolchak off in the best possible light as an investigative reporter."

Rice also asked for the chance to write the sequel. On March 2, ABC signed a contract for an original Kolchak story from Matheson. Rice's letter went unanswered.

Plans for a sequel signaled the end of the *Night Stalker* trail for John Llewellyn Moxey. Dan Curtis wanted to direct the first movie. He would direct the second one.

"Dan really wanted to direct," McGavin explains. "Dan *really* wanted to direct. During the first movie, he'd mumble under his breath to me, 'Will you look at the setup Moxey has here. What's he doing?' And I'd mumble back, 'It'll be fine. It'll be fine.' But that's Dan. He wants to be in charge."

Moxey had no interest in sequels or the later series. "I did the movie and it was just one of those rare films where everything clicked together," he says, "but I wasn't interested in continuing with it in any way. I had nothing against the series. I just had absolutely no interest in being part of it. I felt as if I had done it. *The Night Stalker* was very distinctive and refreshing. Then Darren went ahead and did *The Night Strangler*, which also was very successful. But I didn't want to do the vampire of the week. We'd done it."

Moxey didn't lack for work. After *The Night Stalker,* offers to direct TV movies just kept coming: *Home for the Holidays* (1972), *The Bounty Man* (1972), Gene Roddenberry's *Genesis II* (1973), *A Strange and Deadly Occurrence* (1974), *Conspiracy of Terror* (1975), *Nightmare in Badham County* (1976), *Intimate Strangers* (1977), *Panic in Echo Park* (1977), *The President's Mistress* (1978), *The Power Within* (1979), *Sanctuary of Fear* (1979), *The Children of An Lac* (1980), *Killjoy* (1981), *The Cradle Will Fall* (1983), *Through Naked Eyes* (1983), *When Dreams Come True* (1985), *Blacke's Magic* (the 1986 pilot for the series), *Sadie and Son* (1987), *Lady Mobster* (1988) and *Outback Bound* (1988). He also directed episodes of *Mission: Impossible* and *Charlie's Angels*. Starting in 1984, Moxey was a regular director on Angela Lansbury's hit mystery series, *Murder, She Wrote* (at the helm of eighteen episodes during the CBS show's first seven seasons).

The night of May 6, 1972, was not a good evening for the *Night Stalker* M-Team. McGavin, Matheson and Moxey weren't even nominated for Emmys. As expected, *Brian's Song* took home its share of statuettes. It won for outstanding single program (drama or comedy), best supporting actor in drama (Jack Warden) and writing achievement in drama, adaptation (William Blinn). Keith Michell (*The Six Wives of Henry VIII*) was named best actor in a leading role. Tom Gries won the director's Emmy for a single drama program (for the TV movie *The Glass House*).

If Emmy had no recognition for *The Night Stalker*, other organizations did. Matheson's screenplay won a Writers Guild of America award and the Mystery Writers of America's Edgar for best mystery television feature.

Emmys, however, mattered little to Curtis and Matheson. They were deep into the planning of the next Kolchak caper.

There was one more tribute in 1987. Upstart fourth-network Fox Broadcasting had premiered a horror drama titled *Werewolf*. Chuck Connors (*The Rifleman*) appeared as a mysterious lycanthrope. His name? Janos Skorzeny.

**Carl Kolchak (Darren McGavin) and his editor Tony Vincenzo (Simon Oakland) have one of their usual "slight" disagreements in the newsroom.**

Reporter Kolchak on the prowl with camera in hand.

# Part II

# The Night Strangler

## or, "A Tale of Another City"

*"I came to Seattle for peace and quiet and what do I get?*
*You again and another crazy story."*
— **Tony Vincenzo (Simon Oakland)**
***The Night Strangler* (1973)**

*"Monsters, John. Monsters from the Id."*
— **"Doc" Ostrow (Warren Stevens)**
***Forbidden Planet* (1956)**
**Screenplay by Cyril Hume**

### Original airdate: January 16, 1973

Teleplay by Richard Matheson
Based on some characters created by Jeff Rice
Produced and Directed by Dan Curtis
Music by Robert Cobert
Associate producer: Robert Singer
Director of photography: Robert Hauser, a.s.c.
Production designer: Trevor Williams
Film editor: Folmar Blangsted, a.c.e
Unit production manager/
    Assistant director: Christopher H. Seitz
Script supervisor: Betty Abbott Griffin
Production assistant: Lois Kerst
Makeup artist: William J. Tuttle
Hair stylist: Scotty Rackin
Costume supervisor: John Perry
Men's costumer: Jimmy George

Women's costumer: Barbara Siebert
Transportation manager: Norm Honath
Stunt coordinator: Dick Ziker
Gaffer: Don Johnson
Key grip: Robert Moore
Property master: Robert Anderson
Special effects: Ira Anderson
Construction coordinator: Hank Wynanos
Set decorator: Charles R. Pierce
Sound mixer: Harold Lewis
Assistant editor: Kent Schafer
Music editor: Len Engel
Sound effects: editor: Gary Gerlich
Casting: Hoyt Bowers
Titles, opticals and processing:
    Consolidated Film Industries

Chrysler vehicles provided by Chrysler Corp.
Filmed at 20th Century-Fox Studios
Copyright © 1972 by the American Broadcasting Companies, Inc.

## CAST

Carl Kolchak....................................Darren McGavin
Louise Harper.....................................Jo Ann Pflug
Tony Vincenzo.................................Simon Oakland
Dr. Richard Malcolm...................Richard Anderson
Captain Roscoe Schubert......................Scott Brady
Titus Berry.........................................Wally Cox
Professor Crabwell...................Margaret Hamilton
Llewellyn Crossbinder...................John Carradine
Charisma Beauty..................................Nina Wayne
Tramp.................................................Al Lewis
Dr. Christopher Webb........................Ivor Francis
Wilma Krankheimer.......................Virginia Peters
Janie Watkins....................................Kate Murtagh
Merissa (Ethel Parker)....................Regina Parton
Stacks................................................George Tobias*
Joyce Gabriel........................................Diane Shalet
Policewoman Shelia...........................Anne Randall
Restaurant Woman................. Francoise Birnheim
Underground Tour Guide...............George DiCenzo

\* Although still listed in many cast lists, Tobias does not appear in versions of *The Night Strangler* aired on American television. His scene was cut from both the seventy-four-minute and ninety-minute versions.

**SYNOPSIS:** *The voice is familiar. It belongs to reporter Carl Kolchak: "This is the story behind the most incredible series of murders to ever occur in the city of Seattle, Washington. You never read about them in your local newspapers or heard about them on your local radio or television station. Why? Because the facts were watered down, torn apart and reassembled — in a word, falsified."*

Saturday, April 1: At 2:35 a.m. Merissa (real name Ethel Parker), one of three belly dancers at the Seattle bar Omar's Tent, is attacked by a powerful man dressed in black. The coroner determines that the cause of death was strangulation.

Murder is the last thing on the mind of Tony Vincenzo — "city editor by profession, bilious grouch by disposition" — as he orders a glass of milk at the local press club bar. But murder springs quickly to mind when he hears that familiar voice around the corner. "Oh, no," Tony groans as he hears Carl Kolchak trying to convince a young reporter that, yes, an actual vampire did terrorize Las Vegas.

"Take a look around that corner," Tony tells the bartender, "see if there isn't someone there that looks like he just came from a road company performance of *The Front Page*."

Sure enough, it's Kolchak. Tony now is city editor of the *Seattle Daily Chronicle*. And Kolchak, of course, needs a job. "Get this straight, Mr. Kolchak," warns ever-stern publisher Llewellyn Crossbinder, "no carnival or hoopla tactics on this paper. This isn't Fun Town, U.S.A. This is Seattle."

Warned and hired, Kolchak is put on the story of Ethel Parker, a strangled belly dancer found in an alley. Investigating the murder, Carl meets the other two dancers at Omar's Tent, Charisma Beauty (given name Gladys Weems) and the Princess of the East (better known as Louise Harper). Louise and Carl hit it off. Her mouth moves as fast as her hips. She has a big mouth, Carl has a big mouth. Tony has an ulcer.

Meanwhile, a second strangulation victim has been found — cocktail waitress Gail Manning. The medical examiner's report contains three very disturbing elements. The murderer is incredibly strong. A small amount of blood had been removed by needle from both victims. And, most troubling of all, traces of decomposed flesh were found on both necks — as if they had been strangled by a dead man.

Louise introduces Carl to the underground tour of Old Seattle. In 1889, the Great Seattle Fire leveled much of the city. A new city was built on top of the ruins of the old one. After extensive renovations, tours are conducted through several blocks of the Victorian city beneath the modern Seattle. At the moment, though, the underground is a mere curiosity to Carl Kolchak. A bigger story is taking shape in the basement of the *Chronicle*.

The newspaper's "morgue attendant" (or, if you will, librarian), Titus Berry, discovers that a similar series of strangulations occurred in the Pioneer Square district of Seattle exactly twenty-one years ago. During an eighteen-day period in 1952, six women were found strangled. Then the killer disappeared. But a witness who saw the murderer in 1952 said he had the rotted features of a corpse.

Vincenzo, naturally enough, is reluctant to print Kolchak's story. "Let's not play that stupid game again," the reporter implores his editor.

"Psychologists call it deja vu — the distinct impression of having had the same experience before," Kolchak tells us. "That's what it was, all right, in spades."

But two developments strengthen Kolchak's case: secretary Joyce Gabriel, on the way home from work late at night, sees the killer looming over his third victim, and Titus Berry digs deeper into the files. The good Mr. Berry has found that in 1931, during a period of eighteen days, six women were found strangled in the Pioneer Square area. In 1910, the same thing. The pattern starts in 1889, the year of the great fire. A 1910 witness said that the slayer had "cheekbones protruding through the face."

"Isn't that great?" a delighted Kolchak asks Vincenzo.

When the strangler strikes next, the police arrive in time to surround him. Kolchak arrives in time to witness the escape and nearly get killed. The flash from Kolchak's camera startles the killer and saves the reporter's life. But the strangler easily tosses aside Seattle police officers and scrambles to freedom over a fence.

The fifth victim is Charisma Beauty. Louise Harper, performing on stage at the time, missed the honor by a matter of seconds.

Back at the newspaper, Titus Berry has found another clipping that he thinks will interest Mr. Kolchak. It's an 1880s interview with Mark Twain, who told a local reporter that he had a most interesting conversation with a Seattle physician. Dr. Richard Malcolm, a Union army surgeon during the Civil War and the founder of Seattle's Westside Mercy Hospital, told Twain that the pursuit of physical immortality was completely practical.

This clicks with something told him by Professor Crabwell, a university instructor recommended to Kolchak by Louise Harper. After seeing the strangler fight off the police, Kolchak wanted to know how a man older than ninety could remain strong and vital. Crabwell gave him a quick course in the study of alchemy. Some alchemists, she said, believed an elixir could prolong life. One of the principal ingredients, as if you didn't know, is human blood.

And the Westside Mercy Hospital? It burned to the ground in the great fire of 1889. Malcolm's wife, stepson and stepdaughter died of smoke inhalation. Malcolm disappeared the night of the fire. Berry can find only one picture of Dr. Richard Malcolm.

But in 1910, a Dr. Malcolm Richards appeared on the scene and built a free clinic over the ruins of the Westside Mercy Hospital. Dr. Malcolm Richards disappeared

The spider, Dr. Richard Malcolm (Richard Anderson), leads the badly dressed fly, Carl Kolchak (Darren McGavin), into a web of test tubes and chemicals.

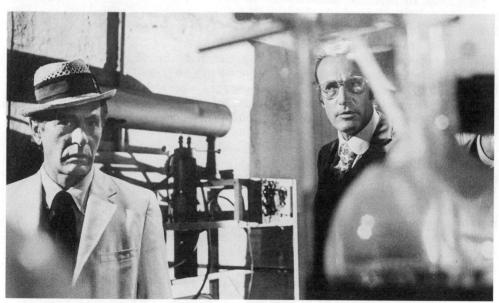

Dr. Richard Malcolm (Richard Anderson) shares his beauty secrets with reporter Carl Kolchak (Darren McGavin) in *The Night Strangler*.

While Carl Kolchak (Darren McGavin) picks up a message on his desk in the newsroom, Janie Watkins (Kate Murtagh) confers with editor Tony Vincenzo (Simon Oakland) in the background.

in 1931. The twenty-one year interludes convince Kolchak that Richard Malcolm and Malcolm Richards are the same man. The reporter also is certain that Malcolm is the strangler terrorizing Seattle.

There is a portrait of Malcolm Richards at the free clinic. If Kolchak is right, it will be identical to his newspaper photograph of Richard Malcolm. It is. What's more, Berry has researched Richard Malcolm's career. Before moving to Seattle, Malcolm was living in New York, where in 1868, six women were strangled to death during an eighteen-day period. That was twenty-one years before the first series of Seattle strangulations in 1889.

Kolchak tells the police that time is running out. Soon, Malcolm will have his sixth victim and disappear for another twenty-one years. A woman going over receipts in a closed restaurant becomes the sixth victim.

Due to pressure from the police, Kolchak is taken off the story. But he refuses to give up. He's sure that Malcolm is hiding in the underground. Searching the basement of the Free Clinic, he finds an entrance to the ruins of Westside Mercy Hospital. Kolchak tells Louise to give him thirty minutes, then call the police. He wants his exclusive.

Kolchak steps into another century. He follows the strains of music to a scene out of *Great Expectations* — a mummified family sits around a dining-room table, frozen in time (1889 to be exact). One plate of food is fresh and hot. It belongs to Dr. Richard Malcolm, who is standing behind Carl Kolchak. Malcolm agrees to give the newshound his story. What difference does it make? He won't be getting back to the twentieth century alive, not after Dr. Malcolm operates on his neck.

Malcolm says he first took the elixir in 1868. But in 1889, his world fell apart. He discovered that the effects of the mixture were not permanent, and the great fire killed his family. At the end of twenty-one years, he starts to age and decay. The restoration process takes eighteen days. Six preparations are required, and the blood elements must be removed from female victims' brains within thirty seconds of death. Malcolm is about to take the sixth and final dose. If he doesn't, the process will quickly reverse itself. As Malcolm reaches for the flask, Kolchak grabs an inkwell and hurls it at the chemicals. The flask breaks and an enraged Malcolm hurls himself at Kolchak. Just when all looks hopeless, Malcolm loosens his grip from Kolchak's throat. The police arrive. Malcolm staggers back. Kolchak gets a good look at him. Malcolm's face is a nightmare of decomposition. Horrible as it is, the face takes on a sad expression. Malcolm gasps out a last word to Kolchak, "Why?" Then he runs to the window and jumps to his death.

The next day, Kolchak learns the true meaning of deja vu. He has been fired. The story will not see print. Tony promises him that he did everything in his power to get the facts in the paper. Kolchak doesn't believe him, until... Cut to Kolchak driving out of town, promising all the way that he'll get the real story out. "If they think they can shut me up," yells Kolchak. "Can anybody shut you up?" asks Tony, who is sitting next to him. Crossbinder also fired Vincenzo. From the back seat, Louise Harper starts a barrage of complaints about being run out of town. "Peace!" pleads Vincenzo as the car fades into the night.

**PRODUCTION HISTORY:** In television, nothing repeats like success. And the ratings success of *The Night Stalker* had ABC thinking sequel almost immediately. Curtis was agreeable if he could direct this one. The formidable challenge of coming up with a second Kolchak caper fell to Richard Matheson. The early going was very tough.

"Dan and I and several others sat in an office at ABC for hours," Matheson recalls, "trying to think up a monster for the second film. Somebody would come up with an idea and somebody wouldn't like it. This went on and on. And at one point, it just struck me as so funny and I said, 'Isn't this ridiculous? Grown men sitting in this big building, trying to decide what would be a good monster.' It seemed so bizarre to me."

Then something clicked in the writer's mind.

"I had seen this underground city while on a trip to Seattle with my wife and kids," Matheson explains. "It isn't as extensive as the film leads you to believe, but I amplified on it and worked with Dan on it. But it took a long time to come up with a good story to go with that. My idea, actually, was that it was Jack the Ripper still alive."

Jack the Ripper? The original night stalker? The idea seemed like a natural, especially since Rice had Kolchak fascinated by the Ripper case in *The Kolchak Papers*. There was just one slight problem. Matheson's close friend and fellow fantasy master Robert Bloch (*Psycho, The Scarf, American Gothic*) had written a story titled "Yours Truly, Jack the Ripper." Would Bloch view this story as dangerously close? There was only one way to find out. Matheson gave his old chum a call and explained the situation.

"I asked him if it would bother him," Matheson says. "I could tell that it would, something about the tone in his voice. So I didn't do it."

Another monster had to be wedded to Seattle's underground. "It took a long time to come up with a good story," Matheson notes.

"Yeah, we worked our tails off on that story," says Curtis. "You know, a good sequel is hard to do. If you don't have a story that's strong enough, why do it? But with Richard Matheson, you're dealing with one of the best people in the business, period. I knew we were in good hands."

Perhaps Jack the Ripper would have been a better payoff for the second movie. Then again, by 1972, Jack already had cut quite a figure in movies and television. Alfred Hitchcock's first suspense film, *The Lodger* (1926), was about a mysterious man (played by Ivor Novello) who just might be Jack the Ripper. *The Lodger* was remade three times, twice under the same title (in 1932 with Novello and in 1944 with Laird Cregar) and as *The Man in the Attic* (Jack Palance in 1954). German director G.W. Pabst had Jack make an appearance in *Pandora's Box* (1928), He got his own movie in 1960, *Jack the Ripper*. He crossed wits with Sherlock Holmes (John Neville) in *A Study in Terror* (1965). And Bloch's "Yours Truly, Jack the Ripper" was turned into a memorable episode of Boris Karloff's *Thriller* (NBC, 1960-62). Bloch revisited the Ripper lore for "Wolf in the Fold," a second-season episode of the original *Star Trek* (NBC, 1966-69). John Fiedler, later Gordy the Ghoul in the *Night Stalker* series, was a sharp guest star for "Wolf in the Fold."

After *The Night Strangler* aired, Jack kept coming back. There was another meeting with Sherlock Holmes (Christopher Plummer this time) in *Murder By Decree* (1979). There was a race through time with H.G. Wells in *Time After Time* (1979). There was *Jack's Back* (1988), a Los Angeles updating. Host Peter Ustinov told us *The Secret Identity of Jack the Ripper* in a live 1988 syndicated special. And Michael Caine chased the Whitechapel murderer through the 1988 miniseries *Jack the Ripper*.

So it's possible that Bloch actually did Matheson an enormous favor. If Jack had slipped into the *Night Stalker* sequel, Kolchak's encounter might have gone down as just one more entry in a crowded field of Ripper retreads. Instead, Matheson dug a little deeper and planted a more original idea in the Seattle underground. Nobody knows for certain what would have happened to a second Kolchak movie with Jack the Ripper as the linchpin. What we do know for certain is that, without Jack the Ripper, *The Night Strangler* was extremely well received and still is considered one of the few Hollywood sequels that approaches the level of an acclaimed predecessor. While Leonard Maltin concedes that the script for *The Night Strangler* is not as tight as the one for *The Night Stalker*, he rates both films in the above- average range in his annually updated *Movie and Video Guide* (known as *TV Movies* in earlier editions).

With the basic story finally set, *TV Guide* announced that Darren McGavin, Simon Oakland, producer Dan Curtis and writer Richard Matheson were reuniting for another ABC movie of the week. Few details were available for the trades and other magazines. Most of the early stories about *The Night Strangler* said it involved a 120-year-old murderer, which was short by several years (the suppressed headline at the end of *The Night Strangler* says he was a 144-year-old killer). And *TV Guide* reported the working title, *Time Killer*.

The twelve-day July shooting schedule began with location filming in Seattle. *Night Stalker* publicist Dan Doran was back for *The Night Strangler*, but other assignments kept him in Los Angeles and away from much of the filming. Rice couldn't afford the stay in Seattle, so he too missed the location shooting this time out. While in Seattle, Curtis and his team grabbed scenes at such landmarks as the Space Needle, Pioneer Square and the downtown monorail system.

Doran and Rice didn't miss much. Seattle was a hectic schedule for Curtis, and the fireworks didn't start until the crew returned to Los Angeles and the 20th Century Fox lot.

By all accounts, *The Night Strangler* couldn't duplicate the happy set run by "that lovely Englishman," John Llewellyn Moxey. The problem wasn't Curtis. The problem wasn't McGavin. The problem was the combination of Curtis and McGavin.

"Dan's a street brawler," McGavin says. "And I'm not bad at brawling myself. So it was not a happy combination, let me put it that way."

Curtis dismisses the squabbles, but he admits they took place: "Look, anytime you have two strong-willed people involved in a project, there are going to be differences of opinion. Often it makes for a better product. You fight and you make up."

Kathie Browne McGavin was around for most of the shoot. "It was happy but strained," she said. "They were two terriers. There wasn't anything really bad about it, but if you put two terriers in the same enclosed area, there's going to be some growling and snapping. That's what happened on *The Night Strangler*. There was no terrible thing that you could put your finger on, but it was strained. You could feel it."

Robert Singer, promoted from assistant to the producer to associate producer for *The Night Strangler*, also recalls strained relations on the set. "Darren and Dan got along much better when Dan was just the producer," he says. "And it was a much tougher movie to shoot."

The strain was eased by another supporting cast of delightful professionals. John Carradine, the horror veteran who had three times donned the cape of Count Dracula (*House of Frankenstein, House of Dracula* and *Billy the Kid vs. Dracula*), was the ideal choice for puritanical publisher Llewellyn Crossbinder. Margaret Hamilton, more than thirty years removed from her legendary stint as the Wicked Witch of the West in *The Wizard of Oz* (1939), was equally perfect for the role of Professor Crabwell (especially since it's difficult to read Jeff Rice's book without seeing Hamilton as Kirsten Helms, the university professor who is the model for Crabwell). Bookish Wally Cox was the only choice to play bookish Titus Berry (the forty-eight-year-old actor died about one month after *The Night Strangler* aired). And Al Lewis, who played the Dracula-inspired Grandpa Munster on *The Munsters* (CBS, 1964-66), was cast as the tramp encountered by Kolchak and Louise Harper in the underground (and later killed by Dr. Richard Malcolm).

Editing for the network time slot meant that most of the scenes with Lewis were cut, making his presence seem almost superfluous. One also suspects that the character of Janie Watkins (labor reporter Janie Carlson in Rice's books) had more to do in the original script. She did. Much of actress Kate Murtagh's material ended up on the cutting room floor, leaving little more than glances between Janie and Carl.

Playing Kolchak's leading lady this time out was Jo Ann Pflug, best known as Lieutenant Dish in director Robert Altman's film version of *M\*A\*S\*H* (1970). It wasn't as easy a part as one might think. Louise Harper had to be at the same time bright, sexy and slightly wacky.

For the relatively brief but crucial role of Dr. Richard Malcolm, Curtis cast a tall prime-time veteran just shy of his forty-sixth birthday. Spotted by MGM executives during a stint at the Laguna Playhouse, New Jersey native Richard Anderson appeared in several notable films of the '50s (*Twelve O'Clock High, Forbidden Planet, The Long Hot Summer, Compulsion, Paths of Glory*). In the '60s, Anderson was more visible on the television screen. By the time *The Night Strangler* came along, the actor had been a regular on four network series: *Bus Stop* (ABC, 1961-62), Gene Roddenberry's *The Lieutenant* (NBC, 1963-64), Lieutenant Steve Drumm for the final season (1965-66) of *Perry Mason* (CBS) and the chief in Burt Reynolds' *Dan August* (ABC, 1970-71). He also had appeared in episodes of *The Big Valley, Ironside, Mannix, The Mod Squad, Land of the Giants, The FBI* and *The Alfred Hitchcock Hour*. Almost at the same time that *The Night Stalker* was being shot, Anderson was playing Bryce Chadwick, the brother killed by Susan Clark in the first-season "Lady in Waiting" episode of *Columbo*. But his greatest prime-time fame was ahead of him. Playing Oscar Goldman in both *The Six Million Dollar Man* (1974-78) and *The Bionic Woman* (1976-78), Anderson would become one of the few actors to star in two series running at the same time.

"Richard Anderson was just wonderful as Malcolm," Matheson enthuses. "He had a wonderful way of suggesting a quiet power. There was a tremendous dignity to his portrayal. He made the monster very human."

It was an interpretation that also greatly pleased the film's director and producer. "In most of my horror films," Curtis explains, "I try to find an additional dimension to the monster. Sometimes you actually end up feeling sorry for him. We certainly did that with Barnabas and Dr. Jekyll. In *Dracula* [the TV movie with Jack Palance], I invented this whole past for him so you could see this once-great warrior. Now that really wasn't possible for Janos Skorzeny, mostly because he doesn't talk and he's not on camera that much. And he's not the central character in *The Night Stalker*. Kolchak is. But that was more of a possibility with Richard Anderson's character. Let's see what makes him tick."

Rice, who was on hand for the Los Angeles filming, was impressed by the way Anderson "played Dr. Malcolm with a subtlety and irony that added immensely to the effectiveness of his role."

Filming continued in downtown Los Angeles, around Hollywood and at 20th Century Fox studios (the backlot was used for some of the Seattle street scenes). The atmospheric Bradbury Building, with its vintage elevator, was used as the part of the Seattle underground near Dr. Malcolm's home and underground clinic. The old United Artists Building, a few blocks away, did double duty as the *Seattle Daily Chronicle* and police headquarters. The incredibly opulent Leon Kaufman mansion in Pacific Palisades was used for part of Malcolm's living quarters. And the mansion's underground garage became Malcolm's laboratory. The Kaufman mansion cost almost two-million dollars to build in 1927. "To make that figure more understandable," Rice comments, "consider that homes in Beverly Hills, built at that time for around $35,000 to $50,000," are worth about $5.5 million today.

The rest of the eerie and impressive Seattle underground set was constructed at 20th Century-Fox.

During a break on July 31, the next-to-last day of shooting, Rice again pitched the idea of regular Kolchak movies. At the time, *Columbo* had completed an incredibly successful first season of seven ninety-minute movies. This seemed like the way to go, and Rice said so to Curtis, McGavin and Herb Jellinek, the ABC vice president in charge of TV movies. Rice was left with the words heard so often by Hollywood hopefuls: "We'll get back to you." He was young enough and naive enough to believe that they would indeed get back to him.

Falling behind schedule, Curtis cut the filming of a time-lapse sequence that would have slowly aged Malcolm into a decayed nightmare. Even though the hours had been brutal, Anderson was disappointed. Oscar-winning makeup wizard William Tuttle (*Seven Faces of Dr. Lao*) was angry. "Never again," he grumbled as he passed Rice on the set.

But a bigger storm was ahead. The long hours, on top of the strain between Curtis and McGavin, finally took its toll. The snapping and growling erupted into something more.

"It was the last night of the shoot at 20th Century-Fox," McGavin recalls. "Dan was berating the crew something awful."

McGavin had had enough. "Dan, don't talk to them that way," the actor said. "Please, you've got a big mouth. They're nice guys and they work their asses off. Knock it off."

Curtis blew up. McGavin, seething inside, maintained a deadly calm exterior. Curtis started another direction.

"The next setup is. . . ."

"That was the last setup, Dan," McGavin informed him.

"What?"

"Good night," McGavin said. "That's it."

"We've got closeups," Curtis argued.

"No, no, we'll go home now," McGavin answered. "You've got enough film. Make your movie. Goodbye."

With that, McGavin and his wife got in their car and went home.

"We went our separate ways," McGavin says, "but we didn't separate on the best of terms. I think that was the last time we saw each other for a long time. Dan, of course, went on to do extraordinarily marvelous things, and we've put our differences behind us. We're older and wiser now."

"Since then," relates Kathie Browne McGavin, "they've talked about it and been together a few times, and I don't think there'd ever be that problem again."

Curtis, to his credit, did not let any of the squabbling color his appreciation of McGavin's talent. Indeed, once *The Night Strangler* was finished and ready for air, its producer-director went out of his way to tell several journalists that McGavin's abilities weren't properly appreciated by Hollywood.

"That's Dan," Matheson says, "in case you hadn't already figured it out. He can scream and yell at you over something, but then it's over. It's finished as far as he's concerned. He doesn't pull any punches. He says what's on his mind. He can battle. But you fight and you go on. He's genuinely surprised if you're still brooding about it the next day. And if he thinks he has gone too far, he can be very. . . well, the word sweet doesn't seem quite right, but I've seen him be very sweet to people. I think the proof is in the number of wonderfully talented people who work with Dan over and over."

That list, of course, includes Richard Matheson.

Edited into a seventy-four-minute package, *The Night Strangler* was scheduled for January 16, 1973 (the closest Tuesday opening to the one-year anniversary of *The Night Stalker*). The ratings were strong (capturing thirty-five percent of the people watching television during that time period), although certainly nothing to compare to the *Night Stalker* numbers.

"The second one was a little more difficult to promote," Doran said. "It wasn't as easily describable. It was a little tougher to get into."

This time, the critics weren't caught napping. Kevin Thomas of the *Los Angeles Times* qualified his favorable review by noting that *The Night Strangler* followed the Hollywood custom "of repeating a successful formula." Even *The New York Times* took notice. In his review, critic Howard Thompson called the TV movie "a yeasty surprise, blending laughs, local color (Seattle) and real chills. Thompson applauded Matheson's script, the "excellent" cast, the designs by Trevor Williams and the photography of Robert Hauser. Even the murders "are staged with deep-freeze taste," the *Times* critic noted. He ended the review with hopes that there would be a third Kolchak movie.

With no third Kolchak movie to air, ABC repeated *The Night Stalker* at 11:30 p.m. Monday, February 26. At the end of *The Night Strangler,* our hero announces that he's heading for New York. It would be more than a year and a half before anyone saw him again.

Like Leonard Maltin, most critics of today give *The Night Strangler* extremely high marks. So do most of the people associated with the production. Numbed by formula sequels with Roman numerals (*Rambo XXIII* and *Friday the 13th: Part IX*), film historians naturally react enthusiastically to a follow-up with some wit, style and energy.

"Stylistically, it holds up very well," says Doran, succinctly summarizing the popular view of *The Night Strangler.*

"I was a big fan of *The Night Stalker,* particularly the first two movies," says Joe Dante, director of such films as *Piranha* (1978), *The Howling* (1981), *Gremlins* (1984), *Innerspace* (1987), *The 'Burbs* (1989), *Gremlins II: The New Batch* (1990) and *Matinee* (1993). "And the second one, *The Night Strangler,* was surprisingly strong — much better than any sequel has a right to be. There were a lot of neat things going on in that."

"Dan did a marvelous job with it," remarks Matheson. "The whole thing had a great feel to it. A lot of people who do sequels just don't want to be bothered. We were still keyed up and in tune with the characters, and we had fun doing it. And it was Dan's first directing job in a TV film, so he really poured himself into it to show what he could do. I added even more humor to it than we had in the first one. I had a lot of fun with it."

Too much fun, says Jeff Rice, who believed that the characters were turning into caricatures. He saw the glimmer of this problem in *The Night Stalker.* He expressed this concern to Herb Jellinek in an October 1972 letter that yet again suggested a series of ninety-minute movies for Carl Kolchak: "I added that Simon Oakland (Vincenzo) be brought back and that the characters of Kolchak and Vincenzo be explored and deepened, especially since Kolchak had tended to become somewhat caricatured in the sequel film."

While conceding that *The Night Strangler* has many strong points, Rice calls it "basically a rehash of the first Kolchak film, with an ages-old strangler draining blood via syringe instead of fang, and the setting changed from Las Vegas to Seattle."

The bitter judgment of a badly treated author who wanted thescreenplay assignment himself? You might be tempted to so dismiss Rice's words if it were not for the complete agreement of one Darren McGavin.

"When ABC wanted to do another *Night Stalker,*" McGavin says, "Dan literally redid the first one in another town. You know what the problem with a sequel is? They don't know how to make a sequel with the character, so what they do is take the formula and redo it. That's why I didn't like *Night Strangler* that much. If you run the two movies consecutively, you say to yourself, 'Wait a minute, I just saw that?' And that's why I didn't want to do a third one at the time. I suppose, as TV movies go, it's all very good, but it was kind of weary and threadbare, even the second time around. It was like we'd done it before. The first one was so original. The second one was the same thing — same structure."

Who's right? Well, everybody is, of course. There is, in the middle of these two sides, a debate that goes to the very soul of television (assuming that the medium has a soul). Network television adores formula. It's safe. It's certainly correct to say that *The Night Strangler* repeats much of the *Night Stalker* formula. It's also correct to say it repeats the formula extremely well. And it's correct to say that the network wanted a TV movie that would repeat the formula. It might even be correct to say that the viewers wanted a film that would repeat the formula (here we are at that soul issue again).

Look, something clever and original comes along. The network is afraid of it. But when the innovative concept works, that's all the network wants. They don't want something even more clever and innovative. They then become afraid of that. Network executives believe that, in prime time, familiarity breeds content. And there's plenty of research to back them up.

A *Columbo* arrives on the scene and breaks all the established network rules. But then, to maintain its success, *Columbo* rarely varies the new formula (which soon becomes an old formula). Do we blame *Columbo* for repeating the formula through more than sixty mysteries? Or do we applaud *Columbo* for treating us to a clever variation on the familiar tune? Pick a side and start arguing. The side you picked probably dictates how you feel about *The Night Strangler.*

*Perry Mason* (CBS, 1957-66) incessantly repeated the same formula for nine seasons. *Mission: Impossible* (CBS, 1966-73) kept the espionage merry-go-round spinning for seven years. Programmers argue that viewers would have resented too much change.

Which leads us to another debate: How should television nurture a success? McGavin would argue that repetition is artistic death. Network executives counter that screwing around with a proven commodity is commercial suicide. Since commercial interests are bound to override artistic concerns, we must evaluate *The Night Strangler* accordingly. It is a brisk, funny, creepy and lively variation on *The Night Stalker.*

McGavin and Rice are on the side of the artistic angels, no question about that. But their visions of originality, like Kolchak's efforts, are certain to be blocked and obscured by the powers that be. So we're left with a very good sequel, if not a great one. McGavin and Rice hoped for more, yet that's more than we can hope for from network television.

You'd like to think that McGavin and Rice are correct about the character sustaining and growing in a different type of suspense story. They are the two people who should know best. But this is a what-if game that ABC was unwilling to play. In fact, given the mind set of the typical network executive, it might be more accurate to say ABC was incapable of playing this game. A programmer grumbles about innovation, then loses sleep over having something as offbeat as *Twin Peaks* or *Murder One* on the prime-time schedule.

And it would be a shame not to have *The Night Strangler.* There are just too many wonderful moments in the sequel. There's the look on Tony Vincenzo's face when he realizes the voice in the bar belongs to Carl Kolchak. It's an acting clinic — hilarious and heartbreaking at the same time. There's the spooky world of the underground. There's Tony giving a tip-of-the-hat acknowledgment to the influence of Hecht and MacArthur's *The Front Page.* There's John Carradine's marvelous face realizing that an employee he doesn't know (Wally Cox) has worked for him for thirty-five years.

There's Margaret Hamilton, not yet Cora the Maxwell House coffee pitcher, holding forth on the mysteries of alchemy. There's Louise Harper taking in the ruin of Tony Vincenzo and asking Kolchak, "What have you done to that poor man?" There's Kate Murtagh's formidable Janie Watkins writing an open challenge to the killer (she'll walk the Pioneer Square district every night, daring him to attack). There's Kolchak's response to that challenge: "He may be sick, but he's not crazy." There's the moment of macabre humor when a morgue attendant (a forerunner of Gordy the Ghoul on the series) takes a bottle of Scotch from Kolchak and pours some in two specimen beakers, which, seconds before, were sitting next to an occupied autopsy table. There's the chillingly malevolent look on Malcolm's face when Kolchak smashes the life-sustaining elixir. There's Richard Anderson's profound and tragic final, "Why?"

We know why, Dr. Malcolm. It's because Carl Kolchak believes in the public's right to know. He believes in this so passionately that he's willing to crawl into the "tomb of old Seattle" to get an exclusive from a killer on the verge of disappearing for another twenty-one years. Yes, above everything else, there's Darren McGavin in perfect sync with Carl Kolchak. Matheson gives him some terrific lines, but, stop the presses, does McGavin know how to deliver them. Facing death (actually told he won't leave the underground alive), Kolchak says, "I'm just a dumb reporter doing his job."

"You grovel nicely," Malcolm says as he agrees to give him the story. If the levels aren't in McGavin's performance, the whole scene doesn't work (and it's just the climax, that's all). Still. . .

Knowing how McGavin views *The Night Strangler*, there's a certain irony to Kolchak's line about experiencing deja vu. "That's what it was, all right, in spades."

## THE COMPLETE NIGHT STRANGLER

Although pleased with *The Night Strangler*, Dan Curtis did not enjoy having to edit the film down to fill a ninety-minute prime-time slot (seventy-four minutes, minus commercials). "That was murder getting that thing down to the time that the network wanted," the director-producer says. "We kept cutting and cutting."

When the twelve-day shoot was completed, Curtis realized he had filmed enough footage for a two-hour movie — without commercials. He had hoped for a two-hour time slot, so the editing process wouldn't be too brutal. The network wouldn't budge past ninety minutes. The *Night Strangler* that aired January 16, 1973, therefore, was an incredibly abbreviated version. All of the scenes with the tramp (Al Lewis), including the one where Kolchak discovers his body, were dropped. The rundown on alchemy by Professor Crabwell (Margaret Hamilton) was reduced to a few lines. And the tour of the Seattle underground led by young George DiCenzo was cut to almost nothing.

A 1965 graduate of the Yale Drama School, DiCenzo landed a job as an assistant to Dan Curtis during the first year of *Dark Shadows*. He had a small part as a deputy in *House of Dark Shadows* (1970). But in 1976, he landed the major role of Los Angeles prosecutor Vincent Bugliosi in the two-part *Helter Skelter*, a four-hour fact-based drama about the arrest and trial of Charles Manson.

Most reference books still list the running time for *The Night Strangler* at seventy-four minutes, and, indeed, this original incarnation shows up quite frequently on local television stations. But ABC Circle Films reinstated much of this original footage for the overseas theatrical release of the sequel. And this version — with Lewis, Hamilton, DiCenzo and Kate Murtagh's Janie Watkins given added screen time — is syndicated to fill the now standard two-hour time slot for movies (it clocks in at ninety minutes, minus commercials). Not quite so frantic, the more-complete *Strangler* is far closer to the vision Curtis had for the sequel.

To some fans, this full-bodied *Night Strangler* is a rumor — a tantalizing possibility that's been talked about for years. Yet this ninety-minute *Night Strangler* has been aired in Cleveland, Detroit and several other major television markets. Still, is there more lurking in the ABC vaults? After all, even at ninety minutes, *The Night Strangler* contains scenes that seem strangely abbreviated. And a complete cast list for the TV movie says that veteran character actor George Tobias (neighbor Abner Kravitz on *Bewitched*) played a character named Stacks. Who is Stacks? In the film and Jeff Rice's novelization of *The Night Strangler*, we learn that he is James Stackhaus, a.k.a. Jimmy Stacks. Mentioned during the scenes between Berry (Wally Cox) and Kolchak, Jimmy Stacks is the Seattle reporter who covered the Pioneer Square killings in the '30s. Okay, so Tobias played Stacks. There's just one problem. Tobias never appears in either the seventy-four minute or ninety-minute version of *The Night Strangler*, and his name is dropped from the end credits. Apparently, a scene was shot with Kolchak tracking down Jimmy Stacks and interviewing him about the murders. ABC isn't sure that this footage still exists. The search, however, will go on for the complete *Night Strangler*.

## KOLCHAK IN PRINT

Movie deals, for the most part, are made on the West Coast. Publishing deals, for the most part, are made on the East Coast. Often, books published on the East Coast are turned into movies on the West Coast. Sometimes, projects developed in the West turn into books published in the East. Working these equations through in 1972, Jeff Rice decided it was time to head East. After *The Night Strangler* finished shooting, Rice went to New York City and found a literary agent to represent him.

The author had been nine months between representation. Working closely with Rice, his new agent soon set up a paperback deal with Pocket Books.

Published in December 1973, *The Night Stalker* was a revised and reworked version of *The Kolchak Papers*. It is particularly illuminating for those who wish to see what was condensed for the movie or left out (including Skorzeny's attack on a drag queen). There are plenty of notes for trivia buffs (McGavin's Kolchak drinks bourbon, Rice's Kolchak drinks Scotch), and the book is far more gritty than fans of the film might expect.

"In fact," Rice says, "Pocket Books insisted I tone down a bit of the vulgarity of language, particularly when Kolchak got hot under the collar, and told me that even though William Peter Blatty threw four-letter words around like grains of rice in *The Exorcist*, I could not do likewise until I had achieved his stature. I was able to re-convert one edited 's.o.b.' back into 'sonofabitch' in the scene where Skorzeny was staked to death because, I insisted, *this* is what would be said under such duress, *not* a letter-abbreviation."

Priced at $1.25, *The Night Stalker* quickly sold out its printing of nearly half a million copies. In January 1974, Pocket Books issued a second Kolchak book (also at $1.25), Rice's novelization of Richard Matheson's screenplay for *The Night Strangler*. Working from the other direction this time (script to novel), Rice again offered a sharper edge and more details.

In deference to McGavin's wardrobe, Rice puts Kolchak in a seersucker suit, but, in other instances, he sticks to the original concepts for the characters. Tony, although given more of a gut, still is pint-sized. Professor Crabwell of the movie is turned back into Kirsten Helms, the character in *The Kolchak Papers*. Kolchak still is smoking cigars. And the name of the publisher is changed from Llewellyn Crossbinder in the movie to Lucius Crossbinder in the book (Rice had used the name Llewellyn Cairncross for the managing editor in *The Night Stalker*).

Such alterations were made necessary when Matheson utilized elements from Rice's original novel for the *Night Strangler* screenplay. So Kirsten Helms does not appear in *The Night Stalker*, but she does show up *The Night Strangler* as Crabwell. Tough labor reporter Janie Carlson, another wonderful character in the first book, does not appear in the *Night Stalker* TV movie, but she does show up in *The Night Strangler* as Janie Watkins (played by Kate Murtagh). The scene in *The Night Stalker* novel where Kolchak hires a student artist to make a sketch of the killer is not in the *Night Stalker* movie. A similar scene, however, does appear in *The Night Strangler*.

Enjoying the luxuries of a novelist, Rice actually improved some areas of the story. Less flighty and more interesting than her movie counterpart, the book's version of Louise Harper has considerably more integrity as a character. And the romance Rice cooks up for Kolchak and Louise is quite touching.

In *The Night Strangler*, Rice says, "Where I had Kolchak falling in love with Louise, the belly dancer, and I'd created a love scene for them in a tub, my publishers wanted it yanked so that they could, with confidence, sell 50,000 copies to the Scholastic Book Club. I turned them down, lost the sale, but saved the soap. . . and the scene. So, in the first film, a love interest was created where only friendship had existed in the novel [between Sam and Carl], seemingly to make it more palatable to the public. In the second film, there was no romance at all, but there was romance in the novel."

Rice had hoped to do more Kolchak novels and novelizations. Despite the fabulous sales for *The Night Stalker* and *The Night Strangler*, and a growing appetite for horror novels in the '70s (Blatty, Tryon, Anne Rice, King), events conspired against Rice. It would be about twenty years before *The Night Stalker* was reprinted and a new Kolchak novel was published, and then, improper distribution kept the books from reaching most fans.

But that's getting ahead of the story. In 1973, when Jeff Rice was working on the novelization of *The Night Strangler*, Richard Matheson was working on a third Kolchak movie.

## WHAT HAPPENED TO THE THIRD MOVIE?

Yes, there was supposed to be a third Kolchak movie. Pleased with *The Night Strangler*, ABC's new vice president in charge of TV movies, Steve Gentry, gave Dan Curtis the green light to develop another script. Curtis gave the green light to Matheson.

"I was a little surprised to get the call," relates Matheson. "McGavin and Curtis had had a falling out, and I wasn't sure they'd work together again. But ABC wanted a third Kolchak movie and Dan wanted to do it."

Swamped with work, however, Matheson wasn't at all sure he could give the script proper attention. So, rather than risk an overload, Matheson brought in his close friend, William F. Nolan (*Logan's Run*).

Jeff Rice, of course, wanted to write the third TV movie. In January 1973, a few days after *The Night Strangler* aired, he asked his new agent in New York to contact Barry Diller of ABC. Rice proposed to write a script set in New York. Diller told the agent to contact Steve Gentry. The agent sent Gentry a letter on February 19. Gentry responded that a third movie was in the works, but Matheson had been given the assignment. Rice and his agent contacted several of the people involved, yet they received much confusing and often conflicting information during the rest of 1973. The end result, however, wasn't tough to figure out. "Once again," Rice says, "I was frozen out of any chance to work on my own creation and also start acquiring a track record as a scriptwriter."

In a September letter to Rice, Matheson revealed that ABC was considering a miniseries of once-a-month Kolchak movies.

Meanwhile, Matheson and Nolan were completing the script for Kolchak's third outing.

"William F. Nolan and I wrote a third script called *The Night Killers*," Matheson says. "It was set in Hawaii, and it was dandy, real dandy. I don't know why they didn't go ahead with it. It was a neat premise for the time. Key politicians were being killed off and replaced by lookalike androids. That was the basic idea. It was very fresh in 1973, but it has been used interminably since. It was a very funny, very fast script, and I tried to talk Dan into making it a number of times."

Curtis did like the script. There was a bigger problem: McGavin *didn't*. The troubles McGavin had with *The Night Strangler* were compounded by *The Night Killers*. The actor just wasn't wild about another fantasy concept.

As late as February 1974, ABC still was thinking that *The Night Killers* could be filmed as a stand-alone sequel or the pilot for a series. ABC even considered the possibility of using another actor as Carl Kolchak. If a series grows out of this, ABC reasoned, the concept is strong enough to stand on its own. Okay, stop. This isn't the first time a network or studio tried to push this idea. Sometimes it works. NBC, for instance, was perfectly willing to shuffle Mark Harmon into *Miami Vice* when Don Johnson was playing the hold-out game. Sure, that time it worked because explosions and fashions and music were more important than character on *Miami Vice*. It didn't work when someone at Universal suggested replacing Peter Falk as *Columbo*. Try to imagine someone else in that raincoat. Universal couldn't do it, either, so, this time, the studio backed down. Can you picture someone other than Raymond Burr as Perry Mason? Hey, they tried Monte Markham in the role, remember? How about Maverick without James Garner? Or Rockford? Somewhere along the line, ABC must have realized that McGavin was Kolchak.

By late February, ABC had to concede that *The Night Killers* was a dead issue. But a series was not.

Since relations with McGavin were frosted, Curtis pursued his own pilot about a writer who investigates the supernatural. Working from a script by Nolan, Curtis produced and directed *The Norliss Tapes* (1973), an enjoyable TV movie starring Roy Thinnes (*The Invaders* and, subsequently, the prime-time version of *Dark Shadows*) as the writer looking into strange occurrences. In the pilot for a possible series, Nolan sent Thinnes after a vampire terrorizing Monterey, California. The supporting cast included Angie Dickinson, Claude Akins (Sheriff Butcher in *The Night Stalker*), Michele Carey, Vonetta McGee, Hurd Hatfield (star of *The Picture of Dorian Gray*) and Don Porter. Although quite good, the TV movie did not get picked up as a series, perhaps because of similarities to *The Night Stalker*, which, ironically, did go to series the following season. Even the title had a familiar ring. At one point, The *Night Stalker* was to be called *The Kolchak Tapes*.

## THE FURTHER ADVENTURES OF DAN CURTIS

Although *The Night Strangler* was the end of the on-screen Curtis-Kolchak connection, it was the beginning of a long association between Dan Curtis and

Richard Matheson. The two Kolchak films also increased the producer-director's standing as television's reigning master of the macabre.

If you flash forward to 1997, you can see that there's a Jekyll-and-Hyde nature to the career of Dan Curtis. Some know him as the Emmy-winning Hollywood producer and director of the 1983 miniseries *The Winds of War* and its 1988-89 sequel, *War and Remembrance* — a staggering forty-seven and a half hours of prime-time ABC television based on Herman Wouk's World War II novels.

Others still think of Dan Curtis as the New York producer who spooked daytime viewers with the supernatural soap opera *Dark Shadows*. In fact, Curtis has said it was his desire to be remembered for more than just *Dark Shadows* that prompted him to try the miniseries form on such a grand scale. Having secured a place in television history beyond Barnabas Collins, the burly Bridgeport native happily agreed to pursue an NBC prime-time revival of *Dark Shadows* in 1991.

But, even if you consider Curtis as merely a merchant of menace, *Dark Shadows* and *The Night Stalker* are only the beginning of a rather distinguished story.

Between *The Night Strangler* and the prime-time version of the Collinsport gang, Curtis made several acclaimed contributions to the horror genre, many in collaboration with Matheson. He did so much that was so good that, in 1978, the *Los Angeles Times* made it official. The newspaper dubbed him television's "master of the macabre."

During the making of his *War* saga, Curtis was reluctant to discuss his decade in the horror field. The success of his miniseries changed all that, and today the curly-haired producer-director has a grand time recalling the years of unleashing witches, werewolves, warlocks, sorcerers, spirits, serpents, vampires, visions and villains.

"I had to shake the *Dark Shadows* image," Curtis says, "not because I wasn't proud of the work I had done, but because I wanted to move on and do other things. I didn't want to try to squeak another door. There's nothing tougher than that.

"I stayed in the field for a while and then I got to the point where I just never wanted to do another scary movie. I could just see that after my whole career, when I was dead, on my tombstone it would say, 'The man who gave us *Dark Shadows*.' I never wanted that to happen."

To recap, by the end of 1973, the Curtis horror resume included the daytime version of *Dark Shadows* (1966-71), *The Strange Case of Dr. Jekyll and Mr. Hyde* (1968), *House of Dark Shadows* (1970), *Night of Dark Shadows* (1971), *The Night Stalker* (1972), *The Night Strangler* (1973) and *The Norliss Tapes* (1973). From this already impressive foundation, Curtis built a towering reputation in the horror field. The horror films and TV movies Curtis directed and/or produced include:

• *Frankenstein* (1973). There would be an amazing total of five television productions from Dan Curtis in 1973. About the same time as *The Night Strangler* and well before *The Norliss Tapes*, his version of *Frankenstein* aired in January in two parts on ABC's late-night *Wide World of Entertainment*. Glenn Jordan, who would later win an Emmy for the TV movie *Promise,* directed. Curtis produced and collaborated with Sam Hall (*Dark Shadows*) on the adaptation of Mary Shelley's novel, Robert Foxworth (later David Selby's co-star on *Falcon Crest*) starred as Dr. Frankenstein and Bo Svenson played his very unKarloff-like creation (sticking closer to Shelley's book). Also in the cast were Susan Strasberg, John Karlen (Willie Loomis on *Dark Shadows*) and Willie Aames. The reviews were good. The *Los Angeles Times* called it ABC's "best shot yet" in its attempt to "woo the midnight audience." *Variety* called it a "decided step forward in latenight entertainment. . . really too good to relegate to the insomniacs." But, within a year, there would be a prime-time version of the story, and the tremendous publicity generated by *Frankenstein: The True Story* (Jack Smight directing a script by Christopher Isherwood) would eclipse the Curtis production. With a bigger budget and bigger names (Leonard Whiting, James Mason, Michael Sarrazin, David McCallum, Jane Seymour, Ralph Richardson, John Gielgud and Agnes Moorehead), *Frankenstein: The True Story* became the 1973 version most people remember.

• *The Picture of Dorian Gray* (1973). Another two-part *ABC Wide World of Entertainment* presentation directed by Jordan and produced by Curtis, this adaptation of Oscar Wilde's story starred Shane Briant, Charles Aidman, Nigel Davenport, Karlen, Fionnula Flanagan, Linda Kelsey (later Billie on *Lou Grant*) and Vanessa Howard. Cobert, as he had done for *The Night Stalker* and *Frankenstein*, supplied the music. John Tomerlin wrote the script.

• *Dracula* (1973). Curtis moved back into prime time as the producer and director of this TV movie aired by CBS. The project reunited Curtis with Palance (his Dr. Jekyll), whose performance caused the *Los Angeles Times* to rave, "if the late Lugosi was the definitive Count Dracula, it's no longer true." The script by Matheson is one of the most-faithful adaptations of Bram Stoker's novel. Palance was supported by Nigel Davenport as Van Helsing, Murray Brown as Jonathan Harker, Simon Ward as Arthur, Fiona Lewis as Lucy, Penelope Horner as Mina and Pamela Brown as Mrs. Westerna. Purists give high marks to both the Curtis *Dracula* and another handsome TV version (with Louis Jourdan as the Count). Both stand up well, even if the definitive *Dracula* is a matter of debate (some side with the 1922 silent *Nosferatu*, others champion Lugosi, John Carradine, Christopher Lee and Frank Langella). Palance again stands tall in pretty elite company, and Curtis has no doubts about his interpretation. "That is the best *Dracula* that was ever made," he says. "In all my horror films, my monster usually is more than something there to kill people. Dracula was an interesting monster because he was an interesting person. You were interested in the code and great past of this noble warrior. Barnabas was always regretful. You certainly felt sorry for Dr. Jekyll. And I always tried to find ways to put humor in, and that's not easy." Drawing on the historical research about Vlad the Impaler, Matheson anticipated a similar connection used by director Francis Ford Coppola for his *Bram Stoker's Dracula* (1992).

• *Scream of the Wolf* (1974). For the first time, the magic seemed to be missing from the Curtis-Matheson connection. Directed and produced by Curtis, this mediocre TV movie starred Peter Graves (*Mission: Impossible*) as a writer investigating mysterious killings (sound familiar?). Clint Walker and Jo Ann Pflug (Louise Harper in *The Night Strangler*) co-starred.

• *The Turn of the Screw* (1974). Continuing his march through the classics of horror literature, Curtis produced and directed this two-part adaptation of the Henry James novel on location in England. Nolan wrote the script for the ABC late-night presentation, which starred Lynn Redgrave as governess Jane Cubberly.

• *Trilogy of Terror* (1975). "That's a classic," a pleased Curtis says of the TV movie anthology he produced and directed. Few would argue with him. Indeed, he and Matheson were back on track with these three stories starring Karen Black as four very different women. The first segment, William F. Nolan's adaptation of Matheson's "Julie," tells of a dowdy college English professor (Black) targeted by a handsome young student. Sharp eyes will spot a brief appearance by Gregory Harrison (four years before *Trapper John, M.D.*) and a nifty in-joke. The movie playing at the drive-in theater is *The Night Stalker*. The second Matheson story, also adapted by Nolan, is "Millicent and Therese," with Black playing sisters (Karlen and George Gaynes, the aging soap star in *Tootsie*, are featured). But the segment most remember is the third, "Amelia" (based on Matheson's "Prey"), which pits Black against a pre-Chuckie devil doll. Stalking Black through her high-rise apartment, the spear-carrying African fetish Zuni doll stole the scary show.

- **Burnt Offerings** (1976). Curtis returned to feature films as the producer and director of this adaptation of Robert Marasco's novel about a couple renting a haunted summer home. Despite an excellent cast (Black, Oliver Reed, Burgess Meredith, Eileen Heck, Bette Davis and Dub Taylor), the results were pedestrian and predictable.

- **Dead of Night** (1977) Curtis recaptured some of the *Trilogy of Terror* magic with this second trilogy TV movie. The screenplay by Matheson starts with "Second Chance," an adaptation of Jack Finney's short story about a time-traveling car (Ed Begley, Jr. stars). Matheson used his own stories for "No Such Thing as a Vampire" (starring Patrick Macnee and Anjanette Comer) and "Bobby," with Lee H. Montgomery as a drowned boy who returns to his mother (Joan Hackett).

About the only non-horror Curtis project between the 1966 premiere of *Dark Shadows* and *Dead of Night* was the 1974 TV movie *Melvin Purvis — G-Man,* with Dale Robertson in top form as the cigar-chomping lawman on the trail of Machine Gun Kelly (Harris Yulin). Curtis produced and directed the breezy script by John Milius (*Conan the Barbarian*). The success of *Purvis* (retitled *The Legend of Machine Gun Kelly*) guaranteed a sequel — the equally fun *The Kansas City Massacre* (1975). Robertson returned as Purvis, who this time was tracking down Pretty Boy Floyd, John Dillinger and Baby Face Nelson.

After *Dead of Night*, Curtis made his decision to break away from the horror field. This effort got off to a tremendous start with the 1978 TV movie *When Every Day Was the Fourth of July,* a touching Depression-era drama that Curtis based on memories of being a boy in Bridgeport. Dean Jones, Yulin and Geoffrey Lewis starred. Curtis directed, produced and narrated the story. And the reviews were almost all raves. Curtis told the *Los Angeles Times* that it was the movie he'd waited twenty years to make. In 1980, Jones and Curtis reunited for a sequel, *The Days of Summer*, which garnered less acclaim.

Both movies were made as part of a $16 million deal Curtis had signed with then-struggling NBC. But it wasn't a completely smooth ride in the post-horror years. Things got rather bumpy when the producer tried to launch the *Love Boat*-type series *Supertrain*, a mega-flop that hastened the fall of NBC boss Fred Silverman. Curtis worked long hours to get *Supertrain* up and running, yet, shortly after its premiere, the network fired him and changed the expensive vehicle's direction. It ran out of steam after a short run (February-July 1979).

That same year, Curtis produced and directed two ho-hum TV movies: *The Last Ride of the Dalton Gang* with Cliff Potts and Randy Quaid (and Curtis veterans Palance, Robertson and Yulin), and *Mrs. R's Daughter,* with Cloris Leachman. Still, the three-hour *Last Ride of the Dalton Gang* was named the outstanding fictional television program in the National Cowboy's Hall of Fame's Western Heritage Awards.

The tenacious Curtis rebounded in 1983 with *The Winds of War*, which starred Robert Mitchum as Captain Victor "Pug" Henry. At $38 million and eighteen hours, it was the longest, most expensive miniseries up to that time. The all-star cast also included Ali MacGraw, Jan-Michael Vincent, Polly Bergen, John Houseman, David Dukes, Topol, Peter Graves, Victoria Tennant and Ralph Bellamy.

The *Winds of War*'s running time and budget were beaten by its sequel, the $104 million, 29 1/2 hour *War and Remembrance*. Many of the major cast members returned, but Jane Seymour replaced MacGraw, John Gielgud replaced Houseman and Hart Bochner replaced Vincent. Curtis picked up an Emmy when *War and Remembrance* beat out *Lonesome Dove* as the best miniseries of the 1988-89 season.

After Emmy night, Curtis had lunch with NBC Entertainment President Brandon Tartikoff, who approached him with the idea of reviving *Dark Shadows* as a prime-time series.

"I think what probably happened was that, after I went off and did *The Winds of War* and *War and Remembrance*," Curtis explains, "I was finally able to shake off this *Dark Shadows* image. It's not like the only thing I've ever done is *Dark Shadows*. I never completely ruled out doing another horror project. If an *Exorcist* had come my way, I would have done it in a second. I certainly never wanted to do *Dark Shadows* again, but for years people have been coming after me to put it back on. My reaction was, why bother? But after *Winds of War* and *War and Remembrance*, I felt like I had accomplished just about everything I had to accomplish in television. And it started all over again — '*Dark Shadows! Dark Shadows! Dark Shadows!*' "

Poorly promoted and badly scheduled, the *Dark Shadows* revival premiered in January 1991 with Ben Cross (*Chariots of Fire*) as Barnabas Collins. The basic story was the same. The big difference, Curtis says, was that the production team "had twenty-five years to look back on it and see the mistakes that we made."

The handsome prime-time series also starred Jean Simmons (*Hamlet, The Robe, Spartacus*) as Elizabeth Collins Stoddard, former horror queen Barbara Steele (*Black Sunday, The Pit and the Pendulum*) as Dr. Julia Hoffman, Roy Thinnes (*The Invaders, The Norliss Tapes*) as Roger Collins, Joseph Gordon-Levitt (five years before becoming Tommy on NBC's *Third Rock from the Sun*) as David Collins and Lysette Anthony (later in the horror spoofs *Dr. Jekyll and Ms. Hyde* and Mel Brooks' *Dracula: Dead and Loving It*) as Angélique.

Curtis says that he would never have done *Dark Shadows* again if he had to come up with "a whole new story — never. If I had to come up with a whole new story, I would have said, 'Fellows, find yourself another lunatic because this one is riding away.' "

Buried on NBC's low-rated Friday lineup, *Dark Shadows* had little chance to build an audience. The network canceled the series after it finished the initial thirteen-hour order.

"I really wasn't looking to put *Dark Shadows* on again," says Curtis. "But I was looking for a way to keep my hand in television, and all the networks were coming after me with offers. So I finally decided, 'What the hell? It might be laughs. Let's go see if it's laughs.' "

In the same "spirit," Curtis agreed to produce, direct and co-write *Trilogy of Terror II*, which aired October 30, 1996, on cable's USA Network. Written with Bill Nolan, the sequel movie starred Lysette Anthony as three different women. Their first segment, "Graveyard Rats," was based on a Henry Kuttner short story. The second was a remake of Matheson's "Bobby." The third, "He Who Kills," was a sequel to "Amelia." Anthony played a museum anthropologist examining the murderous Zuni doll.

"It's murder having to compete with yourself," Curtis says. "That's the scary part. It gave me a little pause to consider that I was competing against a Dan Curtis who was twenty years younger and maybe smarter. Believe me, I didn't like the competition."

Curtis, though, enjoys the challenge of returning to the horror field because "there are so few people who truly comprehend what makes this kind of stuff work. They think anybody can write a horror story. Well, the truth is, anybody *can't* write a horror story. . . Horror stories are the most difficult type of things to do because you need imagination and humor, and you can never make a mistake. The first screwup, you lose all credibility and you're dead with the audience. Most people say, 'Well, it's a ghost, so we can do whatever we want with it.' They're the people who are dead before they start. A logic lapse or the wrong kind of laugh can sink you. Every single word is a deathtrap. So if you can do these kinds of pictures, you can do anything. Most people think just the opposite — that if you can do these kinds of pictures, you can't do anything else. Well, I've proven them wrong."

A few months before *Trilogy of Terror II*, Curtis reacted with a mixture of pride and amazement as fans celebrated the thirtieth anniversary of *Dark Shadows*. "I still get people in the industry wanting me to do *Dark Shadows* again," he says, noting that, after a successful run in syndication and on home video, the series is run twice a day on cable's Sci-Fi Channel. "What's incredible is that these were supposed to be shows seen once and never again. Who the hell watches repeats of a thirty-year-old soap opera?"

Today, therefore, Dan Curtis is proud to say he's the producer who gave us *Dark Shadows, The Night Stalker* and *Trilogy of Terror*. But he takes more pride in *The Winds of War* and *War and Remembrance*.

"People have always said to me since I've finished *War and Remembrance*, 'How are you going to top yourself?' That's crazy. I don't plan to try. There's nothing I can do to top myself. I will never completely recover from it. I'm not destroyed by it, but it's something that will live with me forever. It's always in my mind. The images and moments run through my mind all the time. It will never leave me — never, never. This is something I'll be proud of until the day I go."

**Dan Curtis on location filming his epic miniseries.**

Kolchak in his normal surroundings, the Las Vegas strip, home to hotels, casinos, bars and vampires.

# Part III

# Kolchak: The Night Stalker

## or, "Gone With the Windy City"

*"It's a perfect night for mystery and horror. The air itself is filled with monsters."*
**—Mary Shelley (Elsa Lanchester)**
*The Bride of Frankenstein* **(1935)**

*"Even the moon's frightened of me, frightened to death. The whole world's frightened to death."*
**—Jack Griffin (Claude Rains)**
*The Invisible Man* **(1933)**

## FROM SEQUEL TO SERIES

By late February 1974, even the most optimistic ABC executive could see that *The Night Killers* just wasn't going to happen. At that point, the network shifted its attack to another front – from a Kolchak movie to a Kolchak series.

The point man in this seige was Marty Starger, the president of ABC Entertainment. The object of the seige was Darren McGavin.

ABC was coming down the stretch of what would be a miserable season. The Alphabet Network would place no series in the top ten for the 1973-74 season. In fact, ABC would have only three series in the top twenty, and one of those was the half-season *Monday Night Football*. The one piece of good news was that *Happy Days*, which had premiered in January, was on its way to finishing the season in sixteenth place. The highest-rated series in ABC's roster was the eleventh-place *Six Million Dollar Man*.

The network needed new blood, and McGavin had established himself as one of the most popular actors in television.

"Marty Starger kept calling me and saying, 'Let's do a series, let's do a series,' " recalls McGavin. "I finally said, 'Okay, I'll do a series if you'll give me the franchise on it. Let me produce it.' "

The request took Starger and the Network by surprise. At the time, very few actors produced their own series. Jack Webb was an exception. In the '80's and '90s, this became more common Michael Landon was the producer of *Highway to Heaven*. Carroll O'Connor took control of *In the Heat of the Night*. Peter Falk got a producer's credit on the revival of *Columbo*. Burt Reynolds was listed as one of the producers of *Evening Shade*. Sitcom stars Roseanne, Ellen DeGeneres and Cybill Shepherd each asked for and got a producer's credit. Why would an actor want to take on the headaches of a producer? Well, control and power might have something to do with

**97**

it. They don't call television "the producer's medium" for nothing. And McGavin was adamant. In late 1972, he had set up his own company, Taurean Films, so that he could produce and direct theatrical films and TV movies. The company's first film, *Happy Mother's Day, Love George* (retitled *Run, Stranger, Run*), starred Oscar winner Patricia Neal (*Hud*) and was released to theatres in 1973. McGavin also this horror story about murders at a seaside house. His cast included another Oscar winner, Cloris Leachman (*The Last Picture Show*), Ron Howard (months away from starting his *Happy Days* run) and his *Night Stalker* chum, Simon Oakland. In March of 1974, McGavin was intent on pursuing deals that would allow him to produce, direct and star.

The only way he would climb into Kolchak's seersucker suit again would be if he could produce the series.

"Well, I can't do that," Starger told him.

"Why not?" McGavin asked.

"I just can't," the ABC executive said.

"Okay," McGavin concluded, "then let's not do a series."

The actor had plenty of offers to do TV movies. He didn't need a series. But Martin Starger, like his dear friend and fellow ABC executive Michael Eisner, did not give up easily.

"He must have called me half a dozen times," McGavin says. "He wouldn't let up. Finally, we were at a Sunday evening dinner at [MCA/Universal President] Sid Sheinberg's house. We were at a long dining room table and there were about fourteen people around this table. Sid was at the head of the table, while Marty and I were at the other end, across from each other. Now Marty starts in again."

The subject, of course, was Kolchak.

"Why don't you do the series, for crying out loud?" Starger asked McGavin.

"Marty! Marty!! We're at a social party," McGavin replied. "This is a social evening. Let's not talk business."

"Don't be a schmuck," Starger said, pressing the assault. "Do the series."

"Marty! Knock it off."

The sound of one friend verbally fending off another caught the attention of Sid Sheinberg. "What's going on down there?" demanded the Universal president.

"Nothing, nothing, Sid," McGavin answered, "just a little discussion."

Sheinberg knew better. After dinner, he took McGavin aside and asked, "What was that all about at the dinner table?"

"Oh, Marty wants me to do a series of *The Night Stalker*," McGavin told him. "I don't want to."

"Why not?"

"Because I want to own it," McGavin explained. "I don't want to play around with someone else producing."

The next day, Sheinberg called the actor and said, "Meet me at the studio." Curious, McGavin drove to Universal, then and now, one of the biggest suppliers of network series.

"Why don't we do the series together?" Sheinberg suggested to McGavin. "We'll split it up. You own fifty percent, we'll own fifty percent. The network wants to do it, so do it. Take their money if they want you to do it so bad."

So, it was McGavin's initial understanding that the *Night Stalker* series would proceed as a co-production between Universal and his Taurean Productions. But it didn't quite work out that way. Once he signed to do the series, it became clear that Universal, while certainly offering him profit participation and some ownership in *The Night Stalker*, had no intention of making McGavin the show's official producer. It was not only precisely the situation McGavin wanted to avoid, it was a decision that would doom the series to a year of turmoil and tension.

ABC and Universal, for instance, went public with an announcement that ran as a front-page story in *Variety* on April 24, 1974. There was no mention of a co-production deal with Taurean. There was no mention of McGavin being a producer or executive producer. Indeed, the three-paragraph article, though sparse on details, goes out of its way to mention that no producer had been assigned. Running less than 130 words, the item reported that McGavin would star in the hour series tentatively titled *Night Stalker*. "No producer has been set on the hour series.[Frank] Price [head of television at Universal] will confer with Dan Curtis, who produced the original *Stalker*," Variety reported. "ABC-TV had the initial idea for the project."

Obviously, McGavin's initial "understanding" and the studio's "reality" were in conflict. And conflict would breed conflict. McGavin would fight for the control and power due an executive producer. Studio executives would assign Universal producers to keep control of the series. A power struggle was the inevitable outcome of such a situation.

A promotional release issued by Universal a few days later boasted that "now the adventures of the rugged investigative reporter Carl Kolchak can be seen weekly." This announcement added that Simon Oakland would return as Tony Vincenzo, but, again, the studio made no mention of McGavin being brought on as a producer. Indeed, under the line reading "produced by Universal Television," the studio felt confident enough to add that Dan Curtis would be producing the series.

In April of 1974, therefore, the studio was after Curtis, who, obviously, would insist on calling the shots. Curtis, though, wanted nothing to do with the series. And, considering his strained relationship with McGavin, the odds did not favor his participation reaching beyond an initial conference.

"Sure, they approached me about it," Curtis says. "I thought it was a bad idea. I didn't see how it could be done."

With Curtis out of the picture, Richard Matheson decided to pass on the series.

"If Dan had done the series," says Matheson, "I would have done the series. When I learned that he didn't have involvement in it, I decided not to have involvement in it. Frankly, I was sort of relieved. We'd had so much trouble coming up with a story for *The Night Strangler*. But that was so tough that I couldn't imagine how they could come up with a new monster every week."

Universal offered Matheson the position of story editor on the series. The studio had offered him the same job on *Night Gallery*. Both times, the writer turned them down.

Jeff Rice, who had been proposing a Kolchak series for two years, was in something akin to shock as he read the *Variety* story. He describes his reaction:

"Well! So 'ABC-TV had the initial idea for the project.' I scanned the brief article several times to see who the genius was who came up with this stunning, revolutionary idea out of the blue but could find no one credited with it. Nor, just to add mention of it, could I find, anywhere, a single mention of my name; not as the creator of the original novel which led to the hit movies upon which the series was based, nor even as the creator of the series.

"So that's how I created *Kolchak: The Night Stalker*. It was revelation to me to discover I'd accomplished this marvelous feat after nearly two years of efforts and that I'd done it without even knowing if, when or how I'd done it, and that I had to read it in the trades without finding a single mention of my name.

"Hollywood is a very strange town indeed. At the time I read this story in *Variety*, I was still waiting for payment for my services as a location consultant on the original *Night Stalker* film, money that had been owed to me, at that point, for almost three years. More importantly, however, I still had taken part in no negotiations, made no agreement, and signed no contract conveying to anyone the rights to produce and air such a series; not ABC, which would air it, nor Universal TV, which would produce it."

And, at this point, we must jump all the way back to the original contract negotiated for Rice. No series could be produced without his approval. There also was a long paper trail of correspondence that could document Rice's suggestions for a series.

It is entirely possible that ABC fell on its own bureaucracy. Marty Starger, after all, never had any dealings with Rice. The paper trail ran past several other executives: Allen Epstein, Barry Diller, Herb Jellinek, Steve Gentry, John Angier. And Universal had nothing to do with the two Kolchak movies. This isn't an excuse. It's a possible explanation of the conditions that led to a lawsuit.

Rice can see how he was considered "such a minor point" compared to all the moving and shaking involved. He "could easily understand how forgetting to pay me for the rights to do the series could have occurred. Such is the case, I have discovered, with almost all writers except the most important and highest-paid ones in Hollywood. The writer is the last one to know."

Sometimes, even the highest-paid ones are kept in the dark.

In May 1974, ABC announced its fall schedule. It was McGavin's turn to be caught by surprise. The actor had been hoping the series would start in January 1975 as a midseason replacement. There it was on the fall lineup. They would hit the air in about four months. They had no scripts. No writers had been hired.

McGavin still was opposed to a monster-of-the-week format, but, in a mad dash to get on the air, the series had to fall back on formula.

All right, if it had to be monster-of-the-week, McGavin concluded, the series would rely on suspense and atmosphere. The monsters would be kept in the shadows, he decreed, so viewers wouldn't be looking at a guy in a rubber mask and saying, "There's a guy in a rubber mask."

Under the supervision of Peter Saphier, the vice president of MCA Television, *The Night Stalker* stumbled into production. Most reference books give McGavin the executive producer credit he sought in his early talks with Martin Starger. In truth, no MCA press releases, contracts, on-air credits, scripts or cast lists make any mention of an executive producer — official or unofficial. Yet MCA's biography of McGavin for the *Night Stalker* press kits makes a definite point of mentioning the formation of Taurean Films, proudly proclaiming that the actor would be producing and directing movies for Universal. The studio wasn't shy about acknowledging McGavin's other projects as producer. And this would have been the logical place to embrace a similar intention for the *Night Stalker* series.

What happened to that initial understanding between McGavin and Universal for the series? The deal didn't go through as planned because of "the internal policies of the studio," McGavin says. When asked about those policies by *Scarlet Street* magazine in 1994, he replied, "I don't want to discuss that." Who can blame him?

The "official" executive producer credit does, however, show up in most articles and book chapters on the series. One reason for the confusion is that, on April 11, 1974, thirteen days before the April 24th announcement of a *Night Stalker* series, *Variety* ran a three-paragraph item about Darren McGavin signing "a long-term contract with Universal, a unique deal covering almost every major area of the film entertainment media, Sid Sheinberg, MCA prexy, disclosed yesterday. Deal covers theatrical motion pictures and TV, and stipulates that McGavin's services may be called upon as a writer, producer, director, as well as actor. He also will function in the development of new theatrical and TV projects."

With the *Night Stalker* series announced less than two weeks later, many assumed that this deal covered the ABC show, too. In fact, several newspaper articles over the next few months named McGavin as the program's producer. Reporters for the

*Los Angeles Times*, the *San Diego Union*, the *Chicago Tribune*, the *Chicago Daily News* and the Associated Press interviewed McGavin while he was talking to writers and helping actors. They asked him questions about The *Night Stalker* while sitting in McGavin's production office at Universal. They watched him – "in command," said the reporter for the King Features Syndicate – whip off memos about the direction of the series "to the boys upstairs" in MCA's "black tower" office building. They watched him arrange appearances on the show for actors who were friends. They assumed they were watching the series' studio-picked producer in action — and said so in print. This assumption, coupled with McGavin's strong input into the series, gave rise to the executive producer credit becoming "official."

And, during these first couple of months, McGavin often assumed the duties of an executive producer. Asked to write a theme for the series, composer Gil Mellé was told to report to McGavin. It was with McGavin, not a studio producer, that Mellé planned the title sequence. Universal could alter the deal, but they couldn't stop McGavin from exercising the authority he assumed was his by right. In a town where perception swiftly becomes reality, McGavin was being perceived as the executive producer – credited or not. The actor could not and would not surrender his vision for the character. This was how he could battle for that vision and for what he believed was best for the series.

MCA Television's early press kit for *The Night Stalker*, though, avoids any suggestion of behind-the-scenes input by McGavin. It lists Universal Television as the only production company, Paul Playdon as the producer and David Chase as story editor. Both were hired when McGavin was on location with a film.

Fresh from his stint as producer of Paramount's *The Magician* (NBC's 1973-74 mystery series with Bill Bixby), Playdon was signed to produce McGavin's series. Playdon had been an associate producer on *Cannon* and *Banacek*. He'd also written scripts for *Hawaii Five-O, Mission: Impossible* and *The Wild, Wild West*. Playdon's *Mission: Impossible* credits included the script for the 1969 episode, "The Glass Cage." The director for this caper was John Llewellyn Moxey, who, of course, would go on to helm the first *Night Stalker* movie. The guest cast for the episode included Larry Linville, who would go on to play Mokurji, the pathologist in the 1972 movie that launched Kolchak's career.

"Paul Playdon hired me as story editor," says David Chase, who was then a young freelance writer just establishing himself in Hollywood. "He had read a spec script that I wrote, so we knew each other. I always liked horror movies and I loved *The Night Stalker*, so I was very happy to get the job."

At a June 1974 press conference, television critics were told that McGavin owned a piece of the show. Several wrote in columns filed from Hollywood that McGavin was the series' producer (more fodder for misinformation). It was clear, though, that the star had his own ideas for the program– ideas he could implement by using his "ownership" position and his star status as leverage.

"We're not really trying to do a monster of the week," McGavin told journalists. "We're going to try to retain the elements that made the film a success. We'll deal with innate fears, primal fears lying within all of us.

"One of the story lines concerns a hospital where all sorts of terrible things happen. Kolchak becomes involved and discovers that the hospital was built on the site of an Indian burial ground and is haunted by a spirit that feeds on electrical current.

"We might do another on live amebas dating back five or six million years, and dug out of an Antarctic drilling. What might come of these creatures?

"I have never been a fan of science-fiction movies. They bore the hell out of me. The monsters all have papier-mâché masks, and so forth. We're going to try to avoid showing the monsters."

Even though Universal's internal policies denied him the total control he expected, McGavin worked tirelessly in shaping the series, molding regular characters, suggesting story ideas and lining up actors.

In addition to telling composer Gil Mellé what kind of theme music the series should have, he helped define two regular characters and personally chose the actress to play a journalism intern named Monique Marmelstein. He told Playdon and the writers how the "family" of regulars should be emphasized. He gave the writers at least one idea that became the basis for an episode. This was his series, and he was going to stay on top of it. Under the gun to get the show rolling, McGavin felt it was his responsibility to take charge of the program. Whether Universal came through with the executive producer's title or not, he was often acting like the series' producer.

With Playdon on board as the studio's official producer and with the enthusiastic cooperation of Mayor Richard Daly's film coordinator, McGavin and Kathie Browne checked into Chicago's Drake Hotel for a weekend of filming segments that would be edited into the episodes. Most of these were of Kolchak driving around Chicago. Browne, described by her husband as his "executive associate," worked behind the scenes for most of that grueling season.

The concept of *The Night Stalker* as a series is that Carl Kolchak has landed a job for the Independent News Service (INS) wire bureau in Chicago. He's still bumping into supernatural stories. He's still battling officials wanting to suppress facts. He's still trying to get back to New York. And, of course, he's still working for Tony Vincenzo.

Sounded like fun to most of the TV critics hearing McGavin describe the series. But long hours, internal politics, constant pressure and conflicting visions took their toll.

"It was quite a mess," McGavin recalls. "It wasn't any fun. It was frustrating. What's the name of the series? Guess when it was shot? We started shooting about two in the afternoon and would work for fourteen hours. It was night shooting, which is expensive and means very long hours. The next day, you'd start at four in the afternoon, go fourteen hours, quit at six in the morning, then do it all over again. It was terrible. And we were always under the gun because we didn't have scripts prepared. We'd be out on location for the series, and we'd get rewrites at eleven-thirty at night for scenes we'd shot three hours before. It was a major battle to continue doing it, and I didn't want to continue doing it. There was no structure, nothing to follow. David Chase was the one continuing element through the entire show. He was there from beginning to end."

Filming on the first episode, "The Ripper," started Monday, July 15, continuing through Friday. After the weekend break, director Allen Baron wrapped the shoot on Monday, July 22. On Wednesday, July 31, filming began on the second episode, "The Zombie," directed by Alex Grasshoff.

With another weekend break, this six-day shoot wrapped on August 7. Filming was started on two other episodes while Playdon put the finishing editorial touches on "The Ripper" and "The Zombie." When "The Zombie" print was finished, however, so was Paul Playdon. He and McGavin weren't seeing eye to eye. McGavin didn't feel that Playdon understood the character or the series. The fighting had become too much. Playdon quit over what *Variety* reported as "artistic differences," and, with only two episodes filmed and no backup scripts completed, the series shut down for two weeks.

# PRODUCER OUT, PRODUCER IN

When Paul Playdon left the series, Universal looked around for a new producer. The man chosen to replace him was Cy Chermak, an experienced writer-producer who had been at the helm of such Universal series as *The Virginian, Ironside* and *The New Doctors*. Chermak – who was born September 20, 1929, in Bayonne, New Jersey – was a strong and reliable studio veteran accustomed to tough challenges.

"I had been under contract at Universal for many years at that point," Chermak says. "I first went to work for them in 1962 and ended up staying there fourteen years. I was an alternating producer of *The Virginian*, off and on, for nine seasons. Then I was the executive producer of *Ironside* for seven years, the executive producer of *The New Doctors* for two years and the executive producer of *Amy Prentiss.*"

Created by Chermak's wife, Francine Carroll, *Amy Prentiss* was a series far ahead of its time. Part of NBC's Sunday Mystery Movie package for the 1974-75 season (with *Columbo, McCloud* and *McMillan and Wife),* the police drama boldly moved into prime time with the title character, a thirty-five-year-old widow played by Jessica Walter, as San Francisco's chief of detectives. Although viewers did not immediately respond to a woman in command, Walter's performance was recognized with an Emmy.

Also in the cast was an eleven-year-old Helen Hunt, about twenty years before starring in NBC's *Mad About You.*

"Well, Universal had this show, then called *The Night Stalker*," Chermak explains, "and they were having trouble with it. Paul Playdon, who was a very nice, polite, quiet, well-mannered young man, and a pretty good writer, was having a rough time. He just decided this show was too much. They thought I could help straighten the show out, so Universal asked me to take it over. Not knowing what I was getting myself into, I said yes.

"They needed a strong hand on that show. Darren McGavin had run all over Paul Playdon and they didn't want Darren McGavin producing that show. They wanted me producing that show. I fell right in with their plans."

McGavin, of course, believed he had to "run all over" the studio producers, if just to keep the series on track.

At this point, however, *The Night Stalker* became a Universal series "produced in association with Francy Productions, Inc." Eighteen of the twenty *Night Stalker* episodes (all but the first two) would carry this credit line. Francy (for Fran and Cy) was the production company owned by Francine Carroll and Cy Chermak. Also at this point, Francy was producing *Amy Prentiss*. The assumption that McGavin's company co-produced the *Night Stalker* has given rise to the myth that Francy is owned by the actor. The myth appears as "fact" in most standard reference books.

Unbeknownst to McGavin, Chermak's contract with MCA/Universal granted him the honor of accepting the executive producer credit.

"I was contractually guaranteed the option of taking the title of either producer or executive producer," Chermak says. "I didn't take the executive producer title on *The Night Stalker* because I had no subordinate producers working with me on that show. I did take the executive producer title on Ironside, for instance, because I had three or more alternating producers working with me. When I had producers subordinate to me, I took the executive producer title. Then there was a reason for it."

Ironically, some of the reference books that don't list Darren McGavin as executive producer of *The Night Stalker*, list Cy Chermak as the executive producer (a title he specifically declined). Some of these same reference books also misspell Paul Playdon's name as Playton or Playden.

"There wasn't any need for me take the executive producer title on *The Night Stalker*," Chermak says. "The buck stopped at my office. I oversaw everything from supervising the scripts to okaying the final answer prints. Every draft of every script was gone over with the writer in my office. Every line was approved on my desk. I cut those episodes sitting at the right shoulder of the editor. I approved every answer print.

"I was the top. Now that doesn't mean I didn't have people I had to answer to. I did. They were Frank Price and Sid Sheinberg."

Price, Sheinberg and Chermak were of the opinion that McGavin had pushed Playdon and the series too far in a comedic direction. One of Chermak's mandates as producer was to keep the humor from getting out of hand.

"We felt that the juvenile, sitcom sort of humor was wrong for the show," Chermak says, "particularly in regard to the continuing cast. We wanted to put a stop to that because we felt a series like *The Night Stalker* should be firmly grounded in reality. You had to believe in the people in the INS Newsroom and the way they dealt with the people around them. That reality would make the scary stuff work."

Chermak's young story editor, David Chase, agrees that the series often was more humor than horror: "The original movie was a nice blend of horror and humor. Think about putting a vampire in Las Vegas, which is such a nocturnal and bloodsucking city. It was a real slice of America slapping you in the face. And Kolchak is a real hard-edged reporter. That all really worked. The intent of the series was to bottle that essence and sell it. But it was tough on a weekly basis. Darren liked the characters in the newsroom. We couldn't deliver scary and convincing monsters every week, so it began to head more and more in the direction of a comedy, which was fine with me because that's my bent anyway."

Yet Jeff Rice was sensing something a bit more troubling than the emphasis of humor over horror. He was afraid that his creations were becoming more caricatures than characters. It was a tiny reservation in the first film. It grew into alarm in the second. With the series, "this kind of thing only got worse as time went by."

Chermak, like McGavin, felt blessed to have an actor of Simon Oakland's class and intelligence playing Tony Vincenzo. But before Chermak came on board, McGavin and Playdon had populated Kolchak's world with regular and semi-regular characters prized for their comic possibilities: Jack Grinnage as nerdy reporter Ron Updyke, Ruth McDevitt as elderly Miss Emily Cowles, Carol Ann Susi as bumbling office intern Monique Marmelstein, and John Fiedler as morgue attendant Gordon "Gordy the Ghoul" Spangler. Chermak didn't have a problem with the actors. He had a problem with the way the characters were being used. When it came to this supporting cast, a definite direction had emerged. The players were picked with situation comedy in mind, not a horror drama.

McGavin and Chase don't dispute this.

"The studio wanted a pretty young starlet in the office," McGavin says about the Monique Marmelstein character. "I said, 'No, no. Let's get characters, a human being, not a pretty little contract player swinging her ass around the office.' You need real characters because that part of the show is really a situation comedy. Half of it was an office situation comedy. Humor is important from the first show."

Humor is important, Chermak agrees. But he and McGavin clashed over the type of humor appropriate for the series.

"You absolutely need humor to relieve the tension of horror," Chermak says. "All tension is no tension, just as all pacing is no pacing. I wasn't against humor. I was against situation comedy for this show. We wanted to change from Darren's concept of comedy to my concept of humor. The networks, then as well as today, have a tough time understanding the difference between comedy and humor. We thought we understood the difference very well. And I think we brought in more of the black humor and the inside humor that the college crowd got. That was primarily what I thought would help the show."

Chermak also wanted to vary the show more from a structural standpoint. "Darren had a philosophy about the structure of the show," Chermak explains. "He felt that every episode should follow the same pattern: Kolchak finds out about something, he goes and researches it, he gets himself in hot water, then he finds the solution and that takes us to the conclusion where he doesn't get to print the story. We felt that if we did that, we'd have the audience for only three or four episodes, and then they'd be way ahead of us and know where we were going."

But what didn't change was the tension surrounding the *Night Stalker* series. The long hours and hectic schedules kept nerves on edge. Compounding the problem was the realization that McGavin and Chermak did not get along any better than McGavin and Playdon.

"There were a lot of fights," McGavin recalls. "A lot of fights. Major battles. The scripts were never ready on time. We never had enough time."

David Chase confirms McGavin's bleak description of the series in production.

"Yeah, it was pretty bad," says Chase, now a producer at Lorimar. "There were fights. Paul quit. Cy came on board. There were fights. It was a very expensive show to produce. There were budget restraints. There were brutal hours. Cy Chermak was a very funny guy, a very droll guy. He was really sharp. . . but he and Darren were at odds over the direction for the show."

McGavin believed that Universal executives – and the producers they assigned to *The Night Stalker* – didn't have a good grasp of the Kolchak character and format. The actor believed that the "family" of regulars around Kolchak grounded him in a reality that would make him welcome into TV homes on a weekly basis. McGavin fought against conventional casting choices and for the elements he believed would grant the show longevity. He also contended that staying in the INS newsroom with the regular characters would be an entertaining way to keep costs down on a show that couldn't afford extensive special effects. It would be efficient and entertaining. To McGavin, this was good business and good show business. It would give a horror series a human touch. It would cut expenses. And it would be fun.

Two camps emerged from this power struggle on the Universal lot. Chermak presided over story conferences, production meetings, rewrites, scoring and the editing process. McGavin took the lead on the set. Chermak fought to impose his vision for the series. McGavin fought back, certain that the studio was heading down the wrong path for Kolchak.

"Yes, one of the reasons tensions ran so high on the show was because the relationship between me and Darren deteriorated rapidly," Chermak says. "And everybody knew it. When we were in my office, I was the boss. When they were on the set and I wasn't there, Darren had them doing what he wanted. He never accepted that I was running the show.

"So, aside from the long hours, the people working on this show were torn. It was very tough on them. It really wasn't two camps. That's not quite right. There was one camp, mine, and one actor — a major star — down on the set while I'm frantically preparing the next show. My stomach was constantly churning. I ended up in a hospital room with an ulcer, and I'm sitting there with my wife and (director) Don Weis, talking about what we're going to do on the next show."

Yet Chermak doesn't blame McGavin for trying to pursue his vision of the series. What else should he have done?

"He was not altogether to blame for the situation," Chermak says. "If we were doing this show today, he would be the executive producer in fact and in title, and he would do it the way he wanted. That's just not the way Universal did things in 1974. But you can't blame him for fighting for what he believed was right. Nobody's questioning Darren's sincerity and dedication, or his standing as a star. . . and he was ideal for that role."

In fact, Chermak takes much of the blame on himself. In a town driven by egos and not know for honest self-appraisal, the writer-producer can look back and admit his mistakes.

"I was brought in on Ironside during the first season when it was in trouble," Chermak says. "I subsequently did the same thing on *CHiPs*. I took over that show as executive producer when it was in trouble. I'm something of a play doctor, so I wanted to do the same thing on *Night Stalker*.

"As tough as *The Night Stalker* was, I didn't want to give up on it. I think I let the show down by not being able to get along with Darren. It's as much my fault as his. In those days, I thought it was enough to be talented and you didn't have to get along. That was the biggest mistake I made on *The Night Stalker*. Retrospectively, I realize that my job was to get everyone on the same page. It was my job to make sure we were getting along. I never did that, and it hurt the show. I went in and said I'm the boss. Universal needed evolution. I gave them revolution."

Still, even if McGavin and Chermak had made peace, the technical and budget problems still would have haunted *The Night Stalker.*

"The studio always wanted us to shoot day for night [faking night during daylight hours]," Chermak remembers. "I felt that night for night was what you do on a series like this. If you're going to frighten them, day for night doesn't make it. We just didn't have the budget to do it. We'd get in two or three hours at night and have to quit."

Cutting corners at every turn, Chermak and the production team often would jump from the intense to the absurd during meetings. With no money in the budget for makeup one week, Chermak might ask, "Do we still have the chicken suit from last week? Let's rework that and use it this week."

Chase had to shake his head in amusement over what had to be the silliest production meetings in town. Echoing Matheson's view on the *Night Strangler* planning session, Chase says that "production meetings were just great because what we were talking about was so silly."

Chermak can only shake his head in envy over the technical advances that give an edge to shows like *The X-Files* and the syndicated versions of *Star Trek*. Costly and time-consuming special effects of the '70s can be duplicated on computer screens with a few simple commands.

"Just look at what people are doing with special effects and longer shooting schedules," Chermak says. "If I had had computers and digitalization and blue screen effects, perhaps our show would have been much better — and easier."

Despite his concerns over the direction of the characters and the failure of ABC to secure his permission for a series, Rice was far from unhappy with the presence of a series version of *The Night Stalker*. He had every reason to wish it well.

Pocket Books and MCA Publishing discussed the possibility of Rice turning the series scripts into novels. If they were half as successful as the *Night Stalker* and *Night Strangler* novels, everybody concerned would pick up a nice piece of change. There was talk of a $100,000 advance based on a five-book deal for Rice.

"Things were definitely looking up," Rice says. He talked with Playdon and Chase about script ideas. He talked with Darren McGavin and Kathie Browne about the characters. Any day now, he thought, ABC and Universal will work out the legal agreement to obtain his rights for the series. Any day now, he thought, the call will come to work on scripts for the series. "I really thought they'd come to me since I started the whole thing and knew the characters and their inner workings intimately," Rice says. "I was a fool."

On August 7, 1974, Rice's attorney sent a mailgram to MCA President Sidney Sheinberg. It contained a notification that the Writers Guild of America acknowledged Jeff Rice as the creator of the series. The lawyer also requested that Universal and MCA settle the rights question with his client.

"The telegram was not the threat of a suit," Rice says. "It was simply constructive notice that I had rights to sell that they had not yet purchased. Action on these requests was slow. Reaction was swift.

"I was barred from the lot," Rice recalls. "People around town who had returned my calls were suddenly unavailable. In short order, the deal that had been almost set for me to novelize the series scripts, dissolved in a series of rancorous exchanges between certain people on the west coast and certain others on the east coast."

The one thing nobody could deny Rice was his on-screen credit. On Friday, September 6 (seven days before *The Night Stalker* premiered), an MCA attorney issued a memorandum. Every episode of the series was to carry the same credit line: "Created by Jeff Rice."

Still, Rice was reluctant to file a lawsuit to resolve the rights question. He wanted the series to succeed and, to this end, he prepared lengthy memos for MCA, ABC and the production team. Like McGavin, he opposed a monster-of-the-week format. Rice suggested an approach "that will not limit them to an endless monster hunt but will, in addition, tackle some of the more topical issues of the day." The author also warned against an almost certain "stagnation" and "development of Kolchak and Vincenzo into stereotyped, cardboard, two-dimensional caricatures of human beings instead of the fully-fleshed-out people they are and have a right to be."

By January, with the series going nowhere, Rice still wanted matters settled in a civilized manner. He wanted to negotiate, not litigate. "There was no lawsuit in existence" at that time, Rice says. "I did not want to file a lawsuit. I wanted to write and to save my series (and the value of my property) from destruction and oblivion."

Some reference books claim that Rice's lawsuit hurt an already struggling series. "My attorney and I tried everything we could to avoid a litigation," Rice maintains. He blames ABC and MCA for the litigation: "It was their choice."

The six-count civil suit was filed on Wednesday, March 5, 1975. On Friday, *Daily Variety* reported the filing in a front-page item. On March 18, a column of support for Rice appeared in the *Las Vegas SUN*. It was written by, of all people, the "original Carl Kolchak" — Alan Jarlson. "Jeff Rice, the Las Vegas High School grad-turned-author, was never known as the timid type," Jarlson wrote. "As a reporter for the *Las Vegas SUN* from 1966 to 1968 he gained a fair reputation as a digger, and his aggressiveness nettled not a few public officials who ran their domains like personal fiefdoms. . . His challenges to those who don't hold with the maxim that the public does have a right to know did not go unnoticed by the Nevada State Press Association which honored him as the 'Outstanding Journalist' the last year he plied his trade as a *SUN* staffer."

It took nine months of legal wrangling, depositions, motions and court documents for the parties to reach an agreement. The lawsuit was settled on the day the trial was supposed to begin.

But Rice believes that these victories cost him years of potential income. And still he wanted the series to succeed and improve.

Stuck at ten o'clock Friday nights against a top-twenty show, *Police Woman*, the series faced a ratings future more frightening than any monster Kolchak would encounter. The *Night Stalker* premiered in September, appropriately enough, on Friday the thirteenth.

The title had come to refer to Carl Kolchak, even though Janos Skorzeny was the true title character of the first film. It had happened before in popular culture. *Frankenstein*, the title of Mary Shelley's book, refers to the scientist, not his monster. By the time Boris Karloff made *The Bride of Frankenstein* in 1935, Frankenstein had become the name of the monster. Dashiell Hammett's *The Thin Man* (the murder victim in the book) became the alias for detective Nick Charles.

But just to make things absolutely clear, ABC changed the title at episode five to *Kolchak: The Night Stalker.* Of course, some argued that it made things more confusing since *Kodiak* and *Kojak* also were on that fall schedule.

Interestingly enough, the series was first announced in early 1974 as *Kolchak: The Night Stalker.* By summer, the title had been switched to just *The Night Stalker* to avoid confusion with *Kojak* and *Kodiak.* It was a bit much: *Kojak, Kodiak, Kolchak.* All they needed, McGavin joked, was to be sponsored by Kodak. After four episodes, though, ABC switched back to *Kolchak: The Night Stalker.*

The ratings never got on track after that Friday the thirteenth debut. The second episode, "The Zombie," finished fifty-eight out of sixty-one shows aired that week. *Police Woman* was tenth. The third episode finished sixty out of sixty-three shows. The fifth episode was forty-nine out of sixty. In January 1975, *Kolchak: The Night Stalker* was moved to eight o'clock Friday nights, where it faced even tougher competition: NBC's powerhouse comedy hour of *Sanford and Son* and *Chico and the Man.* How powerful? Well, try silver bullets and wooden stakes and all the garlic you can stand against this: those two comedies were two of that season's three highest-rated series. *Kolchak* stood a better chance against the corrupt officials back in Las Vegas.

"We were killing ourselves," Chase says. "*The Mary Tyler Moore Show* was on at that time. Everybody was talking about it. I never saw it. I was never home to watch *The Mary Tyler Moore Show.* We were too busy."

Still, no matter how bad the power struggles became, McGavin was careful to keep the actors in the dark about behind-the-scenes arguments. If battles were raging, the regulars didn't need to be dragged into the line of fire.

"It was so much fun," says Jack Grinnage, who appeared in eighteen of the twenty episodes as INS reporter Ron Updyke. "It was a very warm, terrific set to be around. I don't know what went on behind the scenes. I know that Cy and Darren didn't get along. There seemed to be a lot of trouble. But the actors weren't ever brought into that. The mood on set was wonderful. Darren was a complete joy to work with—very funny and very supportive. He'd do whatever he could to help you. Simon Oakland and Ruth McDevitt were two of the most beautiful, most professional and most delightful people in the world. It felt like a family. We had such a good time. We really enjoyed each other's company. Whatever trouble there was, Darren never brought into rehearsal or performance. Judging just on that, you wouldn't know there ever was trouble."

"It was wonderful and awful at the same time," says Kathie Browne McGavin. "Everything was so frantic. There was so much to do and so little time. Everybody always was under a lot of pressure. There was lots of location shooting — out at the airport, out in the Valley, out in Pasadena, always some place. I remember the speed, the pace, the energy."

Out of this speed and energy, a sense of fun did emerge among the younger writers guided by Chermak.

"The show was very popular among college students, who picked up on the inside humor," Chermak says. "David Chase was barely out of college himself at the time, so he was close to that. Rudy [Rudolph] Borchert was another key member of the writing staff. He also became a story editor on the show, and he ended up with solo credit on three of the episodes, he wrote a fourth from someone else's story and he co-wrote a fifth. And he made important contributions to several other scripts.

"I remember the 'chicken suit' production meeting David describes. But the truth is that David and Rudy didn't make it to too many production meetings. They were too busy writing and rewriting scripts. They spent most of their time at story conferences or at their typewriters."

Chase, a future Emmy winner, wound up with screen credit on eight of the twenty episodes, most written in collaboration. Borchert had five on-screen credits (the three solos being "The Ripper," "U.F.O." and "The Youth Killer"), but he and Chase had a hand in fashioning "The Devil's Platform" and others.

Once the show was up and running, writing contributions were made by another future Emmy winner, Michael Kozoll (*Hill Street Blues*), and a future Oscar winner, Bob Zemeckis (*Forrest Gump*).

Kozoll, who had less series experience than Chase, co-wrote two of the twenty episodes and co-authored a third that wasn't filmed. Zemeckis, with his partner Bob Gale, revved up "Chopper," one of Chermak's favorite episodes. Both recall working on the show with great fondness.

"There was nothing else like it on the air," Chase says when asked about the hip and playful sensibility that was eased into the scripts. "We knew we were making up this bizarre joke. I hope you can tell there were some people having fun. As a series idea, in retrospect, it was a dead end. It was pretty nutty, if you stop to think about it. This is one show I didn't think about a great deal after it was over. We were moving too fast. I never really evaluated it. I know I never thought about it much as a horror show. It became a comedy. And the humor that took over was sort of a '60s, rock 'n' roll sensibility. And there was a sense of absurdity about the whole thing. [Writers like] Michael and I were of a different generation, and I guess it makes sense that this is what would happen if you [put] us on a horror show at that time of our lives."

After *Kolchak: The Night Stalker*, Chase won a 1978 Emmy as one of the producers of *The Rockford Files*. Two years later, he picked up a second statuette for writing the TV movie *Off the Minnesota Strip*. He also was the producer of the innovative but short-lived CBS series *Almost Grown* (1988). Starting in 1994, he and Stephen J. Cannell reunited as supervising producers of James Garner's new *Rockford* movies.

Kozoll, after working on *Kojak* and *Quincy, M.E.*, took home two 1981 Emmys for producing and co-creating *Hill Street Blues*. But the luster of an Emmy wasn't even the glimmer of a dream for Kozoll in 1974.

"I was a teacher in Northern California," Kozoll recalls, "and, for whatever reason, probably politics, I lost my job. I started watching television and I said, 'I can do that.' So I drove down to Los Angeles and started looking for a job. Cy Chermak and David Chase gave me my first writing jobs. That show literally turned my life around. I was living in my car with my dog at the time. I was taking showers at a cousin's house. I mean, this was scraping by. I was new in town, but I had written some stuff and given it to an agent. There was a spec script for a movie of the week, and Paul Playdon optioned it for ABC. He recommended me to David Chase. It was great that the job turned out to be *The Night Stalker*, but I would have written anything just to make money. I was lucky just to find a place to park on the lot. I had nowhere to put my dog. David let me bring my dog in the office. I have an enormous respect and fondness for David Chase. David is a wonderful writer. . . David was very hip and I had long hair. . . Along the way, I got an apartment, so I'm not kidding. The show turned my life around."

Something in Kolchak touched a kindred spirit in Kozoll, who says he was "a baby writer" when he worked on the series: "I like the show so much because it was about an underdog and the show was truly such an underdog at Universal. You'd tell people at Universal that you were working on *Night Stalker* and they'd get this strange look on their faces. It was such a stepchild of a show. Universal didn't know what they had.

"It was fun. It had none of the pomposity that most television shows had. It had a sense of what its size was... there was a sense of humor and social consciousness in almost every show. It made fun of the establishment, the cops, the government. We did shows about pollution and other issues. It really was quite ahead of its time."

Only the few fans, who turned *Kolchak: The Night Stalker* into a cult show, appreciated this. Not even many of the people connected with the series appreciated this. And *The New York Times* certainly didn't appreciate this. On September 13, 1974, the day *The Night Stalker* premiered, *Times* critic John J. O'Connor (who hadn't written about either of the movies) described the series as "a lumpy mixture of nutty farce and ominous terror." "Nobody will believe it," O'Connor wrote, "not even the producer's immediate family." Then again, in the same column, O'Connor suggested that *The Rockford Files* was "for the severely insatiable." Garner, he said, "is very funny when the routines work, which unfortunately is only about half the time." O'Connor also wrote– in the same column – that the series version of *Planet of the Apes* was "by the same mentality that produced such popular goodies as *Star Trek*."

Other reviews were equally harsh. Lee Winfrey of Knight Newspapers called *The Night Stalker* "quite possibly the worst of all the 25 new television series that began this fall." Noting that McGavin's Kolchak is Polish, Winfrey asked his readers to "please forget he's Polish: think of Copernicus, Chopin, Madame Curie, anything but this ludicrous libel upon an innocent people and what is at least a semirespectable profession." As a representative of both that "innocent people" and that "semirespectable profession," I saw Kolchak as anything but "a ludicrous libel."

Ah, well, *TV Guide* critic Cleveland Amory never even wrote a review of *Kolchak: The Night Stalker.*

In 1974, most hour series produced a season of anywhere from twenty-two to twenty-six episodes. Always behind, *Kolchak: The Night Stalker* managed only twenty. Almost all of these aired in the order they were filmed. The first, "The Ripper," started shooting July 15, 1974. The last, "The Sentry," wrapped things up on February 7, 1975. Each episode was budgeted for a six-day shoot, and only two went longer. "The Vampire" took nine days (September 5, 6, 9, 10, 11, 12, 13, 16 and 17). "Chopper" took seven (starting December 31, 1974, continuing January 1, 2, 3, 6, 7, 8, 1975).

Like the movies, each episode starts with a Kolchak narration. The credits usually flashed on the screen as Kolchak drove around Chicago (for the series, he traded in his blue Camaro convertible for a yellow Mustang convertible). Little bits and pieces about Kolchak's background were dropped into the twenty outings. We see, for instance, that Kolchak knows his way around a darkroom. In the *Night Strangler* novel, Jeff Rice told us that Kolchak was a copy boy in Boston. In "Mr.. R.I.N.G.," Kolchak tells us that he was a cub reporter in Chicago (thus his familiarity with the city). At the end of each episode, our hero talks into his tape recorder, telling whoever will listen how once more the facts were watered down, altered, falsified and suppressed. He is shaken but not stopped. He is beaten up but not beaten. He is down but not out. The right to know is sacred. He will again don his armor of seersucker and helmet of straw. He will again point his lance, which resembles a pen, at a windmill propelled by nothing more than hot air.

# THE GANG OF FOUR

Regardless of how well or ill they were used, the four players hired to support Darren McGavin and Simon Oakland have endeared themselves to each generation of *Kolchak: The Night Stalker* fans. Although two of them appeared in only three of the twenty episodes, they remain the cherished members of Carl's TV "family."

**1.) Jack Grinnage** — After McGavin and Oakland, Grinnage was the closest thing the series had to a regular. Playing the INS newsroom's uptight dork, Ron "Uptight" Updyke, the actor appears in eighteen of the twenty episodes, missing only "The Zombie" and the last one ("The Sentry").

"Actually, I was just supposed to do the first episode," Grinnage says. "Ron was introduced in "The Ripper" as a character who throws up at the sight of blood. I think the character was Darren's idea. Well, they liked the character and wanted to keep him, but my grandmother was ninety at the time and I was taking her to Europe. Now I never had turned down a job in my life, but I told them that I had already planned the trip and was going."

Universal enticed Grinnage to stay by offering him a firm commitment for three episodes.

"Fine," he replied, "but I'm still going to Europe."

Then they offered him seven episodes. Then thirteen. He kept saying no until they offered him a guarantee of every episode for the season. And, if they failed to write his character into an episode, Grinnage still would get paid. It was a run-of-the-series contract, and only McGavin and Oakland had that distinction.

"When I told my grandmother," Grinnage recalls, "she said, 'Dear, I'm not dead yet, we'll go next year.' "

Born and raised in Southern California, Grinnage attended Los Angeles City College, where he became an active member of the drama department. A friend recommended him to an agent, who got him a job on *Father Knows Best*. He played Bud's friend, Claude, for about five episodes, then learned that the role had been recast. Welcome to show business.

But he soon found cause for celebration. Director Nicholas Ray cast him as one of the young hoods in *Rebel Without a Cause* (1955), which starred James Dean, Natalie Wood, Sal Mineo and future *Kolchak: The Night Stalker* guest star Jim Backus. Three years later, he had another supporting role in another film starring a rebel icon of the '50s, *King Creole,* with Elvis Presley and future *Kolchak: The Night Stalker* guest star Carolyn Jones. The director was Michael Curtiz, whose credits included *The Adventures of Robin Hood* (1938) and *Casablanca* (1942).

"And when I worked with Elvis Presley," Grinnage says, "he just wanted to know about James Dean."

In 1961, Grinnage was a regular on NBC's *The Bob Newhart Show*. That same year, he appeared in "The Mind and the Matter," a second-season episode of *The Twilight Zone*. Seven years and several TV roles later, he was playing a gay hairdresser trying to pick up Darren McGavin's David Ross on NBC's *The Outsider*. So Grinnage had been an actor for about twenty years when the role of Ron Updyke came his way.

"One of the two casting people at Universal was Ralph Winters, who had once been my agent," Grinnage says. "I think he was instrumental in getting me the role on *Night Stalker*. There were six people reading for Ron when I auditioned. I have to think that knowing Ralph helped. That and the fact that Darren and I had had such a great time working on *The Outsider*. Both those things had to help."

Jack Grinnage

When cast as Ron, Grinnage was working for the Los Angeles Board of Education. Running the board's drama unit, he took various programs into schools.

"I went to my supervisor and told him I had a series," Grinnage remembers, "and he said, 'Well, let's see what happens.' And what happened was that most of my scenes were shot at night, so I was able to keep my full-time day job while doing the series. That turned out to be a good thing because the series went off the air and I still had to make a living."

Grinnage views his *Night Stalker* experience with great fondness. His co-stars are what made the show special for him.

"Darren couldn't have been nicer," he says. "He'd help you with your lines or anything. He was always there for you. Ruth McDevitt was a dear, as was Carol Ann Susi. I still see Carol Ann, who doesn't live too far from me. We get together for lunch every now and then. She's very funny. We'd get our fan mail delivered on the set, and Carol Ann and I would open our two letters.

"And it was a great honor to work with Simon Oakland. When I was in college, I saw a play called *The Great Sebastian*, with Alfred Lunt and Lynn Fontanne. And Simon Oakland was in the cast. That was really my introduction to theater. So it was an incredible thrill to be actually working with him."

Ron Updyke was supposed to appear in the final episode. Scenes were written for the character, but Grinnage had an offer to do another series. Sure they were going to lose him, the writers cut him out of "The Sentry."

"Then I ended up turning down the other series, anyway," Grinnage says. "After the show left the air, I remained with the Board of Education until Proposition 13 took that job away. But I'd always made props, and I was offered a job at a prop house. So now I do a couple of soap episodes, a commercial, voice-overs, go out on auditions, and then go back to making props. If you saw *In the Line of Fire* with Clint Eastwood and remember the rabbit's foot with the bullets in it, well, I made that!

"I've worked a lot, and I've been lucky that many of the things I was in became cult favorites, like *Rebel Without a Cause* or an Elvis Presley picture. So *The Night Stalker* fits right in with that. And Darren and Kathie remain dear friends. They bought a river barge in France and I spent a month with them. I really enjoy their company."

**2.) Ruth McDevitt** — The only other true regular was veteran character actress Ruth McDevitt, who was forty-five when she made her Broadway debut in the 1940 production of *Absence of a Cello*. Her series experience could be traced all the way back to 1949, when she was a regular on the ill-fated DuMont network's *A Woman to Remember*. She was Mom Peepers for two seasons of Wally Cox's *Mr. Peepers* (NBC, 1953-55). She was Grandma on *Pistols 'n' Petticoats* (CBS, 1966-67). She was the comic relief on *Johnny Cash Presents the Everly Brothers Show*, a 1970 ABC summer series. And she made regular appearances as Jo Nelson for two seasons (1973-75) of *All in the Family* (CBS). Incredibly, by the time *The Night Stalker* found her, McDevitt had been a series regular in four different decades on four different networks. The actress, born Ruth Shoecraft, also appeared in such films as The *Parent Trap* (1961), Alfred Hitchcock's *The Birds* (1963) and *The Out-of-Towners* (1970). She can be seen in the 1964 "Gentleman Caller" episode of *Alfred Hitchcock Presents.*

"Ruth never flubbed a line," Grinnage recalls, "and she never complained, even though she was having trouble getting around by then. She was a real trouper, and she was every bit as sweet as Miss Emily."

Under Chermak's regime and starting with the fifth episode ("The Werewolf"), McDevitt made eleven appearances as sweet-tempered Emily Cowles, who handled such INS chores as society news and the advice-to-the-lovelorn column. But McDevitt actually can be seen in twelve episodes (she played an elderly woman, not Miss Emily, in the series opener).

"Ruth McDevitt was a gem, an absolute gem," Chermak says. "In fact, all of the supporting players – Jack Grinnage, Carol Ann Susi– were very nice, very professional people. I never objected to those characters. We fought over how those characters should be depicted. I wanted to make them more real. Darren wanted them to be more like characters on a sitcom. But the actors themselves were dreams to work with."

**3.) John Fiedler** — Most reference books also list two other regulars: John Fiedler and Carol Ann Susi. In reality, however, each appeared in only three episodes. John Fiedler was a busy character actor known for playing meek, bespectacled fellows in movies and television. When cast as morgue attendant Gordon "Gordy the Ghoul" Spangler on *The Night Stalker*, he was best known for playing wimpy Vinnie in the Broadway and film versions of Neil Simon's *The Odd Couple*. His other notable films included *Twelve Angry Men* (1957), *That Touch of Mink* (1962), *The World of Henry Orient* (1964) and *True Grit* (1969). Fans of Rod Serling's *The Twilight Zone* knew him for two roles, both in episodes written by the anthology series' host – Mr. Dundee in "Night of the Meek" and one of the field reps in "Cavender is Coming." Star Trek fans knew him as Hengist in writer Robert Bloch's *Jack the Ripper* episode, "Wolf in the Fold." His other television credits included episodes of *Thriller, Alfred Hitchcock Presents, I Spy and Columbo*. After *The Night Stalker*, Fiedler earned a place in sitcom history with two memorable roles: Mr. Peterson on *The Bob Newhart Show* (the 1972-78 CBS hit on which Larry Gelman, who played Vinnie in ABC's series version of *The Odd Couple*, also was a regular) and Woody on *Buffalo Bill* (NBC, 1983-84). Playing against the "Vinnie" persona, Fiedler made two memorable trips to Jack Klugman and Tony Randall's *Odd Couple* series: as building manager G. Martin Duke in "Security Arms" and cruel trainer Mr. Hugo in "The Dog Story." He has also supplied the voice of many cartoon characters, most notably Piglet in Disney's *Winnie the Pooh* features.

**4.) Carol Ann Susi** — Spotted by Darren McGavin and Kathie Browne working as a waitress, Susi played Monique Marmelstein, a klutzy intern assigned to the INS bureau through the influence of her powerful uncle.

"I had only been in Hollywood for about six months," the New York-born Susi recalls, "and I'd only done off-off-off-Broadway, so I didn't think I should tell anybody that I was an actress. I didn't think of myself as an actress. I was young and from New York and didn't know any better. Well, I was working as a waitress at this high-priced coffee shop, Hamburger Hamlet, and everybody in the business came in there."

One day in 1974, Darren McGavin and Kathie Browne walked into the restaurant and sat down at one of Susi's tables.

"Are you an actress?" asked McGavin, who, at the time was in the planning stages for a series to be titled *Kolchak: The Night Stalker.*

"No!" the surprised Susi replied. "You gotta know people to do that. I'm not an actress."

Another waitress, overhearing the conversation, decided this was too good an opportunity to pass by. She walked over to the McGavins' table and told them, "Yes, she is an actress. She's just lying to you because she's like that. She denies it."

When Susi returned to the table, McGavin said, "Well, I hear you are an actress."

"I guess I don't want people to know," Susi answered.

"Do you know who I am?" McGavin pressed.

"Yeah, you're Mike Hammer," Susi said, referring to the Mickey Spillane series.

"Yeah," McGavin agreed, "that's right. Well, I'm doing a television series at Universal, and I would love it if you would come audition for me."

Ruth McDevitt

John Fiedler

"Oh, yeah, right!" the incredulous Susi shouted. "Like I'm really going to walk over to Universal and they're going to let me in. Right?"

"No, we'll make sure they let you in," Kathie Browne assured her.

Although still skeptical, Susi showed up for the audition. She was pleased just to get on the Universal lot. The tickled New Yorker was ushered into the presence of producer Play Playdon and director Alex Grasshoff.

"I had nothing at stake," she says. "I never thought I was going to get this job — never! So I read for the part and they told me they had auditioned seventy girls, and I thought, great. But after I read, Darren asked me to stay a little while."

Left waiting in an outer lobby, Susi was overjoyed with the opportunity to read for a series. Then a stern-faced McGavin approached her.

"Well, I hate to tell you this," McGavin started to say.

"Oh, no, that's all right," Susi interrupted him. "I didn't expect to get the part."

"Well, you got the job," McGavin said.

Before Susi's reading, the character was going to be named Allison. She also was going to be tall, blonde and graceful. McGavin convinced Playdon that they should hire somebody short, awkward and very Noo Yawkish. Goodbye, Allison. Hello, Monique.

Susi was told that she would be a semi-regular appearing in most of the episodes. When producer Cy Chermak took over the series for Universal, however, Monique Marmelstein was eliminated from the *Night Stalker* mix.

"It had nothing to do with the actress playing the character," Chermak says. "It had everything to do with how the character was written."

Susi didn't know this at the time. She thought her acting had been judged unacceptable.

"Now I know that people didn't agree on the character," Susi says. "Back then, I thought it was me. I was only twenty-two-years-old. I knew nothing about studio politics. I thought I must be a bad actress. I thought it was me they didn't like – period. I thought my acting must be horrible. I was devastated. That's where you go when you're twenty-two."

She carried around this misconception for five years. She was back working as a waitress when a young writer sat down at one of her tables. The customer looked at Susi and said, "I remember you. You were Monique Marmelstein."

It was David Chase, the story editor on *Kolchak: The Night Stalker.*

Susi began to apologize for being so bad on the series. Chase cheerfully set her straight.

"No, no, you were wonderful," he told her. "Everybody thought so. It just came down from the [MCA Black] Tower that they didn't like the character. They thought you were great."

"You mean it wasn't because I did such a bad job?" Susi asked.

"No!" Chase answered. "You were terrific!"

Even with the years of self-doubt, Susi cherishes *Kolchak: The Night Stalker* as "one of the best acting experiences" of her life.

"Look, I was tickled to be in one of them, let alone three," she says. "It was my first job and I was twenty-two. I was Monique Marmelstein on *The Night Stalker.* I'm very proud I was part of that.

"I used a lot of myself for Monique. I was young. I was from New York. And like Monique, I didn't know what I was doing. I didn't have a clue. But I loved every minute of the show. And I love working with Darren. He couldn't have been nicer to me. He made me feel at ease right away. The first day, he said to me, 'Do you know your lines?' I said, 'Oh, yeah.' He said, 'Good, because I don't know mine, so run them with me.' Then one day they gave us all-new lines to learn, and I panicked. Darren calmed me right down and said, 'Now don't worry, we're just going to learn them,

Carol Ann Susi

you and I, together. It's not our fault we have new lines.' Everybody was very nice to me. They were very patient because they knew I was a complete novice.

"I only met Ruth McDevitt one time. She made a point of telling me how sorry she was that I wouldn't be on the show anymore. She said, 'I was hoping they would make you my granddaughter,' Isn't that sweet? Simon Oakland was a sweet and gentle man. And Jack Grinnage is still a friend. So it was a great place to work. Paul Playdon was very gentle — the complete opposite of Darren, who's very forceful. But Darren knew what he was doing and he taught me a lot about acting."

Susi's favorite episode was her second as Monique, "U.F.O." She particularly likes the scene where an enraged Kolchak learns that Monique had handed over his pictures to government agents.

"When I left the series," Susi says, "I went back to waitressing. Actually, I never left waitressing. I just got the days off to do *Night Stalker*. Darren's wife, Kathie, had told me, 'Don't quit your job yet.' I did keep the job, but the Universal casting people kept calling me with parts in *McMillan and Wife* and all their shows. They were all three-line parts, but I took them. Then I didn't do anything for a long time except waitressing and working with improv groups. That was my oh-victim-me bitter years. What was I bitter about? Around 1983, I woke up and decided I was an actress, not a waitress. I will not die bitter."

Susi started acting classes with Kenneth McMillan (*Ragtime, Eyewitness*): "He was the best. I stayed with him until he died in 1989."

The turning point, though, was the loss of waitressing job in 1985. She took it as a sign. A couple of weeks later, she landed a small role in *Outrageous Fortune*, a comedy starring Bette Midler and Shelley Long. Three weeks after completing work on that film, she was cast in *The Secret of My Success*, a 1987 comedy with Michael J. Fox.

"That started it all again," Susi explains. "I've been working ever since."

She was a regular on *My Kind of Town*, a 1993 situation comedy ordered but never aired by Fox (the seven episodes have only been seen in other countries). She had guest appearances on *NYPD Blue*, *Seinfeld* and *Murphy Brown*. And in 1996, she became a regular on NBC's *Something So Right*, a situation comedy starring Mel Harris and Jere Burns.

"And Something So Right is shot at Universal," says Susi, who also appears in *Batman Forever* (1996). "So it's like going full circle. I always knew I'd work more as I got older. If you're young and a character, it's not so good. If you're older and a character, that's great. Even on *Something So Right*, though, people recognize me as Monique Marmelstein. It totally surprises me that people still love that character and still love that show."

## WHISTLING IN THE DARK

The whistle. Kolchak fans fondly remember the whistle that opened every episode of Universal's *Kolchak: The Night Stalker* series. Reporter Carl Kolchak would stroll into Chicago's INS bureau, whistling a happy little tune. Once he poured himself a cup of coffee, the orchestra would come in, merrily accompanying the whistle. Carl would reach his desk and roll a piece of paper into the typewriter. As he started to type, however, the music would shift to a darker, more ominous tone. The central melody would be repeated, but in a haunting way that suggested danger. It would build and build until a startled Carl glanced over his shoulder. Freeze! Carl's eye, wide with surprise, would remain freeze-framed as the final notes of his new theme music reached their creepy conclusion.

This was the title sequence for Universal's series. The wonderfully atmospheric music was composed by Gil Mellé, whose credits included the theme to Rod Serling's *Night Gallery* (also a Universal horror series) and the all-electronic score for *The Andromeda Strain* (1971). Born in Jersey City, New Jersey, in 1931, Mellé had composed the scores for several Universal projects written by the team of Richard Levinson and William Link: *My Sweet Charlie* (their landmark 1970 TV movie with Patty Duke), *The Psychiatrist* (a 1971 NBC series with Roy Thinnes) and four first-season (1971-72) episodes of *Columbo* (created by Levinson and Link).

When Universal decided to go ahead with a *Kolchak* series, studio executives decreed that new music was in order. Could one of Universal's favorite composers come up with a theme as distinctive and memorable as that written by Robert Cobert for the *Night Stalker* TV movie? This formidable assignment fell into the capable hands of Gil Mellé.

During the summer of 1974, Mellé was told to report for *Night Stalker* duty. He found a harried Darren McGavin in his Universal office. It was at this moment that the composer learned how quickly the theme was needed. How much time did he have to come up with something? Well, McGavin was leaving in a little while to film the series' main-title sequence.

The actor took a few seconds to describe how this sequence would be shot — basically, Kolchak strolling into the INS Newsroom. They wanted something he could whistle on his way to the desk.

"I'm looking forward to working on the project," Mellé said. "When do I start?"

"In twenty minutes," McGavin told him.

Twenty minutes? Twenty minutes to come up with a theme for a network series? What's a composer to do? Casting about for an idea, a scrambling Mellé recalled a secondary musical theme that he had composed for *The Questor Tapes*, producer Gene Roddenberry's 1974 pilot for a Universal series. The recordings would still be in the studio's music library.

Universal already owned the score for *The Questor Tapes*, a project that never went to series. Knowing that Universal also would own whatever music he would do for *The Night Stalker*, Mellé decided this could be the twenty-minute theme he needed. Yes, it just might work.

With no time to spare, Mellé dashed to the music library, located the key passage, dashed back to McGavin and whistled the theme into a tape recorder. Happy with the result, McGavin jumped into a studio golf cart and left for the INS Newsroom set, where a crew was waiting to film the title sequence.

"Gil had always liked that theme, but it had never been properly developed outside of *The Questor Tapes*," says Jon Burlingame, Hollywood's leading expert on music composed for television. "And it wasn't the main theme for *Questor*, it was sort of the secondary theme that kicked in half way through the score of that pilot. Now we're talking about what would become the second half of the theme for *The Night Stalker* — that up and down string thing, after the whistling and the flute stops and the darker portion of the theme kicks in. That's what's out of *The Questor Tapes*. Gil uses that and finds something in the harmony, which he extracts and turns into the whistling thing.

"What's interesting to me about the Mellé theme is that, not unlike what Bob Cobert did for the movie, it is a kind of schizophrenic approach; an upbeat jazz sound mixed with very dark and eerie music. The difference is that it is not integrated, like the Cobert theme is. If you listen to the Mellé theme, there's exactly thirty seconds of the whistling and exactly thirty seconds of the dark stuff. It's an exact fifty-fifty split. It's the light, pleasant tune, which Carl whistles on his way into the newsroom, coupled with the extremely dark something-is-about-to-happen half. It is still a two-pronged approach. but there isn't the integration you get in Cobert's theme.

Although the harmony is the same and the tune is carried through. The sound is what's very different in the Mellé theme. That not a criticism, by the way. It works very well. I just think it's interesting that you have two *Night Stalker* themes that are the same yet different."

Mellé scored the first four episodes of the *Night Stalker* series: "The Ripper," "The Zombie," "U.F.O." and "The Vampire." He quit at this point, weary of the artistic battles between McGavin and Chermak. He left behind a substantial amount of music, though, and excerpts from his scores would be used in most of the remaining sixteen episodes. He shared on-screen credit with other composers on five of those episodes: "The Spanish Moss Murders," "The Energy Eater," "Demon in Lace," "Legacy of Terror" and "The Youth Killer."

The bulk of the music chores fell to his replacement, Jerry Fielding, a Hollywood veteran who had been blacklisted for invoking the Fifth Amendment before the House Un-American Activities Committee in 1953. He rebounded in the early '60s with the score for director Otto Preminger's *Advise and Consent*. Seven years later, his music for director Sam Peckinpah's *The Wild Bunch* (1969) won him an Oscar nomination. He reteamed with Peckinpah in 1971 for *Straw Dogs*. A year later, he composed the score for director Michael Winner's *The Mechanic*. Groucho Marx's first bandleader on *You Bet Your Life*, Fielding had composed the themes to such series as *Hogan's Heroes, Chicago Teddy Bears* and *McMillan and Wife*. After *The Night Stalker*, he would tackle film scores for such directors as Michael Ritchie *(The Bad News Bears)* and Clint Eastwood *(The Outlaw Josey Wales)*. His most Kolchak-like movie was the 1977 thriller, *Demon Seed*. He died in 1980.

Fielding would receive solo credit for ten of the remaining sixteen *Night Stalker* episodes. He shared credit on five other episodes: "The Spanish Moss Murders" (with Mellé and Hal Mooney), "The Energy Eater" (with Mellé and Luchi De Jesus) and three more with just Mellé ("Demon in Lace," "Legacy of Terror" and "The Youth Killer").

A third *Night Stalker* composer, Luchi De Jesus, contributed about fourteen minutes of music to "The Energy Eater." Passages from these compositions were used in eight of the final ten episodes.

The only episode not to bear either Mellé's or Fielding's name was "Horror in the Heights," which is credited to Greig McRitchie.

"Actually, Jerry Fielding scored a total of seven episodes," explains Burlingame, author of *TV's Biggest Hits: The Story of Television Themes from "Dragnet" to "Friends."* "When's Jerry name is the only one on some of those shows, it's because they took what he wrote and used it on the remaining episodes. And he wrote a ton of music for *The Night Stalker*. The score for "The Werewolf" alone is well over thirty minutes.

"And there's some very sophisticated music in what Jerry wrote for those seven episodes. It's as sophisticated as television music got in that era. You hear, for example, some of the complex string writing and harmonics he had done for *Straw Dogs*. He also used *The Night Stalker* as a kind of musical laboratory. You hear in his *Night Stalker* music, embryonic versions of the kinds of writing he would later do for *Demon Seed* and other films, particularly in his use of electronics, strings and jazz textures.

"So, by and large, the music for *The Night Stalker* was the product of Gil Mellé and Jerry Fielding. And Jerry Fielding never just sloughed anything off, and neither did Gil Mellé. In retrospect, it's interesting because these two were both mavericks in the film and television scoring arena. Neither of these guys gave two inches of ground to anybody, and they were way ahead of their time. The choices of Fielding and Mellé, in hindsight, seem perfect for this show."

# KOLCHAK: THE NIGHT STALKER
## (Titled "The Night Stalker" the first four episodes)

**Network: ABC**

Airdates: September 13, 1974 — August 30, 1975
September — December 1974: 10-11 p.m. Fridays
January — August 1975: 8-9 p.m. Fridays

Produced in Association with Francy Productions, Inc. by Universal City Studios, Inc.
(a division of MCA)

**Full Season credits:**

Producers: Paul Playdon (first two episodes)
Cy Chermak (eighteen episodes)
Created by Jeff Rice
Story Consultant: David Chase
Story Editors: David Chase and Rudolph Borchert
Theme composed by Gil Mellé
Set decorations: Robert Freer, Claire P. Brown, Hal Gausman,
Frank J. Rafferty and John M. Dwyer
Assistant directors: David Hawks, Bill Holbrook and John Gaudioso
Unit manager: Ralph Sariego
Film editors: Robert Leeds, Ted Rich, a.c.e., John Elias, J. Howard Terrell,
Anthony Redman Larry Strong, and Edward W. Williams, a.c.e.
Sound: John Kean
Costumes: William Jobe
Titles & Optical Effects: Universal Title
Editorial supervision: Richard Belding
Music supervision: Hal Mooney
Main Title Design: Jack Cole

# Episode #1: "The Ripper"

## Original Airdate: September 13, 1974

Written by Rudolph Borchert
Directed by Allen Baron
Music: Gil Mellé
Director of Photography: Donald Peterman
Art Director: Raymond Beal

### CAST

Carl Kolchak............................................Darren McGavin
Tony Vincenzo..........................................Simon Oakland
Ron Updyke..............................................Jack Grinnage
Jane Plumm...............................................Beatrice Colen
Captain R.M. Warren......................................Ken Lynch

# THE NIGHT STALKER COMPANION

(Cast continued:)

Elderly Woman............................................Ruth McDevitt
The Ripper.................................................Mickey Gilbert
Wax Museum Curator...................................Ivor Francis
Police Detective Susan Cortazzo..............Roberta Collins
Masseuse....................................................Mayra Small
Ellen...........................................................Cathey Paine
Debbie Fielder...........................................Denise Dillaway
Mail Boy.....................................................Ike Jones
Driver..........................................................Clint Young
Driver's Wife...............................................Dulci Jordan
First Museum Patron...............................Lavina Dawson
Second Museum Patron..........................Lilyan MacBride
Second Policeman...................................Donald Mantooth
Cheryl..........................................................Gwyn Karon

**Opening narration:** *"If by chance you happened to be in the Windy City between May 28 and June 2 of this year, you would have had very good reason to be terrified. During this period, Chicago was being stalked by a horror so frightening — so fascinating — that it ranks with the great mysteries of all time. It's been the fictional subject of novels, plays, films, even an opera. Now, here are the true facts."*

**SYNOPSIS**: This is the story behind one of the "great mysteries of all time." At three in the morning on May 21, a go-go dancer named Michelle had just finished what was "really her last number" at the Boom-Boom Room in Milwaukee, Wisconsin. She was stabbed to death by a mysterious figure in black.

Three days later, again in Milwaukee, the shadowy figure pulls a sword out of his cane and makes Debbie Fiedler his next victim. A third victim, Laura Moresco, is found with her throat cut on a Chicago street corner. With the killer in the Windy City, Independent News Service editor Tony Vincenzo assigns the story to Ron "Uptight" Updyke. Veteran crime reporter Carl Kolchak wants the story, but he's too busy filling in for Miss Emily Fenwick, who writes the advice column. Far from pleased, Kolchak gives terse, cynical answers to letters asking Miss Emily for help. Still, while the nerdy Ron may have a superior attitude, he also has a squeamish stomach. "It was horrible," Ron laments to Tony. "May I go home?" So Kolchak is able to connive his way onto the story.

Kolchak sees the suspect jump from a four-story building. He not only survives, he mops up the Chicago streets with the police force. One picture of the murderer shows a rope burn on his neck — like a hangman's rope. Researching a series of Ripper murders, Kolchak finds that authorities tried to hang one Ripper in Germany.

Kolchak's friend, reporter Jane Plumm, has a letter sent to her newspaper by the Ripper, but police won't let it be printed. Although she knows that Kolchak would double-cross his "own fairy godmother for a story," Jane tells him that the letter had a rhyme: "And now a pretty girl will die so Jack can have his kidney pie." The murderer cut out Laura Moresco's kidney, a trick pulled by the original Jack the Ripper.

After killing a fourth victim, the suspect is hit by a car, yet he gets up and walks away.

Pulling the pieces together, Kolchak is convinced that this Ripper is Jack the Ripper, a fiend responsible for the murders of seventy women in eighty years, including the unsolved Whitechapel killings of five prostitutes in 1888. "That would make him older than your suit," Jane tells him, "and that is saying a lot."

Each time the Ripper appears throughout history, his pattern is to claim five victims. Kolchak is determined to stop him before the fifth victim.

Electricity is the only thing that seems to stop this killer, so Kolchak sets an electrical trap near the old house where the Ripper is hiding. Inside the Ripper's lair, Kolchak finds, to his horror, the Ripper. To his greater horror, he finds Jane's body. Running for his life, Kolchak lures the killer into the electrical trap. It works, but the sparks set off a fire that destroys the house and all of the evidence. "How could you explain it?" Kolchak wonders. "Who could explain it?" With a laugh, he tosses off a third and final question, "Who'd believe it?"

**EVALUATION**: Both thematically and stylistically, "The Ripper" relies on techniques established in the two TV movies, *The Night Stalker and The Night Strangler*. Indeed, the episode is something of a combination of elements from *The Night Stalker* (right down to tracking the monster to a spooky old house) and *The Night Strangler*. Still, it is an eerie and well-paced combination. Like several Kolchak episodes, it suffers from the "is something missing?" syndrome. With less than an hour to play with, "The Ripper" never bothers to explain the mysterious connection between Jack and electricity. It doesn't even suggest how the Ripper's life has been unnaturally prolonged. Is this part of the whole electricity angle? And it kills off the extremely likable Jane in a brutally abrupt manner. Kolchak doesn't get the chance to express the merest whiff of sorrow or regret.

ITEM: The very plot Richard Matheson avoided for *The Night Strangler* (because of his friendship with Robert Bloch) was embraced for the series opener.

ITEM: Picking up on the concept of the flawed hero, the climax gives us a Kolchak who's not always smart and not always brave.

ITEM: Captain Warren (Ken Lynch) becomes the first in a long line of police officials infuriated by Kolchak. "You're an absurd man," he tells the reporter. Lynch, who played Sgt. Grover on *McCloud*, already had appeared in episodes of *The Twilight Zone* ("Mr. Denton on Doomsday") and *Star Trek* ("The Devil in the Dark").

ITEM: The unseen (she's on vacation) advice columnist is named Emily Fenwick, but when Ruth McDevitt shows up in the fifth episode as Miss Emily, her name is Edith Cowles (spelled both Cowles and Cowels in different cast lists). In the eighth episode, her name was changed to Emily Cowles, and this it remained for the rest of the series. To add to the confusion, however, McDevitt appears in this first episode as an elderly woman who sends a letter to Miss Emily. The bizarre twist has her sending a letter to herself. Although confusing to viewers who see the episodes out of sequence, it's a touch that somehow fits *The Night Stalker*.

ITEM: Our first glimpse of the INS bureau shows that it's situated by an elevated Chicago rail line. When a train rumbles past, it shakes everything, including Tony Vincenzo's nerves, inside the bureau. The shot of the bureau seen through the windows of a passing train would be used many times in future episodes.

ITEM: In the first series scene between Carl and Tony, they are fighting over Carl's coverage of a bank robbery. "For reasons I have never been able to understand," Carl tells us, "Vincenzo was always confusing my reporter's clever ingenuity with what he calls high-handed lunacy."

**MEMORABLE MOMENT:** Carl hiding in the Ripper's closet. Again and again, the Ripper reaches in for something, his lethal hands passing within inches of Carl's face. If Carl remains silent, he'll be safe. But, finally, he can't take it anymore. He panics, yells out and bolts from the closet.

**MEMORABLE QUOTE:** "I run a lot." (Carl Kolchak when asked why he wears those white sneakers)

Kolchak in the shadow of "The Ripper." Or, reflections in a window glass.
Kolchak prepares to take some photographs.

Kolchak trying not to lose his head in "Chopper."

## Episode #2: "The Zombie"

### Original Airdate: September 20, 1974

Teleplay by Zekial Marko and David Chase
(From a story by Zekial Marko)
Directed by Alex Grasshoff
Music: Gil Mellé
Director of Photography: Alric Edens, a.s.c.
Art Director: Raymond Beal

### CAST

Carl Kolchak..............................................Darren McGavin
Tony Vincenzo............................................Simon Oakland
Monique Marmelstein.............................Carol Ann Susi
Gordon Spangler.......................................John Fiedler
Captain Leo Winwood.............................Charles Aidman
Benjamin Sposato.....................................Joseph Sirola
Victor Friese..............................................Val Bisoglio
Cemetary Caretaker.................................J. Pat O'Malley
Sweetstick Weldon....................................Antonio Fargas
Uncle Filemon...........................................Scatman Crothers
Mamalois "Marie Juliette" Edmonds........Pauline Myers
Francois Edmonds (The Zombie)..................Earl Faison
Poppy...........................................................Roland Bob Harris
The Monk....................................................Ben Frommer
Willie Pike.................................................Gary Baxley
Albert Berg................................................Hank Calia
Jerry...........................................................Chuck Waters

**Opening narration:** *"Popular folklore would have us believe that there exists in the underworld ruthless men who fear nothing. This story should debunk that myth."*

**SYNOPSIS**: Working in the back of a truck, Albert Berg and Willie Pike, two low-level members of a Chicago crime family, are calculating the take from their small-time numbers racket. Their crude counting house is attacked by a seemingly unstoppable force. The police say Willie died from severe blows and label it a gangland slaying.

After filing his story on Willie's death, INS reporter Carl Kolchak arrives on the scene of a standoff between police officers and the Russo brothers, two more members of organized crime. He arrives with the office intern, Monique Marmelstein, in tow. Tony insits that Kolchak be nice to Monique, particularly since her uncle, Abe "the Smiling Cobra" Marmelstein, is the INS boss in New York. The standoff erupts into a vicious gun battle. When Monique runs into the line of fire, Kolchak locks her in the trunk of his yellow Mustang convertible.

The Russo brothers are killed, but the police have declared the site of the gun battle off limits. So Kolchak visits one of his favorite sources, Chicago morgue attendant Gordon "Gordy the Ghoul" Spangler. Gordy, Carl tells us, has "stuck gold in the land of the dead." He runs a lottery based on the birth years of the corpses he watches over. Gordy says that, during the autopsy on the Russo brothers, the coroner asked for the X-rays showing Willie Pike's injuries. Pike, a former boxer, didn't die from severe blows. His spine was snapped. The Russo brothers died the same way. Gordy also tells Kolchak that there's something strange about a third body brought in with the Russo brothers. It's the same body he had in the morgue last week — a body containing six slugs and chicken blood in its ear. The mysterious dead man is a Haitian named Francois Edmonds, who had been an up-and-coming operator in the numbers racket. He's being buried in St. Lucy's Cemetery, but it's the second time he has been put in the same grave. The corpse doesn't stick around this time, either.

Kolchak's investigation of the numbers racket puts him the middle of an escalating war between two rival crime families. The prime suspect is Bernard "Sweetstick" Weldon, Southside numbers boss and bitter enemy of mob boss Benjamin Sposato. Several of Sposato's men, including Al Berg, have had their backs broken by a giant of a man. The giant appears to be the deceased Francois Edmonds.

After spying on a meeting between Sposato and Weldon, Kolchak is nearly killed by the mobsters. The reporter tells Sposato and his right-hand man, Victor Friese, that Edmonds is killing anyone who had anything to do with his death. Friese reminds Sposato that he ordered the hit on Edmonds. The gangsters take the reporter out to St. Lucy's Cemetery and force him to open Edmonds' grave. It is empty. Seconds later, Edmonds appears and kills Friese in the same grisly manner – broken spine.

Kolchak tries to tell the police that Edmonds was the dead man he saw lying in the morgue. For some reason, they find this difficult to believe. He is convinced that Edmonds is a zombie brought back from the dead by voodoo. He is more convinced when Sposato and three of his henchmen are found dead. Their spines have been snapped.

Certain that he has once again stumbled on the supernatural, Kolchak sneaks around the home of voodoo priestess Mamalois Edmonds. To his horror, the reporter sees that she is preparing to send her zombie killer after someone named Kolchak. Armed with the knowledge of how to stop a zombie, our hero confronts the killer in an automobile graveyard.

He succeeds. And if you want proof, you can go out to St. Lucy's Cemetery, where Francois Edmonds has been buried a third time. "Be my guest," Kolchak says, "if you got the nerve."

**EVALUATION**: Not a great episode, but an episode with great moments.

ITEM: Tony has grown fond enough of Kolchak to call him Carl, but, when very angry, he reverts back to Kolchak, as in "KOLCHAK!" He is given ample opportunity in each episode to revert.

ITEM: The episode marked the first of three appearances for both Gordy the Ghoul and Monique Marmelstein. Before heading for his showdown with the zombie, Carl puts Monique in a cab and sends the cab to Brooklyn. Never fear, Monique returns in the next episode.

ITEM: The actor playing Uncle Filemon is Scatman Crothers, whose later fantasy credits would include such films as *The Shining* (1980) and *Twilight Zone: The Movie* (1983). At the time of this episode, he also was playing Louie the garbageman on NBC's *Chico and the Man*, which *Kolchak: The Night Stalker* would later be scheduled against.

ITEM: Speaking of *The Twilight Zone*, the actor playing Captain Leo Winwood is Charles Aidman, who had starred in Richard Matheson's classic "Little Girl Lost" episode of Rod Serling's anthology series. In 1985, Aidman became the narrator of the CBS revival of *The Twilight Zone*.

ITEM: Jack Grinnage's Ron Updyke fails to put in an appearance. The only other episode he missed was the series' finale, "The Sentry."

ITEM: Cast as the cemetary caretaker, J. Pat O'Malley had appeared in countless television shows, including four episodes of *The Twilight Zone* ("The Chaser," "The Fugitive," The Self-Improvement of Salvadore Ross" and "Mr. Garrity and the Graves"). In fact, the "Mr. Garrity" episode featured several actors with Kolchak connections: John Dehner (Captain Rausch in "The Knightly Murders"), Stanley Adams (Fred Hurley in *The Night Stalker* and Louie the bartender in "The Devil's Platform") and Kate Murtagh (Janie Watkins in *The Night Strangler*).

ITEM: Ben Frommer appears as a shady Kolchak informant known as the Monk. Who is he? The writers never again visited this intriguing character. He was truly left in the dark.

ITEM: "The Zombie" is one of three episodes directed by Alex Grasshoff. Only Don Weis and Allen Baron, with four apiece, directed more. Grasshoff's credits also included episodes of *Toma, Movin' On* and *The Rockford Files*. In 1974, he won an Emmy as one of the producers of "Journey to the Outer Limits," a *National Georgraphic* special.

ITEM: Earl Faison, who played the zombie, played professional football with the San Diego Chargers.

ITEM: The episode's climax is one of the show's most chilling.

**MEMORABLE MOMENT:** For David Bianculli, television critic at the *New York Daily News*, the confrontation scene is the series' most memorable moment. "More than fifteen years later," he says, "I still feel squeamish thinking about Kolchak crawling through a car graveyard trying to pour salt into the zombie's mouth and then sewing its lips shut before it could wake up. You're watching and watching and then the zombie's eyes opened!" (The scene originally had the eyes opening as Carl was sewing the mouth shut, but the production team thought this was too much.)

**MEMORABLE QUOTE:** "Captain Leo Winwood and I had a relationship that was long and bloody, like the Crusades, only without the chivalry." (Kolchak on his typically warm and fuzzy relationship with the Chicago police department.)

## Episode #3: "U.F.O."
### (Also known as "They Have Been, They Are, They Will Be . . . ")

### Original Airdate: September 27, 1974

Teleplay by Rudolph Borchert
(From a Story by Dennis Clark)
Directed by Allen Baron
Music: Gil Mellé
Director of Photography: Eduardo Ricci
Art Director: Raymond Beal

### CAST

Carl Kolchak.................................................................. Darren McGavin
Tony Vincenzo................................................................. Simon Oakland
Ron Updyke..................................................................... Jack Grinnage
Monique Marmelstein.......................................................Carol Ann Susi

(Cast continued:)

Gordon Spangler.................................................................... John Fiedler
Captain Quill......................................................................... James Gregory
Dr. Bess Winestock............................................................... Mary Wickes
Alfred Brindle....................................................................Dick Van Patten
Woman Speaker..............................................................Maureen Arthur
Leon Van Heusen......................................................................Tony Rizzo
Stanely Wedemyer..........................................................Rudy Challenger
Howard Gough........................................................................ Phil Leeds
Crowley................................................................... ..........Len Lesser
Waiter............................................................... ...........Fritz Feld
Security Guard Riley..............................................Dennis McCarthy
Keeter Hudson..............................................................Gary Glanz

**Opening narration**: *"I knew this one was more than just the biggest story of my life. It was the biggest story in the lives of everyone on this planet. I fought for the story — fought harder than ever before because I knew it was more than news, much more. I felt people should know about it so they could be prepared when it happened again, if it's possible to be prepared for something like this."*

**SYNOPSIS:** The Lincoln Park Zoo's prized cheetah is missing. The day before, a panther disappeared. INS reporter Carl Kolchak is only interested in the first game of the World Series — until editor Tony Vincenzo threatens to put office intern Monique Marmelstein on the story. He agrees that missing zoo animals are peculiar, even in Chicago, and agrees to look into the mystery.

On his way to the zoo, Kolchak hears a report on his police radio. He can make out an address and the words "officer down," but the rest is garbled by static. The police have an electronics warehouse surrounded. The alarm has been tripped from inside and a guard has been killed. Waiting for something to happen, Kolchak and the police are suddenly thrown back by a powerful blast. The damage is extensive, but all that's missing from the scene is a stack of lead ingots – at least, they're missing once they disappear before the amazed eyes of Kolchak and Captain Quill. As Kolchak is escorted from the scene, he notices four men in suits talking with Quill.

Adding to the puzzle is a series of thefts involving electrical equipment, missing animals, stolen ingots, unseen robbers, hurricane-power winds, stopped watches and electrical equipment. Nothing seems to fit, but Kolchak believes the mysterious incidents are in some way connected. And he believes the men in suits — obviously government agents — have a clue.

At Lincoln Park Zoo, Kolchak is shown the missing animals' cages.

The bars are blasted inward about ten feet across. In the cage, he finds a strange black substance. Dr. Bess Winestock, one of the zoo's veterinarians, tells Kolchak that the animals died of heart attacks.

But in a Chicago suburb, unhappy homeowner Alfred Brindle is trying to tell anyone who will listen that he found a strange black substance on his front lawn. Carl Kolchak is willing to listen. Brindle also tells him that vandals stole his neighbor's stereo system, taking the electronic guts and leaving the rest. On Brindle's lawn, Kolchak finds the same type of black substance he found at the zoo.

Kolchak goes back to the zoo and asks Bess Winestock to analyze the substance. Bess tells Kolchak she doesn't need to do an analysis. It is the same substance found in the cages. It contains bone marrow and digestive acids. Her best guess is that something extracted the bone marrow, ate it and vomited.

Intrigued, Kolchak asks Gordy the Ghoul if he has the autopsy report on the guard killed at the electronics plant. Gordy sneaks a recording of the coroner's autopsy to

Kolchak (Darren McGavin) tries to warn Captain Wells (Henry Jones) that there is a werewolf on board his ship. From Episode # 5 ("The Werewolf").

Kolchak dispatches another vampire, this time under a fiery cross.

Kolchak. Sure enough, it reveals that the human victims had their bone marrow extracted — the same as the dead animals.

The murders and the disturbances are the work of extraterrestrials. Chicago is being visited by temporarily stranded unidentified flying objects.

While at the planetarium, Kolchak is attacked by the unseen force.

The aliens are there for a glimpse at the star charts. Knocked down by the wind force, Kolchak wildly snaps pictures, and the camera's flash seems to drive it away. It's not the light, however, it's the high-pitch whine of the battery recharging that so annoys the alien. Armed with this "weapon," Kolchak can protect himself as he sees the UFO leave Chicago. . . for good?

"What happened?" Kolchak summarizes. "It's all a point of view, really. A traveler has a breakdown, stops to fix it, gets a road map, has a bite to eat and goes on his way. It's happened to all of us. But this traveler happened to be light-years off his course, instead of miles."

**EVALUATION:** The monsters on *The Night Stalker* normally kept to the shadows. In "U.F.O.," the problem was completely averted because we didn't see the alien presence at all (except the final view of the flying saucer, which, even for 1974, looks pretty chintzy). The extraterrestrials are represented, quite eerily, by a wind that grows in intensity, so. . .the episode is one of the series' best. It's cleverly shot, nicely paced and moody, but. . . it's also one of the dumbest. More than usual goes unexplained in this one. It's a bit too convenient for Kolchak to be holding the one thing that will drive off the aliens. Kolchak finds the flying saucer with no difficulty. The whole notion of a stalking unseen alien visitor would be used much more effectively in *Predator* (1987).

ITEM: Chris Carter, creator of *The X-Files*, often says that *Kolchak: The Night Stalker* was the inspiration for his series about paranormal investigations. If so, X would mark this spot in Kolchak's career – the Carl caper most like those pursued by Carter's FBI agents, Scully and Mulder. Other favorite *X-Files* elements include stopped watches, mutilated animals, mysterious men in suits, anti-government paranoia and official suppression of information.

ITEM: Carol Ann Susi makes the second of her three appearances as Monique Marmelstein. But this is her favorite of the three. Hiding in a bathroom stall while Carl berates her for giving away his pictures to government agents, Monique whines magnificently whines: "Be reasonable. What could I do? They had on suits, ties, credentials, they had some forms from the Internal Revenue. They knew all about me. They threatened an audit. . . I had to! They pull an audit on me and I go off the nearest bridge." Afterwards, she tries to console Kolchak by saying, "They didn't look that good."

ITEM: Gordy, making his second of three appearances, is thinking of changing the "stiffs lottery" from birth year to time of death.

ITEM: The episode contains one of the series' comic high points. Seated in his INS office, Tony Vincenzo is about to enjoy a gourmet dinner. He clearly loves to eat, and here is a table of delights. Kolchak bursts in with the latest gory details of the case. Tony is torn between professional duty and personal pleasure. Heck, he's a tough veteran journalist. He can tackle both at the same time. He insists that Kolchak give him the details, no matter how nauseating. While Tony continues the meal, Kolchak continues running through the facts. Tony tries to maintain his gruff editor's exterior. It's a losing battle. The effects of this struggle are on his stomach, but they can be seen on his face. It's the type of very human moment that Simon Oakland could put across in beautiful fashion.

ITEM: German character actor Fritz Feld, who worked until he was almost ninety, has a cameo as the waiter serving Tony the dinner. Often armed with his trademark hand-to-mouth pop (imitating the opening of a champagne cork), Feld appeared in such films as *Bringing Up Baby* (1938), *The Phantom of the Opera* (1943), *The Secret Life of Walter Mitty* (1947), *Mexican Hayride* (1948, with Abbott & Costello), *Barefoot in the Park* (1967) and *The Sunshine Boys* (1975).

ITEM: The strong supporting cast also includes James Gregory (Inspector Luger on *Barney Miller*), who had appeared in the "Where is Everybody?" pilot episode of *The Twilight Zone* (and in a third-season episode, "The Passerby"), and Mary Wickes, who contributed wonderful supporting comic performances to such films as *The Man Who Came to Dinner* (1942), *Who Done It?* (1942, one of Abbott & Costello's best), *White Christmas* (1952) and *Sister Act* (1992). In addition to appearing in memorable episodes of *I Love Lucy, Alfred Hitchcock Presents, F Troop* and *Columbo,* she was a regular on an amazing total of nine series, the last of which was ABC's *Father Dowling Mysteries.*

**MEMORABLE QUOTE:** "Don't be stupid, please!" (Kolchak to police officers.)

## Episode #4: "The Vampire"

### Original Airdate: October 4, 1974

Teleplay by David Chase
(From a story by Bill Stratton)
Directed by Don Weis
Music: Gil Mellé
Director of Photography: Ronald W. Browne
Art Director: Raymond Beal

### CAST

Carl Kolchak............................................................... Darren McGavin
Tony Vincenzo.......................................................... ....Simon Oakland
Ron Updyke............................................................. Jack Grinnage
Faye Kruger............................................................Kath leen Nolan
Catherine Rawlins....................................................Suzanne Charny
Lieutenant Jack Matteo...........................................William Daniels
Ichabod Grace............................................................ Jan Murray
Jim "The Swede" Brytowski...........................................Larry Storch
Deputy Sample...........................................................John Doucette
Gingrich...................................................................Milt Kamen
Girl........................................................................Anne Whitfield
Man.........................................................................Army Archerd
Woman.................................................................. ...Selma Archerd
Chandra.............................................................. .....Noel de Souza
First Reporter...................................................... ...Bill Baldwin
Second Reporter.......................................................Scott Douglas
Third Reporter.........................................................Alyscia Maxwell
Hotel Manager.........................................................St uart Nisbet
Bellboy................................................................. .......Howard Gray
Man talking.............................................................. Jimmy Joyce
Elena Munoz........................................................Biene Blechscmidt
Linda Courtner........................................................Betty Endicott
Andrew Garth..........................................................Tony Epper
Stacker Schumaker......................................................Rand Warren

**133**

**Opening narration:** *"They were tearing up an old road to lay more freeway a few miles south of Las Vegas. The state of Nevada's Department of Highway's digging would be a help to thousands of motorists. But to one other person, it would turn out to be a nightmare."*

**SYNOPSIS**: The nightmare begins when airline stewardess Elena Munoz misses a detour sign and blows a tire on a jagged rock. To her horror, she sees two hands digging their way through the dirt. The police dismiss her as a crank.

Back in Chicago, Jim "The Swede" Brytowski, an old reporter buddy from Las Vegas, is breezing through the Windy City for a quick visit. Swede tells Carl Kolchak about a series of three strange murders stretching along the road from Las Vegas to Los Angeles. Now a TV newsman named James Bright, the Swede snares Kolchak's interest with the strangest item of all — the bodies were drained of blood. Whoever or whatever the killer is, the path is heading to Los Angeles.

Having seen the work of a vampire in Las Vegas, Kolchak is eager to snoop around Los Angeles. Tony agrees to send him to do a story on a trendy transcendental meditation guru. Once in Southern California, however, Kolchak forgets about the guru and starts investigating the murders. Lieutenant Matteo believes that the vampire killings are nothing more sinister than ritual killings being committed by a cult of Satan worshipers. Matteo also believes that Kolchak is a nut.

But the reporter from Chicago knows the telltale signs from Las Vegas: drained bodies, puncture marks on the victims' necks, night killings.

When four hulks — professional football players, no less — are wiped out by the female suspect, Catherine Rawlins, Kolchak is determined to set up a late-night meeting with the vampire posing as a prostitute.

With the help of Faye Kruger, a realtor who wants to be a journalist, Kolchak finds the vampire's house. When he loses his protective cross, the reporter nearly loses his life. But he manages to lure Catherine to a huge cross that's been soaked with gasoline. Kolchak sets the giant cross on fire and drives a wooden stake through the immobilized vampire's heart.

**EVALUATION:** Starting Catherine Rawlins in Las Vegas gives the episode a nice link with the original *Night Stalker* story. Although derivative, it stands (or stalks) as one of the series' five best episodes.

ITEM: "The Vampire" certainly contains one of the program's most striking and memorable images — the giant flaming cross that traps Catherine Rawlins. "For some reason, 'The Vampire' really works for me," producer Cy Chermak says. "I think it's my favorite of the episodes. I love the cross burning. There is a little bit of a controversy over whose idea that was, but that can happen after twenty-three years. I thought it was my idea. Rudy Borchert says he thinks it was his idea, and it might very well have been."

ITEM: Chermak also likes the moment when Kolchak thrusts a cross at a sweet-faced prostitute, thinking she's a vampire. "All right, which freako scene is this?" she asks.

ITEM: The episode also contains a fiendishly clever surprise. Knowing there's a vampire on the loose, we're treated to a clever scene that neatly turns the tables on our expectations. Catherine Rawlins (Suzanne Charny) enters a room, followed by a dark man we just know is the vampire. We think she's the next victim. Surprise! She's the vampire. Although the episode does borrow heavily from the films, at least a female vampire gives it a little fresh blood (heh, heh, heh).

ITEM: Comedian Larry Storch (*F Troop*) manages to turn his brief scene into a sharp piece of satire on TV journalism.

ITEM: Hollywood columnist Army Archerd has a cameo appearance as a prospective buyer for the guru's house (a set that Universal already had used in two

*Columbo* episodes). But *Night Stalker* got first use of Archerd, who didn't make his *Columbo* cameo until a year later (in the "Forgotten Lady" episode).

ITEM: Between his Tony-winning Broadway run as John Adams in *1776* and his Emmy-winning stint as Dr. Mark Craig on NBC's *St. Elsewhere*, William Daniels played a police detective for this episode. It would be seventeen years before McGavin and Daniels again worked together. "That's the way it is in this business," McGavin says. They reteamed for Arthur Miller's *Clara*, a one-act play presented by cable's Arts & Entertainment Network in 1991. Ironically, Daniels again was cast as a world-weary detective. "I kept wanting to tell Bill how to do it," says McGavin, who has played his share of world-weary detectives. Daniels enjoyed both projects with McGavin, but, obviously, the chance to work on a Miller play offered a little more dramatic bite than working on a vampire investigation.

ITEM: This was the first of four episodes directed by TV veteran Don Weis. His long list of credits include four episodes of *Alfred Hitchcock Presents* ("The Big Switch," "The Pearl Necklace," "A Secret Life" and "First-Class Honeymoon"). A film director in the '50s and '60s, he became one of the busiest TV directors of the '70s and '80s, helming episodes of *M*A*S*H, Remington Steele, Ironside, Petrocelli, It Takes a Thief, Happy Days, The Courtship of Eddie's Father, Hawaii Five-0, Mannix, The Magician, Planet of the Apes, Charlie's Angels, Fantasy Island, The Love Boat* and *Hill Street Blues.* For the big screen, he directed *A Slight Case of Larceny* (1953), *The Affairs of Dobie Gillis* (1953), *The Gene Krupa Story* (1959) and *Critic's Choice* (a 1963 teaming of Bob Hope and Lucille Ball). "This was a show that needed strong directors," Chermak says, "and Don Weis was perfect. He was the kind of director who didn't take any crap from anybody. I relied very heavily on Don Weis. I knew I could count on him. We had other strong directors on the show, like Mike Caffey and Vince McEveety, but they only did one episode each. Don did four." Weis worked so hard on this episode that he took a room in the Beverly Wilshire Hotel rather than drive home to Malibu.

**MEMORABLE QUOTE:** "You should meet my boss. He'd turn Buddha into a chain-smoker." (Carl Kolchak on Tony Vincenzo)

**MEMORABLE QUOTE:** "I'm tired of it, Kolchak, I am fed up! I've got a brother-in-law who's got a fourteen-year-old kid he's always bailing out of juvenile hall, but I've got you and you are worse!" (Tony Vincenzo on Carl Kolchak)

# Episode #5: "The Werewolf"

## Original Airdate: November 1, 1974

Written by David Chase & Paul Playdon
Directed by Allen Baron
Music: Jerry Fielding
Director of Photography: Ronald W. Browne
Art Director: Raymond Beal

## CAST

| | |
|---|---|
| Carl Kolchak | Darren McGavin |
| Tony Vincenzo | Simon Oakland |
| Ron Updyke | Jack Grinnage |
| Edith Cowels | Ruth McDevitt |
| Mel Tarter | Dick Gautier |
| Captain Julian Wells | Henry Jones |
| Paula Griffin | Nita Talbot |
| Bernhardt Stieglitz | Eric Braeden |
| Wendy | Jackie Russell |
| George Levitt | Lewis Charles |
| Hallem | Bob Hastings |
| Dr. Alan Ross | Barry Cahill |
| Gribbs | Dort Clark |
| Radio Man | Heath Jobes |
| Jay Remy | Jim Hawkins |
| Lois Prysock | Lyn Guild |
| Sailor | Steve Marlow |
| Bernie Efron | Ray Ballard |

**Opening narration:** *"Admittedly the story you are about to read is bizarre, incredible. Those of you who wish to being unsettled, who wish to avoid thinking, will label it insane. And though you the reader would find these facts almost impossible to substantiate, that does not change their nature. Facts they are. I know. I saw them happen."*

**SYNOPSIS:** Chicago is in the grips of a terrible snow storm, but spirits are high at the INS Christmas party. Editor Tony Vincenzo is about to leave on his first vacation in five years. He is going to take the last voyage of the good ship Hanover, which will head for the scrap heap after a final swinging-singles cruise.

To further improve the normally gruff editor's mood, the company has agreed to underwrite the vacation. A few stories will take care of Tony's INS obligation.

In the middle of singing Yuletide favorites, the INS employees have little interest in a news item out of Montana. Earlier in the month, a family of four was found slaughtered. The coroner concluded that the family was attacked by wolves, even though no wolf had been spotted in the area since 1948. Despite the wolf's nasty reputation, in the entire history of North America there is not one documented case of a wolf attacking and killing a human being.

These gruesome slayings couldn't be farther away from the glad tidings in the INS newsroom. But Tony is about to be attacked by a different type of wolf pack. The INS auditors are on their way to Chicago, and, vacation plans or not, he must be there to go over the books. With most of the staff fighting a flu bug, Tony has no choice. He sends Carl Kolchak on the last cruise of the S.S. Hanover.

Tony warns Carl to stick to happy nostalgia and the singles scene.

But, then again, what could go wrong on the grand old luxury liner?

Well, when the first full moon appears, so does a werewolf. A woman is brutally mauled, then three crewmen are found torn apart on the bridge. Afraid the panic will spread to the passengers, Captain Wells does everything in his power to keep Kolchak away from the facts.

Meanwhile, swinging simpleton Mel Tarter introduces Kolchak to movie nut Paula Griffin. Mel thinks that Carl's name is Cal and that the term for the press is the Fifth Column, not the Fourth Estate. Paula is a wealth of movie trivia, including how to kill a werewolf (a silver bullet, of course).

Paula is more than willing to help Carl slip past Captain Wells, who is threatening to toss the reporter in irons. Kolchak manages to fashion a proper bullet by "borrowing" the silver buttons off the captain's dress uniform. He is able to slip by the crew members, and manages to come face to snout with the werewolf. The lycanthrope, by the way, is Bernhardt Stieglitz, a NATO officer once stationed in Montana.

**EVALUATION:** Like too many *Kolchak* episodes, this one ends abruptly. And it was tough to keep the wayfaring werewolf in-the shadows for long. Too bad. He's a pretty moth-eaten-looking beast. Considering the great strides in werewolf makeup (*An American Werewolf in London, The Howling,* Fox's *Werewolf* series), this one looks like a costume-party joker. The idea of being trapped on an ocean liner with a werewolf has possibilities (narrow corridors, following a full moon, nowhere to go), but the episode's monster is more laughable than terrifying. When the fur flies, this one looks pretty flea-bitten — more loopy than lupo.

ITEM: The wolf in ship's cabins was played by Eric Braeden, who was no newcomer to fantasy. He had been Professor Forbin in *Colossus: The Forbin Project* (1970) and Dr. Hasslein in *Escape From the Planet of the Apes* (1971). For several years, he has played Victor on the CBS soap opera *The Young and the Restless.*

ITEM: Dick Gautier was between stints as Hymie the Robot on *Get Smart* and Robin Hood on ABC's *When Things Were Rotten,* the short-lived Sherwood Forest spoof from writer-producer Mel Brooks.

ITEM: The season before *Kolchak: Night Stalker* aired on ABC, Nita Talbot starred in *Here We Go Again,* a short-lived situation comedy on the Alphabet Network. One of her co-stars was Dick Gautier.

ITEM: Captain Wells was played by well-traveled character actor Henry Jones, whose films included *The Bad Seed* (1956), *Vertigo* (1958) and *Butch Cassidy and the Sundance Kid* (1969). A Tony winner for the Broadway production of *Sunrise at Campobello* (1958), he appeared as angel J. Hardy Hempstead in 1960 "Mr. Beavis" episode of *The Twilight Zone.*

ITEM: Ruth McDevitt makes her first appearance as a *Night Stalker* regular, but in one of those failures of continuity certain to keep trivia experts up nights, she's billed as Edith Cowels (note the spelling of the last name) and she writes the riddles feature. In later episodes, however, the spelling of the last name was changed and she got a new first name and a new job. She became, with no explanation, EmiIy Cowles, advice columnist and society writer. Confused? Well, in the first episode, we are told that the name of the advice columnist is Emily Fenwick. McDevitt appeared in that episode, but not as Emily Fenwick, Emily Cowles or Edith Cowels. Got it straight now? Continuity wasn't always the Kolchak team's strong suit.

ITEM: Bob Hastings, who plays one of the ship's officers, was accustomed to naval uniforms. He had played Lieutenant Elroy Carpenter for four seasons on *McHale's Navy* (ABC, 1962-66),

**MEMORABLE EXCHANGE:** Tony: "How come you never get sick, Kolchak?" Carl: "I must live right, sir."

# Episode #6: "Fire Fall"
## (also known as "The Doppleganger")

### Original Airdate: November 8, 1974

# THE NIGHT STALKER COMPANION

Written by Bill S. Ballinger
Directed by Don Weis
Music: Jerry Fielding
Director of Photography: Ronald W. Browne

## CAST

| | |
|---|---|
| Carl Kolchak | Darren McGavin |
| Tony Vicenzo | Simon Oakland |
| Ron Updyke | Jack Grinnage |
| Monique Marmelstein | Carol Ann Susi |
| Ryder Bond | Fred Beir |
| Sergeant Mayer | Philip Carey |
| Maria | Madlyn Rue |
| Cardinale | David Doyle |
| Dr. Shropell | Alice Backes |
| Mrs. Sherman | Carol Veazie |
| Bert, the stage manager | Gary Glanz |
| Felicia Porter | Patricia Porter |
| Young Man | Marcus Smith |
| George Mason | Joshua Shelley |
| Woman | Martha Manor |
| Mrs. Markoff | Virginia Vincent |
| Doctor | Lenore Kasdorf |

**Opening narration:** *"Remember the penny arcades that used to be so much fun when you were a kid? For a handful of coins you could test your strength, your skill at a pinball machine. Those arcades were a lot of things to a lot of kids, but there was one particular arcade that represented something special for me. It was here that began one of the most terrifying experiences of my life."*

**SYNOPSIS:** Rabino's Arcade in Chicago – a regular bag-man's drop, narcotics pickup and all-purpose meeting place for gangsters – is the site of a hit on Frankie Markoff, a convicted arsonist. He is gunned down while playing his favorite pinball game.

On his way to an appointment, internationally respected symphony conductor Ryder Bond cuts off the hearse carrying the body of Frankie Markoff. Shortly after this "crossing of paths," George Mason, first violinist and concert master of the Great Lakes Symphony, is killed in his apartment. The cause of death seems to be spontaneous combustion. Mrs. Sherman, a tenant walking her dog outside Mason's apartment at the time, sees a ghost-like figure. But it's the ghost of someone very much alive – Ryder Bond.

The next day, after seeing what looks like Ryder's ghost, music "groupie" Felicia Porter is killed while sitting by a hotel pool. Again, it seems to be a case of spontaneous combustion. A woman who hears her screams thinks she caught a glimpse of Ryder Bond.

But there are dozens of witnesses who say the conductor was with them at the time of these deaths.

A research scientist named Cardinale tells Kolchak that it sounds like someone has their hands on a lethal chemical perfected by the military.

Then a third associate of the conductor is turned into a pillar of fire.

The Chicago police have no idea what's causing these instantaneously flaming corpses, but the common theme is Ryder Bond. Each time, Bond seems to have been near the scene of the incinerations. Each time, there are other witnesses that say he was nowhere near these infernos.

Kolchak decides to confront Bond directly. But the conductor disappears before him and the room bursts into flames. Puzzled by these physical impossibilities,

138

Kolchak concludes that the intense heat must stem from powerful unnatural forces. And that unnatural force is identified by a gypsy named Maria. It is a doppleganger that is enveloping Bond's associates in flames and reducing them to ashes. Maria tells Kolchak that a doppleganger is a restless, malicious ghost trying to take over the living body of someone he or she admired before death. In this case, the object of admiration and possession is Ryder Bond, a renowned prodigy at fourteen and a famous conductor at forty. The spirit will take on the appearance of the person in preparation for the ultimate takeover.

The doppleganger can only attack when people are asleep, although it is forbidden to enter holy ground. Bond admits to Kolchak that he has been catching fleeting glimpses of his own image. He agrees to let Kolchak take him to a Catholic cathedral.

Frankie Markoff's widow tells Kolchak that her husband wasn't exactly "burning with ambition," but his one great love was classical music.

Fighting sleep and fatigue, Kolchak places his own life in jeopardy by trying to convince the restless spirit that he is not and never will be Ryder Bond.

Faced with proof of its death, the spirit will return to its proper sphere.

**EVALUATION:** Although the supernatural aspects aren't well thought out in "Fire Fall," the episode does sizzle with eerie touches. Consistent? No, but it tosses off spooky sparks on its way to a paranoia-drenched conclusion. Along with "U.F.O." and "Mr. R.I.N.G.," this is the episode most like an *X-Files* investigation.

ITEM: Sadly, "Fire Fall" marked the last appearance of Carol Ann Susi's Monique Marmelstein.

ITEM: "Fire Fall" was the second of four episodes (after "The Vampire" and before "The Trevi Collection" and "Demon in Lace") directed by Don Weis. Only Allen Baron directed as many ("The Ripper," "U.F.O.," "The Werewolf" and "The Devil's Platform"). In fact, four men — Weis, Baron, Alex Grasshoff and Dan McDougall – directed thirteen of the twenty Kolchak episodes.

ITEM: David Doyle was two years away from a lucrative run on *Charlie's Angels* (ABC, 1976-81) as Bosley, a character created for Tom Bosley, who appears in the last episode of *Kolchak: The Night Stalker* ("The Sentry"). Bosley was busy playing Howard Cunningham on ABC's *Happy Days* (1974-84). Before his death in 1997, Doyle won a new generation of fans as the voice of Grandpa on Nickelodeon's animated *Rugrats*.

ITEM: Madlyn Rhue, who plays Kolchak's gypsy friend, is known to *Star Trek* fans as Marla McGivers in "Space Seed," the 1967 episode that introduced Ricardo Montalban as Khan.

ITEM: "Fire Fall" was the first of two Kolchak scripts to bear the name Bill S. Ballinger, a writer whose credits include six episodes of *Alfred Hitchcock Presents*.

ITEM: Tony gets off one of his best lines of the series: "Kolchak, when you get back to the swindle and fraud story, write about how you're employed here. Which is one of the biggest swindles in memory."

**MEMORABLE QUOTE:** "It was here that began one of the most terrifying experiences of my life." (Another one?)

# Episode #7: "The Devil's Platform"

## Original Airdate: November 15, 1974

Teleplay by Donn Mullally (From a story by Tim Maschler)
(On-screen writing credit not given to Norm Liebmann,
Larry Markes, David Chase and Rudy Borchert)
Directed by Allen Baron
Music: Jerry Fielding
Director of Photography: Ronald W. Browne
Art Director: William H. Tuntke

## CAST

| | |
|---|---|
| Carl Kolchak | Darren McGavin |
| Tony Vincenzo | Simon Oakland |
| Ron Updyke | Jack Grinnage |
| Emily Cowels | Ruth McDevitt |
| Robert W. Palmer | Tom Skerritt |
| Susan Driscoll | Julie Gregg |
| Lorraine Palmer | Ellen Weston |
| Senator James Talbot | John Myhers |
| Dr. Kline | Jeanne Cooper |
| Officer Hale | William Mims |
| Louie the Bartender | Stanley Adams |
| Stephen Wald | Dick Patterson |
| Park Policeman | Robert DoQui |
| Television Announcer | Bill Welsh |
| Television Reporter | Keith Walker |
| First Policeman | Bruce Powers |
| Second Policeman | Ross Sherman |
| Mailman | Sam Edwards |
| First Maintenance Engineer | Ike Jones |
| Second Maintenance Engineer | John Dennis |

**Opening narration:** *"The old cliché that politics makes strange bedfellows is only too true. At one time or another, various and sundry politicians have found themselves, when it proved expedient, of course, sharing a blanket with the military, organized crime, disgruntled, gun-toting dairy farmers, the church, famous athletes, the comedians, the list is endless. But there was a senatorial race not so long ago right here in Illinois, where the strangest bedfellow of all was found under the sheets. The strangest and certainly the most terrifying."*

**SYNOPSIS:** Robert Palmer is a dashing young politician whose fast rise to prominence has propelled him into a race for a Senate seat. A mysterious car crash claims the life of a major contributor to Palmer's opponent, incumbent Senator Talbot. A boat explosion kills two more people close to Talbot.

All of a sudden, Palmer has bolted out of obscurity to become the favorite to unseat the incumbent. But Palmer's campaign manager, Stephen Wald, is about to derail the crafty politician's hopes. Wald is threatening to expose all of the bribery and extortion in Palmer's past. The two men get into an elevator. Waiting for the elevator in the lobby is INS reporter Carl Kolchak. The cables snap. The elevator crashes. Wald is killed. But in the place of Palmer's body is a snarling hound from hell. The vicious beast leaps at Kolchak, who grabs what he believes is the dog's license. It's actually a Satanic medallion. "Some advice for pedestrians!" he tells us. "When you're run over by a strange dog and you can't get his number, at least get his license tag."

When Kolchak's photographs of the elevator crash are developed, the dog can be seen with glowing red eyes. Yet the image of the devil dog fades and disappears. Palmer also seems to have disappeared. No one can find him.

During a visit to Palmer's home, Kolchak again is hounded by the murderous mutt. This time, however, it takes back the medallion. A few seconds later, Palmer makes an appearance at his front door.

Palmer, of course, is a politician who's literally in league with the devil. In return for success and power, he's sold his soul to Satan. When Susan Driscoll tells the candidate that she knows about the evidence that was in Stephen Wald's briefcase, Palmer again transforms himself into the hell hound. Police shoot the dog six times, but it doesn't stop.

Then Senator Talbot is killed in a head-on crash. Kolchak knows he must stop Palmer. Sneaking into the politician's house, the reporter witnesses a bizarre ritual. Palmer brags about his unholy bargain. He tempts Kolchak with promises of a Pulitzer Prize and—what he desires most—a return to New York City with a job on a major daily newspaper. Kolchak refuses and manages to destroy the medallion when Palmer is in his canine form. The beast immediately turns into a friendly pooch. But no one ever saw Robert Palmer. . . again.

**EVALUATION:** No less than six writers worked on "The Devil's Platform," and it shows. The problem isn't the story, it's the structure. Still, the episode has a certain amount of fun a notion that average viewer is more than willing to accept — that a politician has sold his soul to the devil.

ITEM: The premise may be memorable, but it made no impression on guest star Tom Skerritt. "I really have no memory of that show at all," says the actor who played Dallas in director Ridley Scott's *Alien* (1979) and Reverand Maclean in Robert Redford's *A River Runs Through It* (1992). "I was doing a lot of episodic television at that time. I was very busy. I was going from one show to another, and a lot of it blurs together. I just don't remember doing that one. Sorry." Far more memorable was Skerritt's Emmy-winning role of Jimmy Brock on *Picket Fences*. Other notable parts include Duke Forrest in *M*A*S*H* (1970), Wayne in *The Turning Point* (1977), the uncle in *Poltergeist III* (1988), Drum in *Steel Magnolias* (1989) and Evan Drake on NBC's *Cheers*.

ITEM: To add to the Miss Emily confusion, Ruth McDevitt is billed as Edith Cowels, but Carl calls her Emily.

ITEM: In addition to the obvious point made by having a politician in league with the devil, the episode contains some of the series' snappiest exchanges. "You know, I once thought of entering the priesthood," Tony says. Kolchak quickly responds: "Then the Inquisition ended and all the fun went out of it for you." Not bad, Carl.

ITEM: The episode also includes some wonderful material about Kolchak's shabby pork-pie straw hat. Back from a trip to Europe, Miss Emily has brought Carl a dashing new chapeau. Clearly uncomfortable, he can't wait to switch back to his old standby. Tony is disgusted by what he calls that "bird-feeder hat." "What don't you like about this hat?" Kolchak asks him. "What's under it," Tony responds. Not bad, Tony....

ITEM: The "devil dog" is a Rottweiler, the breed of dog used for the same purpose by director Richard Donner in *The Omen* (1976).

ITEM: Stanley Adams, who plays Louie the Bartender in "The Devil's Platform," became the first actor, other than Darren McGavin and Simon Oakland, to appear in *The Night Stalker* movie and series.

ITEM: "The Devil's Platform" was the fourth and final episode directed by Allen Baron. He had directed four of the first seven episodes.

Looming over Kolchak in "Bad Medicine," future James Bond adversary Richard Kiel makes the first of two appearances as a *Night Stalker* monster.

Did you R. I. N. G.? Carl meets "Mr. R. I. N. G.," one of the few
*Kolchak* creatures not kept in the shadows.

**MEMORABLE QUOTE:** "There's two things that just can't be rushed — anyone who is paid by the hour and an office-building elevator." (The wit and wisdom of Carl Kolchak) "That's what's wrong with this country, nobody cares." (More wit and wisdom of Carl Kolchak)

## Episode #8: "Bad Medicine"
### (also known as "The Diablero")

### Original Airdate: November 29, 1974

Written by L. Ford Neale and John Huff
Directed by Alex Grasshoff
Music: Jerry Fielding
Director of Photography: Ronald W. Browne
Art Director: Raymond Beal

### CAST

| | |
|---|---|
| Carl Kolchak | Darren McGavin |
| Tony Vincenzo | Simon Oakland |
| Ron Updyke | Jack Grinnage |
| Emily Cowles | Ruth McDevitt |
| Captain Joe Baker | Ramon Bieri |
| Dr. Agnes Temple | Alice Ghostley |
| Charles Rolling Thunder | Victor Jory |
| The Indian (Diablero) | Richard Kiel |
| Albert Delgado | Mavin Kaplan |
| George M. Schwartz | James Griffith |
| Ballistics Man | Dennis McCarthy |
| Auctioneer | David Lewis |
| Guard (Night Watchman) | Morris Buchanan |
| Hostess | Madilyn Clark |
| First Reporter | Keith Walker |
| Second Reporter | Bill Deiz |
| First Policeman (Mason) | Alex Sharp |
| Mrs. Rhonda June Marsky (Adele Saperstein) | Lois January |
| Mrs. Luci Lapont Addison | Barbara Morrison |
| Mrs. Charlotte Elaine Van Piet | Riza Royce |
| Chauffer | Ernie Robinson |
| Desk Officer | Troy Melton |
| Second Policeman (Crowley) | Walt Davis |
| Oriental Man | Arthur Wong |
| Auction Guard | Richard Geary |
| Police Detective | Bob Golden |

**Opening narration:** *"F. Scott Fitzgerald once wrote, 'The rich are different than you and me.' They sure are. They got more money. But there wasn't enough money in the world to save some of the members of Chicago's upper crust from a fiendish force so dark, it can only be called diabolic."*

**SYNOPSIS:** Several of Chicago's wealthiest women are being murdered by a stalking creature that takes different animal forms. One sees the creature as a bird. Another sees it as coyote. In each case, however, the creature turns into a towering

American Indian capable of holding his helpless victim in a hypnotic trance. After stealing the most expensive gems, the diabolic giant killer vanishes into thin air. The deaths are called suicides by the police, but INS reporter Carl Kolchak knows these are murders when he learns about the missing jewels. Following a police alert to a gem exchange building, Kolchak sees the evil and powerful spirit in action. The police find two guards shot dead with their own guns. The chase leads to the roof, where Kolchak and the police watch as a seven-foot Indian jumps off the roof. But when they look to the sidewalk, nothing is there. Once again, the eerie presence has vanished.

At an exhibit of Native American artifacts, Kolchak recognizes the outfit worn by the Indian at the gem exchange. It is the costume of a tribal sorcerer. An elderly Indian, Charles Rolling Thunder, tells Kolchak the legend of the Diablero, an ancient sorcerer who was able to assume different animal forms. According to the legend, the Diablero was part of a cliff-dwelling tribe. After using his magic for evil, the Diablero was cursed to travel through history as a spirit until he had rebuilt the treasure stolen from the tribe.

The eyes are everything to the Diablero. With them, he can transfix his victims. But his eyes also are the secret to his defeat. Bright light will temporarily blind him and break his power. He will be destroyed if he gazes at his own reflection. Knowing that the Diablero is a cliff dweller, Kolchak heads to the top of the tallest unfinished building in Chicago. He's armed with his camera's flash and a mirror. The reporter is forced to improvise his battle strategy, but, faced with his own reflection, the Diablero turns into dust.

**EVALUATION**: The Diablero is a powerful presence, but, in the politically correct '90s, the episode's depiction of Native American characters seems a little too "old Hollywood."

ITEM: Ramon Bieri, who plays Captain Joe Baker in this episode, returned nine episodes later for "Legacy of Terror." Even though again cast as a police officer, the second time he played Captain Webster. Go figure.

ITEM: No, that's not Ted Cassidy (Lurch on *The Addams Family*) playing the Diablero. That's Richard Kiel, best known as Jaws in the James Bond films *The Spy Who Loved Me* (1977) and *Moonraker* (1979). His fantasy credits extended all the way back to his outing as the Kanamit in the classic "To Serve Man" episode of *The Twilight Zone* (twelve years before "Bad Medicine"). In 1990, he co-wrote and produced *The Giant of Thunder Mountain,* a family film about the friendship between a little girl and a reclusive mountain man.

ITEM: Yes, that is veteran character actor Victor Jory playing Charles Rolling Thunder. One of the screen's great villains, Jory was Injun Joe in *The Adventures of Tom Sawyer* (1938) and Jonas Wilkerson in *Gone With the Wind* (1939). Yet his roles ranged from Oberon in *A Midsummer Night's Dream* (1935) to Captain Keller in *The Miracle Worker* (1962).

ITEM: Before playing Dr. Agnes Temple, Alice Ghostley had made regular appearances on ABC's *Bewitched* as Esmerelda. She also had co-starred with William Daniels (Lt. Matteo in "The Vampire") on the short-lived situation comedy *Captain Nice* (NBC, 1967). She later made regular appearances on the acclaimed CBS comedy, *Designing Women.*

ITEM: Marvin Kaplan, the comic actor playing jewel-thief-turned-barber Albert Delgado, played Henry for eight years on *Alice* (CBS, 1977-85). He has supplied the voices of many cartoon characters, including Choo Choo on *Top Cat* (ABC, 1961-62).

ITEM: Look closely at the supposedly dead police dog at the gem exchange. He doesn't play dead long enough. Before the camera cuts away, he moves his head.

**145**

**MEMORABLE QUOTE:** Carl to INS dark-room staffer complaining about developing pictures: "Why don't you stay in here a little longer and develop a personality."

## Episode #9: "The Spanish Moss Murders"

### Original Airdate: December 6, 1974

Written by Al Friedman and David Chase
(From a story by Al Friedman)
Directed by Gordon Hessler
Music: Gil Mellé, Jerry Fielding and Hal Moone
Director of Photography: Ronald W. Browne
Art Director: Raymond Beal

### CAST

Carl Kolchak............................................................. Darren McGavin
Tony Vincenzo........................................................ ...Simon Oakland
Ron Updyke............................................................ Jack Grinnage
Emily Cowles......................................................... Ruth McDevitt
Captain Joe Siska.................................................Keenan Wynn
Dr. Aaron Pollack.................................................Severn Darden
Jean (The Fiddler)...............................................Randy Boone
Pepe LaRue (Morris Shapiro)....................................Johnny Silver
Dr. Hollenbeck...................................................... Virginia Gregg
Henri Villon........................................................ ...Maurice Marsac
Michelle Kelly......................................................Roberta Dean
Sergeant Villaverde............................................ .....Rudy Diaz
Joe, the apartment superintendent....................................Ned Glass
The Bayou Monster (Peremalfait)................................Richard Kiel
Record Producer.....................................................Brian Avery
Natalie, the lab assistant........................................Elisabeth Brooks
Sleep Subject......................................................Donald Mantooth
Officer Johnson...................................................James La Sane
First Reporter....................................................... .....Bill Deiz
Second Reporter....................................................Frieda Rentie

**Opening narration:** *"Maybe you have to brush with death before you can really reflect on life — on the people and times that really meant something to you, like childhood, dreams of sailing on silver seas and wooden shoes, visions of sugar plums dancing. Silver seas, sugar plums. The visions, the nightmares of a child are perhaps the most frightening and horrifying. . . Some people who were in Chicago during the first stifling hot weeks of July would say that were so. . . if they were still alive."*

**SYNOPSIS**: Lab assistant Michelle Kelly is found murdered. A little later, a restaurant's chef is killed. Found at the scene of both mysterious deaths is a strange green substance. The slimy stuff is swamp moss not common to the Chicago area.

The trail leads to the dream research laboratory of Dr. Aaron Pollack. It's at the lab that Kolchak and Captain Joe Siska find the logical suspect. But Paul Langois has the perfect alibi. Part of Pollack's medical experiment, Paul has been asleep for six weeks. Not ready to give up, Kolchak talks to Paul's friends and associates. Pepe

LaRue (real name Morris Shapiro), a street musician, tells Kolchak the legend of peremalfait, a Cajun bogeyman.

Kolchak realizes that Paul, a man of incredible temper, is summoning up pere-malfait — a swamp monster — from the strong emotions of his unconscious mind. His dream has become a nightmare for Chicago. Even when Paul dies, though, peremalfait has become strong enough to exist independently, and its next target is a certain snooping reporter.

Since the bayou monster probably will head for the sewer system, Kolchak heads for a showdown armed with the one weapon that can kill peremalfait — a stake fashioned from a bayou gum tree.

**EVALUATION:** The balanced mixture of suspense, atmosphere, terror and comedy makes this episode one of the series' finest outings. Only "Horror in the Heights" was a better realization of *Kolchak: The Night Stalker* could have been on a weekly (not weakly) basis.

ITEM: Richard Kiel makes his second appearance as a *Night Stalker* monster.

ITEM: Keenan Wynn, one of Hollywood's best character actors, makes his first of two appearances as Captain Joe Siska. He has several wonderful moments as a frustrated police officer barely controlling his rage at Kolchak. In 1958, he played a compulsive gambler in "A Dip in the Pool," an *Alfred Hitchcock Presents* episode based on a Roald Dahl story. He also appeared, with his father, Ed Wynn, in the original TV production of Rod Serling's *Requiem for a Heavyweight*. And he was the writer in "A World of His Own," the 1960 *Twilight Zone* episode that ended the first season.

ITEM: Virginia Gregg's long list of TV credits included episodes of *Dragnet, The Twilight Zone, Alfred Hitchcock Present, The Addams Family* and *Mission: Impossible*.

ITEM: Severn Darden, who plays Dr. Aaron Pollack, appeared in such films as *They Shoot Horses, Don't They* (1970), *Conquest of the Planet of the Apes* (1972), *Battle for the Planet of the Apes* (1973), *The Day of the Dolphin* (1973), *Saturday the 14th* (1981), *Real Genius* (1985) and *Back to School* (1986). He also was a regular on the short-lived 1980 science-ficiton series, *Beyond Westworld* (1980).

ITEM: Gordon Hessler was a Kolchak director with creepy experience. He was a story editor and associate producer on *Alfred Hitchcock Presents*. He directed an episode of *Tales of the Unexpected*. And his films included *The Oblong Box* (1969), *Scream and Scream Again* (1970), *Cry of the Banshee* (1970) and *Murders in the Rue Morgue* (1971).

ITEM: No scene better illustrates the walk between humor and horror than the one where Kolchak realizes that peremalfait is after him. As he babbles in panic to Tony, the scene becomes both funny and genuinely terrifying.

ITEM: Simon Oakland also has his share of snappy lines. Shown a fuzzy picture of the bayou monster, Tony says, "What is that, Salvador Dali's bar mitzvah picture?"

**MEMORABLE EXCHANGE**:
KOLCHAK: "Whatever happened to 'I'm okay, you're okay?' "
SISKA: "Well, to tell you the truth, you're not okay. The people in group therapy didn't tell me I was ever going to meet anybody as un-okay as you are."

**MEMORABLE QUOTE:** "There's nothing under the sun that I fear as much as I fear dentist appointments." (And this from a man who has tangled with vampires, werewolves, zombies and Tony Vincenzo.)

## Episode #10: "The Energy Eater"
### (also known as "Matchemonedo")

### Original Airdate: December 13, 1974

Teleplay by Arthur Rowe and Rudolph Borchert
(on-screen credit not given to Robert Earll)
(From a story by Arthur Rowe)
Directed by Alex Grasshoff
Music: Gil Mellé, Jerry Fielding and Luchi De Jesus
Director of Photography: Ronald W. Browne

### CAST

| | |
|---|---|
| Carl Kolchak | Darren McGavin |
| Tony Vincenzo | Simon Oakland |
| Ron Updyke | Jack Grinnage |
| Emily Cowles | Ruth McDevitt |
| Jim Elkhorn | William Smith |
| Nurse Janice Eisen | Elaine Giftos |
| Walter Green | Michael Strong |
| Dr. Ralph Carrie | John Alvin |
| Frank Wesley | Michael Fox |
| Diana Lanier | Joyce Jillson |
| Don Kibbey | Tom Drake |
| Captain Webster | Robert Yuro |
| Dr. Hartfield | Robert Cornthwaite |
| Laurie | Barbara Graham |
| Janitor | John Mitchum |
| Receptionist | Ella Edwards |
| Policeman | Bob Golden |
| First Girl (Claudia Granoff) | Melissa Greene |
| Second Girl | Dianne Harper |

**Opening narration:** *"The city of Chicago sparkles with architectural monuments to man's achievement, his artistic aspirations, his quest for the truth, his respect for the law. . . Now a different sort of monument. . .There is a theory that dying institutions erect their own mausoleums before they die. This particular monument was to be a hospital and research center dedicated to extending the life of man, improving the quality of that life. It succeeded instead in introducing a new horror, a new way of death, a mystery."*

**SYNOPSIS**: INS reporter Carl Kolchak is on his way to cover the dedication of a new lakefront hospital. The construction was rocky, delayed by the mysterious deaths of two Native American members of the high-steel crew. The deaths were all the more puzzling because the Indians are ideal high-rise construction workers — perfect balance and no fear of heights.

During the dedication service, a maintenance worker is killed by a surge of electrical energy. In the basement, Kolchak notices several cracked walls and an unusually high temperature. Then the walls start shaking.

Kolchak takes architectural engineer Don Kibbey down to the hospital's basement. Kibbey confirms there's a problem, but he doesn't know what it is. They get a clue when the lights start begin shaking and exploding.

Nurse Eisen confirms that there have been unexplained deaths. Each of the victims had a connection with electrical equipment.

There were no documented irregularities during the hospital's construction, so Kolchak tracks down the Native American crew that left the job after several accidents and the two fatalities. Once the Native American high-steel workers walked off the job, the hospital was completed without further tragedy. Since the dedication, however, the building has been plagued by one disaster after another: the cracking and buckling walls, malfunctions, light systems blown out and an electrical system gone haywire. It's only the beginning. The mysterious electrical deaths continue — staff members and patients.

The Native American workers will only talk through their shaman and crew chief, womanizing Jim Elkhorn. "It's tribal business," Elkhorn tells Kolchak. "I don't discuss that with reporters or outsiders." When pressed for an answer, Elkhorn only says, "Matchemonedo, he killed my men."

With Janice Eisen's help, Kolchak gets Elkhorn to talk. He explains that Matchemonedo is an ancient, powerful and invisible bear god that once lived on the site where the hospital was built. The construction awakened the slumbering presence and unleashed its malignant fury.

When Elkhorn tries to calm the restless spirit, he and Kolchak hear a loud humming sound, followed by buzzing, rumbling and sparks. Since police are at a loss to explain the deaths and unusual phenomena, it's up to Kolchak and Elkhorn to subdue the malevolent force that seems to thrive on electrical energy. Their research shows that Matchemonedo is only active in summer months. During the winter, it hibernates — like a bear. They suggest a massive refrigeration system. Elkhorn calls it quits at this point, but

Kolchak is determined to get a picture of Matchemonedo. He takes cameras with special film to the hospital basement, not knowing that hospital executives have taken his advice on refrigeration. It works — for now. And it almost kills Kolchak, who wakes up, with frostbite, in another hospital. His unfocused eyes make out a bear-like presence casting a shadow over him. It isn't Mathemonedo. It's Tony Vincenzo.

**EVALUATION:** One of the weakest *Kolchak* episodes, "The Energy Eater" is repetitious, derivative and badly paced. The mixture of legend and electricity is anything but shocking. And the ending is sudden and unsatisfying.

ITEM: The last of three episodes directed by Alex Grasshoff, "The Energy Eater" was the director's second story about a Native American legend. Also a writer and producer, Grasshoff has captured three Academy Award nominations for documentaries.

ITEM: Best known as Joe Riley on *Laredo* (NBC, 1965-67), William Smith mixed it up with Clint Eastwood for the climactic bare-fisted brawl of *Any Which Way You Can* (1980).

ITEM: Another invisible force again skirted the need for cooking up a monster for, say, Richard Kiel to play. The episode also is given a boost by the visits to impressive high-rise construction sites. It needs all the help it can get.

**MEMORABLE QUOTE:** "What would you say if I told you there was a force beyond your comprehension trying to destroy this hospital?" (I'd say it was business as usual on Carl's beat.)

## Episode #11: "Horror in the Heights"
### (also known as "The Rakshasa")

### Original Airdate: December 20, 1974

Written by Jimmy Sangster
Directed by Michael T. Caffey
Music: Greg McRitchie
Director of Photography: Ronald W. Browne
Art Director: Raymond Beal

### CAST

| | |
|---|---|
| Carl Kolchak | Darren McGavin |
| Tony Vincenzo | Simon Oakland |
| Ron Updyke | Jack Grinnage |
| Emily Cowles | Ruth McDevitt |
| Harry Starman | Phil Silvers |
| Elderly Hindu Ali Lakshmi | Abraham Sofaer |
| Museum Curator Lane Marriot | Murray Matheson |
| Julius "Buck" Fineman | Benny Rubin |
| Barry the Waiter | Barry Gordon |
| Officer York | Shelly Novack |
| Sol Goldstein | Herb Vigran |
| Joe | Ned Glass |
| Frank Rivas | Jim Goodwin |
| Charlie | John Bleifer |
| Officer Boxman | Eric Server |
| Mrs. Miriam Goldstein | Naomi Stevens |
| Officer Thomas | Robert Karnes |
| Officer Prodman | Paul Sorensen |

**Opening narration:** *"There are sections of Chicago the guidebooks don't refer to. You can't blame them, really. The guidebook's function is to sell the glamour and excitement of our Windy City, and whichever way you dress it up, old age is neither glamorous nor exciting. Roosevelt Heights used to be a plush neighborhood, but the plush neighbors moved uptown, leaving the old people, and old people don't move easily. They become set in their surroundings. Their friends live next door. They've been going to the same store for twenty-five years. And, probably most important of all, they can't afford to relocate, even if they wanted to. The battle of fixed income versus galloping inflation never ends. But even inflation took a back seat here in Roosevelt Heights as a far greater fear overtook the residents, a terror which effectively dwarfed everything else."*

**SYNOPSIS:** The mysterious deaths of senior citizens pulls INS reporter Carl Kolchak into the plight of a low-income neighborhood, Roosevelt Heights. Harry Starman, the friend of a recent victim, believes the grisly murders are the work of a Nazi group stirring up anti-Semitism. As proof, he shows Kolchak swastikas painted all over the neighborhood.

But the swastika is a symbol that appears in several cultures. Centuries before Hitler appropriated the symbol, it was used by the Greeks, Navaho Indians, Aztecs, Mayans, Pueblos and Dakotas. Following the symbols, Kolchak finds an elderly Hindu. At first, the reporter thinks that this old man is in some way responsible for the deaths. During another visit, however, the elderly Hindu tells Kolchak about the Rakshasa, an evil spirit that appears to its victims as the likeness of a trusted friend.

Wooed into the arms of the demon, they are chewed to pieces. The old man gives Kolchak a special crossbow that can kill the Rakshasa, if you have the nerve to shoot the person to whom you've given your trust. Kolchak believes he's safe because he doesn't trust anybody.

Ah, but there is one person. Down a dark alley shuffles the sweet and loving figure of Miss Emily. Carl tells her to stop. He knows it's the Rakshasa. But maybe not. He implores her to stop. It keeps coming. "I'm gonna have to shoot you," he warns her in an almost-caring voice. He shoots.

Later, he'd like to tell Miss Emily that he trusts her so much that the beast took her form. But he'd also have to tell her that he shot her with a crossbow.

**EVALUATION**: If the series had to stake (pardon the expression) it's entire reputation on one episode, this outing would be it. They never topped "Horror in the Heights," a title that refers to the neighborhood Roosevelt Heights.

ITEM: This was the only episode written by Jimmy Sangster, the horror veteran whose credits included *The Curse of Frankenstein* (1957), *Blood of the Vampire* (1958), *Horror of Dracula* (1958), *The Mummy* (1959), *The Brides of Dracula* (1960) and *Maniac* (1962). The Hammer graduate was an ideal *Night Stalker* contributor.

ITEM: More than just a good horror story, the episode manages to slip in statements about senior citizens, anti-Semitism, urban renewal and trust in cynical times.

ITEM: And you just must like an episode that has Tony describe a picture of the monster as "Bongo the chimp with fangs. " Well, it does.

ITEM: And you also must like an episode that has Kolchak tell a young policeman, "Son, I've seen more dead bodies than you've had TV dinners." You tell him, Carl.

ITEM: And you must like an episode that contains an in-joke referring to a previous Kolchak caper. One of the four poker players in the opening sequence is named Joe (played by Ned Glass). The same character had shown up in "The Spanish Moss Murders" as an apartment superintendent. Kolchak gets information out of Joe by telling him he works for the Health Department. When Harry Starman mentions the Health Department in "Horror in the Heights," Joe thinks he recognizes Kolchak. "Didn't you used to work for the Health Department?" he asks. Kolchak tells him that was his brother. The double-play put Glass into what are probably the series' two best episodes.

ITEM: Always a busy supporting player, Murray Matheson was the Clown in Rod Serling's "Five Characters in Search of an Exit" episode of *The Twilight Zone*.

ITEM: Burmese actor Abraham Sofaer was in the "Mighty Casey" episode of The *Twilight Zone*, Robert Bloch's "Change of Heart" episode of *Alfred Hitchcock Presents* and the "Charlie X" episode of *Star Trek*. Born in 1896, he made his London stage debut in 1921 and his film debut (*Dreyfus*) in 1931. Talk about your veteran character actors.

ITEM: Barry Gordon, who makes a brief appearance as the waiter, later won fame as lawyer Gary Rabinowitz on *Archie Bunker's Place*, as president of the Screen Actors Guild and as the cartoon voice of Donatello, one of the *Teenage Mutant Ninja Turtles*. As a child actor, Gordon appeared in two 1960 episodes of *Alfred Hitchcock Presents*, "The Day of the Bullet" (by *Kolchak* writer Bill S. Ballinger) and "The Contest of Aaron Gold."

ITEM: Benny Rubin, a regular member of Jack Benny's radio show family, had his own NBC comedy/variety series in the spring of 1949. But the real slice of TV history was Sergeant Ernie Bilko himself, Phil Silvers.

ITEM: Another familiar face to TV viewers was Herb Vigran, who played everything from gangsters to judges in episodes of *The Jack Benny Show, I Love Lucy* and *Gunsmoke*. He also was restaurant owner Novello in *White Christmas*. And, of course, he seemed to be the crook every other week on *The Adventures of Superman*. Actually, Vigran only appeared in six of the *Superman* episodes (even he thought he'd done more than a dozen).

ITEM: With Silvers, Rubin and Vigran in the cast, "Horror in the Heights" is probably the most extreme example of the series' fondness for casting comedians and comic actors. The mirthful parade through *Kolchak: The Night Stalker* also included Scatman Crothers ("The Zombie"), Mary Wickes and Dick Van Patten ("U.F.O."), Jan Murray and Larry Storch ("The Vampire"), Dick Gautier and Bob Hastings ("The Werewolf"), Alice Ghostley and Marvin Kaplan ("Bad Medicine"), Pat Harrington and Jamie Farr ("Primal Scream"), Jim Backus and Jesse White ("Chopper") and Jackie Vernon ("Demon in Lace").

ITEM: The only episode written by Sangster also was the only episode directed by Michael T. Caffey. "Mike Caffey was an extremely strong director, very tough," producer Cy Chermak says. "He could ball up his fist and pick you off the ground by your shirt front. He could have done more. I would have love for him to have done more, but he didn't need the aggravation. I think his attitude was, 'Who needs it?' "

ITEM: Miss Emily reveals that she's working at INS to get material and experience for a detective novel. She can work on a typewriter and the paper is free. It's a good attitude for a professional writer, Carl tells her.

**MEMORABLE QUOTE:** "We all have rats, sir. You should see the one I work for." (Carl Kolchak on you-know-who)

## Episode #12: "Mr. R.I.N G."

### Original Airdate: January 10, 1975

Written by L. Ford Neale and John Huff
Directed by Gene Levitt
Music: Jerry Fielding
Director of Photography: Ronald W. Browne
Art Director: Raymond Beal

### CAST

| | |
|---|---|
| Carl Kolchak | Darren McGavin |
| Tony Vincenzo | Simon Oakland |
| Mrs. Walker | Julie Adams |
| Ron Updyke | Jack Grinnage |
| Emily Cowles | Ruth McDevitt |
| Leslie Dwyer | Corrine Michaels |
| Captain Akins | Bert Freed |
| Mr. R.I.N.G. | Craig Baxley |
| Bernard Carmichael | Robert Easton |
| Senator Duncan Stephens | Henry Beckman |
| Librarian Miss Byrett | Maidie Norman |
| Colonel Wright | Myron Healy |
| Peters | Bruce Powers |
| Policeman | Vince Howard |
| Man | Read Morgan |
| Miss Barham | Gail Bonney |
| Guard | Donald Barry |

**Opening narration:** *"I don't know when exactly I was in this office last. Someways, it seems like I never left. But, no, that's not right. For at least a few days I was away, far away, in the hands of men with no faces and no names. They broke me down, broke my story down, telling me how it hadn't happened the way I claimed. At least, I think that what they did, between injections. Memories fade fast enough without chemical help, but if I don't tell this story now, I don't think I ever will."*

**SYNOPSIS**: A groggy, disoriented and drugged Carl Kolchak tries to recall the events of the last few days. The story starts in a laboratory. While working on a top-secret project at a high-security military institute, Nobel Prize winner Professor Avery Walker is attacked and killed by a rampaging computerized robot. The android escapes from the grounds and attacks a postal worker.

Meanwhile, the official cause of death for Avery Walker is listed as a heart attack. INS editor Tony Vincenzo assigns the obituary to Carl Kolchak.

Walker's widow doesn't seem very upset. Drinking heavily, she lets slip a few details about her late husband's hush-hush government project. She also tells him the name of Leslie Dwyer, the computer expert who was working with Avery. The project was something called R.I.N.G.

With these few details, Kolchak confronts Leslie Dwyer. She claims to have no knowledge of R.I.N.G., but the reporter can tell he's touched a nerve.

Dressed in the clothes of the postal worker, the robot steals a novelty mask and some undertaker's wax from a mortuary. Covering its face of circuits, the android fashions a crude human face from the mask and wax. The more Kolchak kicks around the story, the more official pressure is brought on Tony, who isn't sure what's so important about a "glorified adding machine."

Carl tells Tony that it is their duty to find out how tax dollars are being spent. It's the public's right to know.

When Leslie Dwyer turns up missing, Kolchak traces her to an isolated mansion. He also finds R.I.N.G. Needing guidance, the sophisticated robot found the scientist and asked for her help. Dwyer tells Kolchak that R.I.N.G. stands for Robomatic Internalized Nerve Ganglia. This is a robot programmed with intellect and a survival instinct. When Walker was told to dismantle it, the robot killed him because it didn't want to die. Although R.I.N.G.'s knowledge is vast, it has the emotional development of a child. Just when Kolchak is convinced that R.I.N.G. can be controlled, the military surrounds the house and shoots the robot. Kolchak is given a mind-fogging drug, yet he tries to talk the details into his tape recorder before they fade completely.

**EVALUATION:** Like "U.F.O." and "Fire Fall," this is an episode that could have influenced *The X-Files*. With its story about a hush-hush government project, the eerie tale creeps along knee-deep in paranoia. It does, however, creep when it should move at a brisker pace.

ITEM: Julie Adams, who plays Mrs. Walker, was the leading lady swept off her feet by *The Creature from the Black Lagoon* in 1954.

ITEM: Bert Freed, who plays Captain Akins, was the first actor to play Lieutenant Columbo. Freed played the seemingly inept police detective for "Enough Rope," a live television production of NBC's *The Chevy Mystery Show*. Writers Richard Levinson and William Link turned "Enough Rope" into the stage play *Prescription: Murder*, and Oscar winner Thomas Mitchell became the second *Columbo*. Levinson and Link then turned their play into a TV movie. That's when Peter Falk climbed into the raincoat.

ITEM: Henry Beckman's credits included two episodes of *The Munsters*, which, like *Kolchak: The Night Stalker*, was shot at Universal.

Once a witch, always a witch. Beautiful Lara Parker, Angélique on *Dark Shadows,* plays witch Madelaine on "The Trevi Collection."

Did anyone get the number of that succubus?
That's Teddie Blue as "The Demon in Lace" (episode #16).

ITEM: Robert Easton, who also guest starred on *The Munsters* (as bumpkin basketball star Moose Mallory), got his start playing country-fried rubes of dubious intellect. As Luke in the Abbott & Costello comedy *Comin' Round the Mountain,* he uttered that classic line: "I'm teched. I got kicked in the head by a mule." Escaping stereotype, Easton has become Hollywood's leading dialect coach.

ITEM: "Mr. R.I.N.G." is a good example of how the supporting characters were minimized in later episodes. Ron Updyke is seen in the first few moments. He waves good-bye to Carl and says, "I'm going home to my city by the bay." That's it. He's not seen again in the episode. "In the first draft of that script, Ron had a much bigger role," Jack Grinnage says. "When we got to the final version, I was left with a line about going home to San Francisco."

ITEM: But Ron's departure does set up a funny moment. Carl can't figure out why Ron is so happy. It couldn't be a big story or a raise. What could it be? Miss Emily supplies the obvious reason for Ron's euphoria: "You're in trouble."

**MEMORABLE QUOTE**: "I've got a feeling it'll make Watergate look like a pie fight." (Kolchak describing a story to Tony Vincenzo)

## Episode #13: "Primal Scream"
### (also known as "The Humanoids")

### Original Airdate: January 17, 1975

Written by Bill S. Ballinger and David Chase
Directed by Robert Scheerer
Music: Jerry Fielding
Director of Photography: Ronald W. Browne
Art Director: Raymond Beal

### CAST

| | |
|---|---|
| Carl Kolchak | Darren McGavin |
| Tony Vincenzo | Simon Oakland |
| Ron Updyke | Jack Grinnage |
| Captain Maurice Molnar | John Marley |
| Thomas Kitzmiller | Pat Harrington |
| Dr. Helen Lynch | Katharine Woodville |
| Dr. Fisk | Lindsay Workman |
| Jack Burton | Jamie Farr |
| Dr. Peel | Regis J. Cordic |
| Dr. Cowan | Byron Morrow |
| The Secretary | Barbara Rhoades |
| Rosetta Mason | Jeanie Bell |
| Nils | Al Checco |
| Landlady | Sandra Gould |
| Policeman | Vince Howard |
| The Humanoid | Gary Baxley |
| Woman | Barbara Luddy |
| Humane Society Man | Paul Picerni |
| Barney | Arnold Williams |
| Dr. Jules Copenick | Paul Baxley |
| Robert Gurney | Craig Baxley |
| William Pratt | Chuck Waters |

**Opening narration:** *"During World War II, close to this very spot, science bore a child that changed the course of human relations and, to this day, threatens to end human history. It was called, innocuously enough, the Manhattan project and it grew into the terror we all have come to know as the hydrogen bomb. But this year, only a stone's throw from here, science delivered a new child."*

**SYNOPSIS:** Investigating the gruesome death of a research scientist, INS reporter Carl Kolchak ends up getting the royal runaround in the office of public relations officer Thomas Kitzmiller. Hardly satisfied with the oil company's official explanations, Kolchak manages to sneak through security barriers to interview Dr. Helen Lynch, another scientist on the project.

Lynch tells the journalist about the experiment. One of the oil conglomerate's Arctic expeditions had brought back a frozen core sample of soil for analysis. The sample is found to contain living cells that are millions of years old. When the scientific team thawed the cells, they "started to exhibit biological functions." In other words, the cells started to reproduce. The cells rapidly developed into a form of life from the Ice Age — a prehistoric apelike creature with a voracious appetite for flesh.

Again and again, the creature strikes, leaving behind a grisly trail of torn limbs. One witness describes the beast as half-man, half-gorilla.

Trying to find a logical place where the creature remains hidden during the day, Kolchak heads into the tunnels beneath a Chicago sports stadium.

**EVALUATION:** The ending is reminiscent of "The Spanish Moss Murders." Dr. Helen Lynch is reminiscent of Leslie Dwyer in "Mr. R.I.N.G." John Marley's Captain Molnar is reminiscent of many of his police predecessors. And the episode is a good example of humor working far better than horror.

ITEM: Still, the humor does work well. The episode, in addition to the obvious slaps at the oil companies, contains some of the series' more whimsical touches. One of the creature's victims is watching a Universal horror film with the Mummy. Another victim is named William Pratt. Boris Karloff's real name was William Henry Pratt. While playful, these in-jokes also remind us that Universal was the studio that gave us Lugosi's *Dracula* and Karloff's *Frankenstein*.

ITEM: The most playful scene, however, is the one in which the ever-serious Ron Updyke tells Carl and Tony a very somber story about a piecost. Finally, Tony takes the bait. "What's a piecost?" he asks. "About eighty-nine cents," Ron answers.

"I heard that joke in the second grade," story editor David Chase says. "I just threw it in. It's this little moment of absurdity. I mean, why is this reporter telling a grammar-school joke?

"I always sort of looked at the INS newsroom as a family, with Tony as the bellowing father. Kolchak became the naughty boy, always a little out of place. Ron was the good boy. Emily was the favorite aunt or sweet grandmother."

Jack Grinnage also singles out the piecost joke as a favorite moment: "Darren, Simon Oakland and I had so much fun with that scene. We just laughed so hard after finishing that."

ITEM: And the jokes keep flying. When Kolchak smells something like mildew, Captain Molnar suggests it's his undershirt. "Maybe it's your jokes," Carl shoots back.

ITEM: Jamie Farr, who appears as a biology teacher, already had made a name for himself as Corporal Maxwell Klinger on *M\*A\*S\*H*.

ITEM: A month before this episode aired, Pat Harrington had started his nine-year run as Schneider the super on *One Day at a Time*. Already a TV veteran, Harrington was a member of Steve Allen's resident company.

ITEM: Captain Molnar was hardly the first or last cop played by John Marley. His most notable film roles were Frankie Ballou in *Cat Ballou* (1965), Ali MacGraw's father in *Love Story* (1970) and Jack Woltz in *The Godfather* (1972).

ITEM: Written by story editor Chase and Bill S. Ballinger (who had received solo credit on "Fire Fall"), "Primal Sceam" had its origins in a suggestion made by Darren McGavin. Even before Playdon was signed on as the first producer, McGavin was on a plane to Australia when he read a Time magazine piece about core samples being taken from Antarctic ice.

The samples contained amebas thousands of years old and still alive. When asked by reporters at the first Kolchak press conference about story ideas, McGavin said they might do one about a hospital built over an Indian burial ground ["Bad Medicine"] and another "on live amebas dating back five or six million years, and dug out of an Antarctic drilling."

**MEMORABLE QUOTE:** "Now you saw that thing and I saw it, and that was not just any ape. I mean, that wasn't just J. Fred Muggs out there, dressed in a tutu and drooling for the public and playing on a unicycle. That was some creature!" (Kolchak on gorilla my dreams)

## Episode #14: "The Trevi Collection"

### Original Airdate: January 24, 1975

Written by Rudolph Borchert
Directed by Don Weis
Music: Jerry Fielding
Director of Photography: Ronald W. Browne
Art Director: Raymond Beal

### CAST

| | |
|---|---|
| Carl Kolchak | Darren McGavin |
| Tony Vincenzo | Simon Oakland |
| Ron Updyke | Jack Grinnage |
| Emily Cowles | Ruth McDevitt |
| Madame Trevi | Nina Foch |
| Madelaine | Lara Parker |
| Lecturer | Marvin Miller |
| Doctor | Bernie Kopell |
| Griselda | Priscilla Morrill |
| Superintendant | Douglas V. Fowley |
| Photographer | Peter Leeds |
| Mickey Patchek | Chuck Waters |
| First Hood | Richard Bakalyan |
| Second Hood | Henry Slate |
| Melody Sedgwick | Bev erly Gill |
| The Man | Henry Brandon |
| The Figure | Dennis McCarthy |
| Ariel | Diane Quick |
| Model Agency Manager | George Chandler |

**Opening narration:** *"Tuesday, May 2, one p.m. Mickey Patchek was a dealer, a snitch, a peddler of information. His clothes were as cheap as his reputation. So when he phoned me with some information to sell, I was surprised that he wanted to meet me in the heart of Chicago's chichi high-fashion district. What started out as a mild surprise culminated in stark-raving terror."*

**SYNOPSIS:** INS reporter Carl Kolchak tries to meet snitch Mickey Patchek at Madame Trevi's fashion salon. Kolchak sees Mickey sneak upstairs during a fashion show. Thinking that Mickey has given him the slip, Kolchak decides to leave. He goes out the door in time to see Mickey's body thrown from the salon's top floor. The information peddler is killed when he lands on the roof of a parked car.

Trouble seems to gravitate around Madame Trevi and her salon. That same day, one of her leading models, Ariel, has her face clawed by a cat.

Kolchak is contacted by Murray Vernon, a rival snitch offering the same evidence Mickey was selling. Before he can tell Kolchak anything, however, Murray is gunned down by mobsters. But the gangsters are sure that Murray gave Kolchak the information. They give him sixty hours to hand over the evidence.

That night, another Trevi model, Melody Sedgwick, is scalded to death in her shower.

The mysterious deaths — not to mention his need to track down Mickey's information for the gangsters — lead Kolchak back to the fashion salon of Madame Trevi, a businesswoman known to be conniving and ruthless. But is she ruthless enough to resort to murder? The police believe that the murdered men were fashion spies caught in the act of stealing designs.

Although one of Madame Trevi's models, Madelaine, offers to help Carl Kolchak, the INS reporter senses that she's not telling him everything. High fashion is a multimillion-dollar world, so perhaps Madame Trevi would kill to protect hers. The scenario is sinister, but it's hardly mysterious. Then Madelaine tells Kolchak that the deaths are supernatural. Madame Trevi, Madelaine says, is a witch using dark powers to take over the entire industry. Kolchak finds it difficult to believe until he is almost run down by a car — a car with nobody in it. Observing the attack from an upstairs window of her salon is Madame Trevi.

Kolchak visits a coven of witches to gain more information, but, after he leaves, we see that Madelaine is the witch. She has used her powers to control Madame Trevi and to eliminate the top models in front of her.

Using a mojo bag for protection, Kolchak sets out to destroy Madelaine's power by publicly accusing her of being a witch.

**EVALUATION:** Not a bad witches' brew for the series, although not as strong as, say, "Horror in the Heights" and "The Spanish Moss Murders."

ITEM: Carl Kolchak in the world of high fashion? Writer Rudolph Borchert even had Carl lecture Tony about sprucing up his wardrobe.

ITEM: Carl also is greatly amused when Tony admits that he has a brother-in-law named Rocco in the venetian-blind business.

ITEM: Again seeking out minimalist horror effects, the production team makes eerie use of animated mannequins by suggesting an impending attack through camera angles and slight movements.

ITEM: Lara Parker, who had played the witch Angélique on *Dark Shadows*, was a natural choice for the role of the witch Madelaine. "I don't think it had anything to do with me being cast," Parker says. "I auditioned for the part and got it. But I think all of the *Dark Shadows* fans were thrilled to see me as something supernatural. I remember Darren McGavin telling me, 'Nobody really understands the style of this thing. It has to be played seriously, and then the horror will come out naturally.' It was sort of ironic because I'd been doing that type of show for five years." But the grueling hours and overworking had taken their toll on the cast members and production crew, so Parker wasn't walking into the happiest of TV experiences. "Darren McGavin was working very, very hard," she says, "so he was sort of withdrawn and not very accessible during that episode. Yes, we worked at night. And, yes, the hours were long. They'd already done more than half of the episodes at that point, and I think nerves were a little frayed around the edges. But it was a nice part, a fun part. I had my head held under water. I had purple spots all over my face while I turned into a raving maniac. I had to freak out, yelling and screaming. I'm very game. . .but, long hours and all, he wasn't very nice to work with. He was very short-tempered. When I'd be doing the yelling, he'd be saying, 'Stop that, don't do that, don't do it that way.' He kept trying to tell me how to play a witch. It was a fun part, but, to be honest, it wasn't the most fun acting experience I ever had."

ITEM: Bernie Kopell, who made appearances as the evil Siegfried on *Get Smart*, plays a doctor. Two years after this episode, he started a lucrative nine-year cruise as the ship's doctor on *The Love Boat*.

ITEM: Marvin Miller, who has one scene as the lecturer on witchcraft, was best known as Mr. Michael Anthony, the financial representative who, for five years of *The Millionaire* (CBS, 1955-60), gave away a million tax-free dollars on behalf of billionaire John Beresford Tipton.

ITEM: Nina Foch, who plays Madame Trevi, had the ideal preparation for a *Kolchak* episode. Two her first films were *The Return of the Vampire* (1943), with Bela Lugosi, and *Cry of the Werewolf* (1944). In 1945, she appeared in *A Song to Remember,* the film that marked the screen debut of young Darren McGavin. Her movie credits also include *An American in Paris* (1951), *The Ten Commandments* (1956) and *Spartacus* (1960). After her *Kolchak* gig, she played Dr. Julia Moorehouse in ABC's *Shadow Chasers,* a 1985-86 *Ghostbusters*-inspired series about two paranormal investigators (Dennis Dugan and Trevor Eve).

ITEM: Unlike most *Kolchak* episodes, "The Trevi Collection" plunges right into the story with Carl giving a date and time and place for the first mysterious circumstance. Usually, this information was provided after a more general opening narration that established the mood. Then Carl would launch into the date-time-place spiel. "The Trevi Collection" skips the talking-into-the-tape-recorder opening and cuts right to the chase.

**MEMORABLE QUOTE:** "Dying and maiming were coming into vogue in the fashion world." (Kolchak on "The Trevi Collection")

## Episode #15: "Chopper"

### Original Airdate: January 31, 1975

Written by Steve Fisher, David Chase, Bob Gale and Robert Zemeckis
(From a story by Robert Zemeckis and Bob Gale)
Directed by Bruce Kessler
Music: Jerry Fielding
Director of Photography: Ronald W. Browne
Art Director: Raymond Beal

## CAST

Carl Kolchak............................. ..................................... Darren McGavin
Tony Vincenzo.................................................................. .....Simon Oakland
Ron Updyke..................................... .................................. Jack Grinnage
Emily Cowles................................................................ Ruth McDevitt
Herb Bresson...................... .................................................. Jim Backus
Lila Morton..................................................................S haron Farrell
Captain Jonas.................... ..................................... Larry Linville
Henry "Studs" Spake.......................................................Art Metrano
Professor Eli Strig...........................................................Jay Robinson
Norman Kahill...............................................................Frank Aletter
Neil, the morgue attendant..........................................Steve Franken
Watchman................................................................ ....Jesse White
George (Second Watchman)...........................................Jimmy Joyce
Electric Larry................................................................ Joey Aresco
Headless Rider (Harold "Swordman" Baker)................Steve Boyum
Nurse................................................................ ..Brunetta Barnett
Mrs. Rita Baker............... ...............................................Fern Barry
Otto................................................................ ......Jack Bernardi
Snow White........................... ........................................Jim Malinda
Beaner................................................................ ...Jimmy Murphy
Claude......................... ........................................Ralph Montgomery

**Opening narration:** *"The teenage years: sixteen candles, fervent passions, aimless joyrides and the forbidden taste of beer. A time the world allows for sowing one's wild oats. But for some individuals I came to know in this summer of their discontent, it had been a time when they had sown the seeds of their own destruction."*

**SYNOPSIS**: The story opens on a sunny April day at the Cook County Warehouse and Impound Yard, a Chicago landmark in the middle of a controversy. A powerful real-estate developer has purchased one of the area's largest cemeteries. He plans to build condominiums, and the excavated coffins are being temporarily stored at the warehouse.

Shortly after the cemetery's former residents have been moved to this vast structure on Chicago's outskirts, widow Rita Baker sees a headless motorcycle rider break through her garage door. The next day, cab driver Joseph Morton is stuck down by the headless motorcycle rider.

Police Captain Jonas is determined to keep the grisly details from a snooping Carl Kolchak. The youngest captain on the force, the ambitious Jonas is sure that his predecessors just didn't know how to handle Kolchak. He sets the tone for their relationship by having the reporter's yellow Mustang towed away from the crime scene. Kolchak sets the tone by tricking Jonas into betraying key pieces of information.

Morgue attendant Neil tells Kolchak that Morton was beheaded by a sword. Motorcycle dealer Herb Bresson tells Kolchak that the tire tread left at the scene is from a '50s bike.

The next day, Henry "Studs" Spake is attacked by the mysterious rider. He saves himself by climbing a telephone poll. Studs was Morton's best friend. Both rode with the Jokers, one of the area's two major biker gangs in the '50s. At Morton's funeral, Kolchak meets both Studs and the grieving widow, Lila.

After breaking into the Cook County Warehouse and Impound Yard, Studs is beheaded by the sword-wielding biker. Kolchak, not far behind him, gets a picture of the gruesome greaser.

**161**

Investigating the puzzling deaths of these middle-aged men, Kolchak discovers that each was a former member of the Jokers. He also learns that, in 1956, the decapitated body of Harold "the Swordman" Baker was found by the police. His head was not found.

A third victim, Lila Morton's sister, is struck down. She, too, once rode with the Jokers. Kolchak finds Lila in a panic, packing to leave town. Lila tells the reporter that Joe, Studs and the Jokers set up a booby trap for Swordman Baker. They just meant to knock Baker off his bike. The trap was too high, however, and the Swordman lost his head.

Turk, one of the jolly Jokers, kept the Swordman's head as a trophy, until the headless rider played a joke of his own. He made Turk his first victim — nineteen years ago. Studs figured out that the Swordman would stop killing if his head and body were reunited. So Studs took the canister with the head to the Swordsman's grave. That stopped the postmortem motorcycle rides. The killings started again when the cemetery was disturbed. The head and body must have separated in the move. Studs had gone there to locate the canister and put it with the proper coffin. To keep the Swordman from eliminating all the motorcycle gang members responsible for his beheading (including Lila), Kolchak heads for the warehouse to finish what Studs started. He must again put his life in jeopardy to rid the streets of Chicago of this vengeful corpse from the '50s.

**EVALUATION:** "Chopper" would be one of the series' best episodes. . . if only the hammy headless rider didn't look so obviously like a stunt man with a jacket pulled over his head and phony shoulders. As producer Cy Chermak points out, twenty years later, special-effects wizards could make the rider look frighteningly real. Still, plenty goes right in story, which is why both Chermak and Chase single it out as a favorite.

"I thought it was very well written," Chermak says. "The dark humor is really something, but I hate the visual. It looked silly. Today, with digitalization, you could do that effect one, two, three."

ITEM: Following Stanley Adams, Larry Linville became the second cast member from the original *Night Stalker* movie to make a guest appearance in an episode of the series.

ITEM: The supporting cast of "Chopper" represents a great deal of television history: Jim Backus (the voice of *Mr. Magoo*, his series ranged from *I Married Joan* to *Gilligan's Island*), Linville (Major Frank Burns on *M\*A\*S\*H*), Steve Franken (Chatsworth Osborne, Jr. on *The Many Loves of Dobie Gillis*) and Jesse White (the original Maytag repairman in the commercials).

ITEM: Franken, though, was filling in for Fiedler. Neil the morgue attendant seems to be a fun, but he's no Gordy the Ghoul.

ITEM: Jesse White got his start as Mr. Wilson in the Broadway and film versions of *Harvey*. In 1956, he appeared with Henry Jones (Captain Wells in "Werewolf") in *The Bad Seed*. His other notable movies include *Bedtime for Bonzo* (1951), *Death of a Salesman* (1951) and *Matinee* (an underrated 1993 film from director and *Kolchak* fan Joe Dante).

ITEM: One of the contributing writers to "Chopper" was a recent graduate of USC's School of Cinema, Robert Zemeckis. A Chicago native, Zemeckis went to Universal to observe the making of a TV series, *McCloud*. Then in his early twenties, Zemeckis and collaborator Robert Gale wrote a script for *McCloud*. They also took a whack at *Kolchak*.

"Bob Gale and I worked on a couple of ideas for *The Night Stalker*," Zemeckis recalls, "and they produced one. It was my first professional sale. So I guess you could stay it all started with *Kolchak*."

"We knew they needed ideas and scripts. The show had trouble because they needed a new monster every week. And after they had done a werewolf, a vampire and zombie, they said, 'Oh, no, we're running out of monsters.' So Bob and I saw this and thought, if we could create a folklore that they could plug into the series, we might get our first sale. We started out with a sort of 'Legend of Sleepy Hollow' thing, and we combined that with the '50s biker idea. And they bought it. I thought it came off very funny. They kept all the main elements of the story. The rewriting that was done was because we didn't understand the limitations of television.

"Obviously, I've always loved this kind of stuff, but that's not why we wrote 'Chopper.' We did it because we perceived this vacuum. Now I tell students, 'Don't try to sell a spec script to a hit show. They have a staff of writers and more scripts than they know what do with. Sell one to a show that's having trouble finding writers.' That was *Night Stalker*. If you come along with the right idea, they'll recognize that it's good for their show."

Zemeckis and Gale then sold their *McCloud* script. Then they sold one to *Get Christie Love* (ABC, 1974-75). In 1978, Zemeckis turned to directing with *I Wanna Hold Your Hand*. The rest of the resume speaks for itself: *Used Cars* (1980), *Romancing the Stone* (1984), the *Back to the Future* trilogy (1985, 1989, 1990 and shot at Universal) and *Who Framed Roger Rabbit* (1988). Zemeckis also has directed episodes of a series he executive produces for Home Box Office, *Tales from the Crypt* (a horror anthology you know Carl Kolchak would appreciate). On March 27, 1995, he walked on the stage of the Shrine Auditorium in Los Angeles to pick up his Oscar for directing *Forrest Gump*. The hit film also won Academy Awards for best picture, best actor (Tom Hanks), screenplay, film editing and visual effects. And it all started with a headless motorcycle rider.

"That episode was one of my favorites," David Chase. "It's typical of what the young writers, like Bob Zemeckis, would come up with. It was a '60s rock 'n' roll joke. It was wild — a headless biker riding around."

ITEM: Simon Oakland, in typically wonderful form, has a blast with Tony's restricted diet. Released from the hospital with a churning ulcer, Tony must try to keep his temper while keeping away from spicy food.

**MEMORABLE QUOTE:** Kolchak, when Captain Jonas says a motorcycle rider has taken it into his head to start a killing spree: "He certainly hasn't taken it into his head, because he has no head!"

"All I know is what has to be done"! (A Carl credo)

# Episode #16: "Demon in Lace"

## Original Airdate: February 7, 1975

Written by Stephen Lord & Michael Kozoll and David Chase
(From a story by Stephen Lord)
Directed by Don Weis
Music: Gil Mellé and Jerry Fielding
Director of Photography: Ronald W. Browne
Art Director: Raymond Beal

## CAST

| | |
|---|---|
| Carl Kolchak | Darren McGavin |
| Tony Vincenzo | Simon Oakland |
| Ron Updyke | Jack Grinnage |
| Emily Cowles | Ruth McDevitt |
| Captain Joe Siska | Keenan Wynn |
| Professor C. Evan Spate | Andrew Prine |
| Rosalind Winters | Kristina Holland |
| Registrar | Carolyn Jones |
| Coach Toomey | Jackie Vernon |
| Mark Hansen | John Elerick |
| Mike Thompson | Ben Masters |
| Coroner | Davis Roberts |
| Dr. Salem Mozart | Milton Parsons |
| Craig Donnelly | Steve Stafford |
| Tim Brennan | Donald Mantooth |
| Spanish Woman | Carmen Zapata |
| Maria Venegas | Maria Grimm |
| The Landlord | Carlos Molina |
| Betty Walker | Margaret Impert |
| Don Rhiner | Snag Werris |
| Girl (Marlene Franks) | Iris Edwards |
| Demon | Teddie Blue |

**Opening narration:** *"It was Goethe who said we love girls for what they are. Well, even the great Goethe could have learned something from the tale that took place on the campus of Illinois State Tech."*

**SYNOPSIS:** Handsome college men are being found dead on the campus of Illinois State Technical College. While Carl Kolchak's old friend Captain Joe Siska investigates the puzzling deaths for the police, Rosalind Winters, a reporter for the college newspaper, agrees to help the INS representative.

The cause of the killings is a succubus, a demon that takes female form. In this case, the succubus is taking possession of attractive young women so it can lure young men into a deadly embrace.

The college students are dying of heart attacks, the coroner determines, but they are being literally scared to death. The succubus sucks the life force right out of them. Once the demon lures a young man into its embrace of death, it reveals its true nature to the victim. The presence is so overpowering and the demon so repulsive that the result is heart failure.

Snooping around the campus, Kolchak learns that Professor C. Evan Spate is working on a tablet he found in Mesopotamia. It has ancient symbols that explain the power of the succubus. More than that, however, the succubus presides over the mystical tablet. The only way to destroy the power of the succubus is to destroy this priceless relic.

**EVALUATION:** Good scares. Good sense of humor. Good atmosphere. Good fun. Good episode.

ITEM: Keenan Wynn makes his second appearance as Captain Joe Siska, whose therapy is completely destroyed by one Carl Kolchak (there couldn't be two). Wynn's many films include *The Hucksters* (1947), *The Three Musketeers* (1948), *Angels in the Outfield* (1951), *Kiss Me Kate* (1953), *The Great Man* (1956), *Dr. Strangelove* (1964), *Finian's Rainbow* (1968), *Nashville* (1975) and *Piranha* (1978).

ITEM: "Demon in Lace" was the last of four episodes directed by Don Weis.

ITEM: How's this for an appropriate guest star? Carolyn Jones, best known as Morticia Addams on *The Addams Family*, as the Registrar.

ITEM: Cast as the tuna-touting coach, Jackie Vernon continued the march of comedians through the series.

ITEM: Ben Masters, cast as a student, went on to co-star with Kate Mulgrew (later Captain Kathryn Janeway on *Star Trek: Voyager*) in ABC's 1988 medical drama, *Heartbeat*.

ITEM: Tony reveals that in college he played drums in a group called Tony Vincenzo and his Neopolitans. In real life, Simon Oakland was an accomplished violinist.

**MEMORABLE QUOTE:** "Another vanishing corpse, Tony. I tell you, we're in luck! It's terrific!" (Carl soberly pondering the pursuit of journalistic excellence)

# Episode #17: "Legacy of Terror"
## (Also known as "Lord of the Smoking Mirror")

### Original Airdate: February 14, 1975

Written by Arthur Rowe
Directed by Don McDougall
Music: Gil Mellé and Jerry Fielding
Director of photography: Ronald W. Browne
Art Director: Raymond Beal

### CAST

| | |
|---|---|
| Carl Kolchak | Darren McGavin |
| Tony Vincenzo | Simon Oakland |
| Ron Updyke | Jack Grinnage |
| Captain Webster | Ramon Bieri |
| Tillie Jones | Pippa Scott |
| Mr. Eddy | Sorrell Booke |
| Professor Jamie Rodriguez | Victor Campos |
| Pepe Torres | Erik Estrada |
| George Andrews | Carlos Romero |
| Vicky | Sondra Currie |
| Rita Torres | Mina Vasquez |
| Sergeant Rolf Anderson | Craig Baxley |
| Captain Madge Timmins | Udana Power |
| Professor Jones | Robert Casper |
| Major Taylor | Scott Douglas |
| Lona | Dorrie Thomson |
| Nina | Merrie Lynn Ross |
| Medical Examiner | Pitt Herbert |
| Officer Lyons | Cal Bartlett |
| Andrew Gomez | Ernesto Macias |
| Nanautzin (The Mummy) | Mickey Gilbert |
| Officer Smith | Ron Stein |
| Officer Olson | Gene Le Bell |
| Mrs. Torres | Alma Beltran |

**Opening narration:** *"Among the philosophers, the great thinkers and the common Joes of this world, no question is more controversial than truth. Remarkable as it may seem, I can attest that the following events did occur, whether you believe them to be true or not."*

**SYNOPSIS:** While Tony is trying to enjoy a convention at the Sherwood Hotel, Carl Kolchak is investigating the deaths of a star fullback and a Green Beret officer. Neither should have been easy to overpower, yet each victim was quickly subdued. Both had their hearts cut out in a ritualistic manner.

Two more deaths follow. Again, the hearts are cut out. Witnesses describe the killer as a huge eagle-like creature. The trail of evidence leads to the hotel. In the building's basement storeroom, Kolchak finds the mummified remains of a 500-year-old Aztec warrior. The mummy's costume includes feathers similar to those found at the murder scenes.

Hoping to put the pieces together, Kolchak consults Professor Jamie Rodriguez, a historian specializing in Aztec culture. The pieces are bizarre and centuries old, but they fit.

In the sixteenth century, the Aztec empire fell under the force of Spanish armies. The Aztec sun worshippers started a bloody cycle in 1507. Every fifty-two years, the mummy of an Aztec warrior rises and claims five victims. A blood sacrifice is needed for sustenance. This is the ninth phase of the cycle. The tenth, in the year 2027, will complete the cycle — the Aztec millennium.

The first four victims are taken by the mummy. The fifth must be a sacrifice made willingly. The mummy has claimed four victims: the fullback, the Green Beret officer, an Air Force pilot and a policeman. Who is the victim willing to surrender his life?

Kolchak is certain it's Pepe Torres, a young man always surrounded by beautiful women. Pepe tells Kolchak he has agreed to be the sacrifice. In return, he's been granted every luxury, every wish. Until the day of the ancient sacrificial ceremony, Pepe will live like a prince. Kolchak's only hope of saving himself and stopping the cycle is to convince Pepe that he's made a bad deal. If he can just delay the rites of sacrifice, the mummy's power will be broken.

**EVALUATION:** Some nifty moments, but this one unravels like a loosely wrapped mummy.

ITEM: Yes, that's Erik Estrada, the future *CHiPs* star, as Pepe. And, yes, Cy Chermak would later produce *CHiPs*.

ITEM: Yes, that's Sorrell Booke, the future Boss Hogg on *The Dukes of Hazzard*, as the taxidermist rather sensitive about the poor image of taxidermists.

ITEM: In another one of those "go-figure" continuity problems with the series, Ramon Bieri makes his second appearance as a police captain. In "Bad Medicine," though, he played Captain Joe Baker. This time, he's Captain Webster. Of course, there was a Captain Webster in "The Energy Eater," but he was played by Robert Yuro.

ITEM: Mickey Gilbert, who played "The Ripper" in the first *Kolchak* episode, returns to play the mummy. That earns him a tie for most appearances as a Kolchak creature. Also with two monsters apiece are Richard Kiel (in "Bad Medicine" and "The Spanish Moss Murders") and Craig Baxley (the title roles of "Mr. R.I.N.G." and "The Sentry"). But Craig Baxley does appear in "Legacy of Terror"— as Rolf Anderson, the Green Beret who becomes one of the sacrificial victims. The stunt specialist appeared in a fourth *Kolchak* episode, "Primal Scream," but not as the monster. That distinction fell to another member of the flying Baxley family, Gary. Another Baxley, Paul, played Dr. Jules Copenik in "Primal Scream."

ITEM: Look closely at the final few seconds of "Legacy of Terror." Gilbert's dormant mummy opens its eyes during the fade-out. Intentional? Either way, it's a spooky moment.

ITEM: And I'll bet you thought there were just two Kolchak TV movies, right? The *Night Stalker* and *The Night Strangler*, right? Well, not quite. There are two more TV movies out there — sort of. In 1976, a year after the series left the air, Universal decided to edit four of the episodes into two TV movies for syndication. So, with Kolchak bouncing between two cases, the sixteenth and seventeenth episodes —"Demon in Lace" and "Legacy of Terror" — became *Demon and the Mummy*. The sixth and tenth episodes — "Fire Fall" (or "The Doppleganger") and "The Energy Eater" (or "Matchemonedo") — became *Crackle of Death*. Darren McGavin was called in to loop connecting dialogue. Jack Grinnage and Simon Oakland were called back to overdub a few lines of dialogue. With no other bridging material, however, the films never seem more than two hastily slapped-together movies. The editing at times is sloppy. The dubbing frequently is poor. And the cutting between two cases often is confusing. In *Demon and the Mummy*, for instance, the action shifts between heart attacks on the campus and hearts cut out near the hotel. These movies were not made because the original *Kolchak* order was cut from twenty-two to twenty. "They were made for the same reason all pictures are made," says Harry Tatelman, vice president of Universal Pictures Television, "to make money." Yet the syndicated presence of these two movies yanked the four episodes out of MCA's *Kolchak* package for local stations and cable channels. They were not seen when CBS made *Kolchak: The Night Stalker* part of its late-night lineup. They were not seen when cable's Sci-Fi Channel aired the series (although Sci-Fi did pick up the two 1976 movies for occasional showings). They would remain "lost episodes" until the Columbia House Video Library put out all twenty episodes — complete and uncut — in its Collector's Edition series.

**MEMORABLE QUOTE:** "I promised I'd show up with a haircut, new hat and pressed suit....but I lie a lot." (Kolchak prepares for a convention appearance)

# Episode #18: "The Knightly Murders"

## Original Airdate: March 7, 1975

Written by Michael Kozoll and David Chase
(From a story by Paul Magistretti)
Directed by Vincent McEveety
Music: Jerry Fielding
Director of Photography: Ronald W. Browne
Art Director: Raymond Beal

## CAST

| | |
|---|---|
| Carl Kolchak | Darren McGavin |
| Tony Vincenzo | Simon Oakland |
| Ron Updyke | Jack Grinnage |
| Captain Vernon Rausch | John Dehner |
| Mendel Boggs | Hans Conried |
| Minervo Musso | Lieux Dressler |
| Ralph Danvers | Jeff Donnell |
| Coat of Arms Dealer (Roger) | Robert Emhardt |
| Maura | Lucille Benson |
| Pop Stenvold | Shug Fisher |
| Leo J. Ramutka | Jim Drum |
| Charles Johnson (Butler) | Bryan O'Byrne |
| Lester Nash (morgue assistant) | Don Carter |
| Bruce Krause (telephone repairman) | Sidney Clute |
| Brewster Hocking | William O'Connell |
| Sergeant Buxbaum | Gregg Palmer |
| First Reporter | Ed McReady |
| Freshman Reporter | Alyscia Maxwell |

**Opening narration:** *"Tuesday, 11:15 p.m. If you know anything about Chicago politics, you'll understand why a sixty-three-year-old ward captain was braving the ungentle hour and less gentle streets. You see, ward captain Leo J. Ramutka was returning home from a wake — an auf Wiedersehen to a loyal registered voter he knew would one day meet him in that great polling station in the sky. What ward captain Ramutka failed to foresee was just how soon that meeting would be."*

**SYNOPSIS:** Returning from that wake, ward captain Leo J. Ramutka is murdered as he walks through the door of his home. The means of death is what particularly troubles the police. Ramutka was gunned down with a medieval crossbow. A puzzling series of murders follows — deaths by jousting lance, arrow and mace. It seems to be the work of an unchivalrous and distinctly errant knight errant. So Kolchak must become the knight stalker.

The trail leads to a museum filled with medieval weapons, armor and artifacts. The curator, Mendel Boggs, is upset because there are plans to turn a section of the museum into a discotheque. Boggs becomes a primary suspect. All of the mysterious assailant's victims were involved in the project.

While trying to warn a potential victim, Kolchak sees the murderous knight in action. The next day, he identifies the suit of armor as one at the museum.

Digging into the history books, Kolchak learns that the armor belonged to a twelfth-century French knight who was violently opposed to pleasure in any form. With a historian's help, Kolchak pieces together a startling theory. Plans to turn the museum into a disco have disturbed the spirit of the Black Cross Knight. This angry spirit has reentered his suit of armor to strike down those who would transform a somber museum into a house of gaiety, laughter and pleasure. The only weapon that could pierce the evil knight's cursed armor was a battle-ax blessed by Pope Gregory.

**EVALUATION:** One of the best. Certainly not as good as "Horror in the Heights" and "The Spanish Moss Murders," but up there with "The Vampire" and "The Zombie."

**ITEM:** John Dehner is in typically fine form as the flattering, grandiloquent Captain Vernon Rausch, a police officer who is all style and no substance. Dehner also contributed wonderfully droll portrayals to episodes of *The Twilight Zone* ("The Lonely," "The Jungle," "Mr. Garrity and the Graves"), *Columbo* ("Swan Song" and

"Last Salute to the Commodore"), *The Andy Griffith Show* ("Aunt Bee's Medicine Man") and *Mission: Impossible* ("The Contender"). Between 1960 and 1983, he was a regular on ten network series.

ITEM: Also adding several moments of fun to the episode is Hans Conried, best known as Uncle Tonoose on *The Danny Thomas Show* (*Make Room for Daddy*). Animation fans know him as the voice behind Captain Hook in *Peter Pan* and Snidley Whiplash on *Rocky and His Friends*. Dr. Seuss fans know him as the cruel music teacher in the film version of *The 5,000 Fingers of Dr. T.* (1953) and the narrator of the TV version of *Horton Hears a Who*.

ITEM: It was in this episode that Carl Kolchak made his most definite statements about being Polish. Strolling into a coat-of-arms store, he's attacked by the smooth-talking proprietors. Oh, they say after he tells them that Kolchak is Polish, "you must be descended from Archbishop Kolchak of Cracow." Kolchak doesn't think that's likely. Well, they say, maybe you're a descendant of Baron Kolchak, "the Lion of Warsaw." He ends up buying a "Kolchak" coat of arms.

ITEM: For the second time, we get a young stand-in for Gordy the Ghoul.

ITEM: This was the only episode directed by Vincent McEveety, the television veteran whose long list of credits includes several episodes of Gunsmoke and Murder, She Wrote. He also directed such Disney comedies as *The Strongest Man in the World* (1975), *Gus* (1976) and *The Apple Dumpling Gang Rides Again* (1979). His cast for *The Strongest Man in the World* included Phil Silvers, Dick Van Patten and James Gregory, all of whom appeared in episodes of *Kolchak: The Night Stalker*.

**MEMORABLE QUOTE:** "Why do I always feel like I don't belong here?" (Tony Vincenzo on his general state of confusion in the INS newsroom)

# Episode #19: "The Youth Killer"

## Original Airdate: March 14, 1975

Written by Rudolph Borchert
Directed by Don McDougall
Music: Gil Mellé and Jerry Fielding
Director of Photography: Ronald W. Browne
Art Director: Raymond Beal

### CAST

| | |
|---|---|
| Carl Kolchak | Darren McGavin |
| Tony Vincenzo | Simon Oakland |
| Ron Updyke | Jack Grinnage |
| Emily Cowles | Ruth McDevitt |
| Gordon Spangler | John Fiedler |
| Helen | Cathy Lee Crosby |
| Sergeant J. Orkin | Dwayne Hickman |
| Bella Sarkof | Kathleen Freeman |
| Kaz Kazantarkis (Cab Driver) | Demosthenes |
| Lance Mervin | Michael Richardson |
| Lance's Mother | Penny Stanton |

(Cast continued:)

Conventioneer......................................................... Eddie Firestone
Landlord................................................................ James Murtaugh
Secretary................................................................ .......Joss White
First Young Man.....................................................James Ingersoll
Second Young Man...........................................................Reb Brown

**Opening narration:** *"Nowhere in man's history does he display more tenacity, more perseverance, than in his search for eternal youth. Halting the relentless process of aging has been a constant dream of man's. . . and of woman's."*

**SYNOPSIS:** Four young swinging singles have disappeared, and INS reporter Carl Kolchak believes there's a connection with the discovery of the bodies of four very old people. Could these beautiful young people be dying from instant aging?

There is a connection. Each of the four victims was a client of the same computer-dating service. Kolchak follows the trail to the computer-matching service, which is run by a beautiful woman whose features resemble those of statues of Helen of Troy.

A scholar specializing in Greek mythology tells Kolchak that the goddess Hecate promised Helen of Troy eternal youth if she continued to offer young people as sacrifices. So Kolchak believes that the wrinkled, aged corpses are the missing young people, stripped of their youth. And the Helen running the computer business is actually Helen of Troy.

**EVALUATION:** Despite some nice touches, like the lap dissolve sequence that ages a runner from twenty-two to ninety, the episode runs out of gas. The buildup is good. The payoff is weak. And some of the age makeup is poor, even by 1975 standards.

ITEM: After enduring Gordy the Ghoul wannabes in "Chopper" and "The Knightly Murders," we are treated to John Fiedler's return as our favorite morgue attendant. With Fiedler back in the fold, this episode comes closest to having the entire cast of regulars and semi-regulars. Only Carol Ann Susi's Monique Marmelstein is missing.

ITEM: Dwayne Hickman, best known as television's *Dobie Gillis*, became a successful programming executive at CBS. In *Cat Ballou* (1965), he shared scenes with John Marley (Captain Molnar in "Primal Scream"). On *Dobie Gillis*, he shared scenes with Steve Franken (the morgue attendant in "Chopper").

ITEM: Moving from the realm of the incredible in "The Youth Killer," Cathy Lee Crosby became one of the hosts of ABC's *That's Incredible!* (1980-84).

ITEM: At the time of this episode, the actor billed as Demosthenes was playing Detective Stavros on *Kojak*. His real name was George Savalas, brother of series star Telly Savalas.

ITEM: Busy character actress Kathleen Freeman has been a guest star on dozens of situation comedies. She also has been a regular on several series, including Sandy Duncan's *Funny Face* (CBS, 1971). One of her co-stars was Henry Beckman, Senator Stephens in "Mr. R.I.N.G."

**MEMORABLE QUOTE:** "I work all the time." (a Kolchak understatement)

# Episode #20: "The Sentry"

## Original Airdate: March 28, 1975

Written by L. Ford Neale and John Huff
Directed by Seymour Robbie
Music: Jerry Fielding
Director of Photography: Ronald W. Browne
Art Director: Raymond Beal

## CAST

| | |
|---|---|
| Carl Kolchak | Darren McGavin |
| Tony Vincenzo | Simon Oakland |
| Lieutenant Irene Lamont | Kathie Browne |
| Dr. James Verhyden | Albert Paulsen |
| Jack Flaherty | Tom Bosley |
| Dr. Lamar Beckwith | John Hoyt |
| Ted Chapman | Frank Campanella |
| Colonel Brody | Frank Marth |
| Arnie Wisemore | Cliff Norton |
| Ruth Van Galen | Margaret Avery |
| First Detective | Lew Brown |
| First Reporter (Brian) | Keith Walker |
| Second Reporter (Ed) | Bill Deiz |
| Dr. Phillips | Greg Finley |
| Dr. Gordon | Tom Moses |
| The Sentry | Craig Baxley |
| Receptionist | Kelly Wilder |

**Opening narration**: *"This is one story I may not get to file in person, so I'll have to talk fast because it's after me."*

**SYNOPSIS:** In the deep labyrinth of caverns and storage caves underneath Merrymount Archive, Inc., an ancient lizard-like creature is killing workers and scientists. The reptilian being is on a rampage because seismologists working in the underground storage complex have removed several of its eggs. Geologists believe these are rocks to be studied. Kolchak, sensing a coverup, sneaks into an autopsy and then into Merrymount. He's determined to discover the cause of these mysterious deaths. Once inside, Kolchak heads for the deepest part of the underground installation.

The reporter realizes that the so-called monster is a type of prehistoric guardian protecting the eggs. The bizarre slayings were triggered when man invaded its world. To prove his theory, Kolchak will need to get dangerously close to this reptilian creature fighting for survival. Our last glimpse, appropriately enough, is Kolchak talking into his tape recorder about the inevitable coverup. This is where we came in — the tape recorder and warnings of a coverup opening *The Night Stalker* in 1972. "Take my advice," Kolchak says about things that go bump in the night, "run to the nearest exit."

**EVALUATION:** With these words, after twenty-two supernatural encounters, Carl Kolchak ended his prime-time career. *Star Trek* fans noticed the resemblance between this finale and the Horta episode, "Devil in the Dark." It was a weak finale with one very strong element — the presence of Darren McGavin's wife, Kathie Browne. If you're thinking nepotism, forget it. When they married on New Year's Eve 1969, Browne had her own list of acting credits, which included episodes of *The Alfred Hitchcock Hour* ("Bed of Roses" and "Wally the Beard") and *Star Trek* ("Wink of an Eye"). She also had been a regular on two series: *Slattery's People* (CBS, 1964-65) and *Hondo* (ABC, 1967). Far more than a curiosity, her Lieutenant Lamont would have made an interesting recurring character. Obviously ambitious and all steel under that soft exterior, Lamont isn't above using her feminine charms to get what she wants. Now here's an intriguing twist: Carl Kolchak, played by her husband, is the only male in the episode wise to her game and immune to her wiles. "Hey, ease up on her, Kolchak," one moonstruck reporter says, "she's just doing her job." An amazed Kolchak grumbles back, "Yeah, sure, yeah, so was Adolph Eichmann." If *Kolchak: The Night Stalker* had remained on the air, this character would have been worth exploring in more of a three-dimensional way — a strong and smart woman who knows she must play some games to survive on a man's police force.

ITEM: Also in the cast was John Hoyt, an actor whose films range (and I mean range) from Joseph L. Mankiewicz's *Julius Caesar* (1953) to the science-fiction sex spoof *Flesh Gordon* (1974). His television roles include Dr. Knox in "The McGregor Affair," a 1964 episode of *The Alfred Hitchcock Hour*, and Dr. Philip Boyce in "The Menagerie," the *Star Trek* pilot turned into a two-part first-season episode. He also was in "Will the Real Martian Please Stand Up," a 1961 episode of *The Twilight Zone*.

ITEM: That's Margaret Avery, ten years before her role as Shug in director Steven Spielberg's *The Color Purple*, playing Ruth Van Galen.

ITEM: Unlike most *Kolchak* episodes, "The Sentry" opens with a action sequence of sorts — Kolchak racing through the Merrymount Archive tunnels in a golf cart.

ITEM: The lobby of Universal City's landmark MCA Black Tower office building doubles for the lobby of Merrymount Archive. This was a typical cost-cutting maneuver with Universal television shows. You can spot the Black Tower lobby and elevator bank in other *Kolchak* episodes, too.

ITEM: Kolchak's Mustang picks up a nickname — "the Yellow Submarine."

ITEM: Eight days after this last *Kolchak* episode aired, McGavin was honored with the Count Dracula Society's Ann Radcliffe Award. This was the thirteenth year that the society recognized chilling achievement in film, television and literature. One of the hosts for the evening was Janos Skorzeny himself, Barry Atwater.

**MEMORABLE QUOTE**: "It's after me." (It could be any episode, but it's Carl Kolchak in "The Sentry.")

## THE KOLCHAK COLLAPSE

Let us once and for all bury the myth that Fred Silverman killed *Kolchak: The Night Stalker*. Yes, it is true that the hot young programmer left CBS to become president of ABC Entertainment in 1975. It is also true that under his direction ABC went to number one in the ratings for the first time in television history. And it's true that the network went to the top with such junk as *Three's Company, Charlie's Angels* and *The Love Boat*. If you are looking for other cultural crimes to place at Silverman's doorstep, consider that in the late '70s he jumped to NBC, where he tried such masterworks as *Pink Lady & Jeff, Kate Loves a Mystery* and *Supertrain*.

But the *Kolchak* corpse must be removed from his front stoop. Many reference books blame Silverman for the Kolchak cancellation. Some go so far as to chalk up the cancellation to Silverman's alleged hatred of fantasy and science fiction. Yet Silverman tried *Buck Rogers in the 25th Century* when he was at NBC. More to the point, however, Silverman didn't join ABC until June 1975, well after *Kolchak: The Night Stalker* shut down production and accepted a cancellation notice.

What killed *Kolchak*? Low ratings certainly had a great deal to do with its demise. Stuck in a poor time slot against fierce NBC competition (all four of NBC's Friday series made that season's top fifteen), *Kolchak: The Night Stalker* didn't crack the top fifty. Out of eighty-four series aired during the 1974-75 season, *Kolchak* finished a miserable seventy-fourth. It averaged only 13.6 percent of all television homes (the top show of that season, *All in the Family*, averaged 30.2 percent). Only one series in the bottom twenty was renewed, and that was a little cop comedy in its first season —*Barney Miller*. All of the other series with less than a fifteen rating, including *The Night Stalker*, were canceled. So, whether Silverman liked the show or not, it had almost no chance of seeing a second season.

And whether Silverman had been the new boss or Martin Starger had stayed, a certain amount of cleaning house would have occurred. The 1974-75 season was a total disaster for ABC. Deep in third place, the Alphabet Network couldn't place one series in the season's top fifteen. Only three ABC series made the top thirty.

"That was a real low point for the company," says ABC publicist Dan Doran. "Nobody wanted to look at the ratings. Yes, *Kolchak* failed, but everything was failing at the time."

The last stake in the Silverman legend is driven by Carl Kolchak himself – Darren McGavin.

"Do you want to know who canceled this series?" the actor says. "I canceled it. I was tired. I wasn't having any fun. I couldn't face another season of it. So I called [Universal TV boss] Frank Price and said, 'I want out.' He said, 'Well, ABC has to decide. . .' So I called Marty Starger and said, 'I want out.' He said, 'Well, we need to talk to Universal. . .' I said, 'Look, will you two get together and cancel this thing.' The next day I got the phone call telling me I was free."

A February 1975 interview with columnist Ward H. Mosby of *The Milwaukee Journal* confirms McGavin's disenchantment. "I hope they cancel this show as quickly as they can and get it out of their corporate, pinheaded minds," he told Mosby. "This is not the show I started out to do, and rather than try to pump life with a hypodermic needle into something that's just dying, I'd rather bury it and put it out of its misery."

McGavin told the journalist that his disenchantment started "about the third show" and went "steadily downhill." He estimated that fans were seeing only sixty percent of the show's potential. Profit participation or not, the actor was "fearful they'll pick up this show for next year. If they do, they're in for a rude shock." His biggest gripe was that the scripts were getting to the cast and crew so late: "Many people should have the script for production meetings with key people. By delaying, all of those people are going crazy. It makes them look bad. It destroys pride in people's work. Same with the directors. No time to think."

Meanwhile, Chase describes a writing staff that was "killing themselves."

Unable to write or contribute to the series, Rice felt frustrated and helpless as *Kolchak* moved week to week toward inevitable cancellation. Watching the show in a graveyard time slot "and knowing the competition it was up against," Rice says, "was like watching one's child with a foot stuck in a railroad track, seeing a freight train bearing down on him, and being too far away to do anything about it."

At Universal, only a few voices of sorrow could be heard.

"When the show was canceled, there was a wrap party," Michael Kozoll recalls. "Almost nobody attended."

You might be thinking that, after all the fighting and a trip to the hospital, Cy Chermak would have been glad to see *Kolchak: The Night Stalker* get canceled. You'd be thinking wrong.

"I was relieved to have the all the stress come to an end, but I wasn't happy to see the series come to an end," the producer says. "I wanted to make it work. And I thought it deserved a second season to find an audience. I thought it deserved a chance. Most shows need at least two seasons to click with the audience and get things on track."

He's right, you know. Some of television's most-celebrated series were slow starters on the verge of cancellation after one season. Three notable examples: *The Dick Van Dyke Show, The Twilight Zone* and *Hill Street Blues.* Many series not facing cancellation after one season still don't hit their creative stride until the second year.

"I don't like to give up," Chermak says. "I thought we could have learned a lot from that first season. I felt we would have clicked with the audience in the second season. And in 1997, I think I was right. Look, the show is still running on the Sci-Fi Channel. People are buying the tapes. It's a cult success with only twenty episodes. There are fans all over the world. There's this guy named Dawidziak who's writing a book about it. So, yes, I think I was right. It should have been given another chance."

## UNPRODUCED KOLCHAK

Most of Carl Kolchak's stories never made it to print. And some of his adventures didn't make it to the screen. On March 12, 1975, *Daily Variety* reported that ABC and Universal had agreed to cut the twenty-two episode *Kolchak: The Night Stalker* order by two. Just a little more than two weeks later, on March 28, the twentieth and final original episode, "The Sentry," completed that reduced order.

"ABC had already decided to cancel show and we were running behind anyway," producer Cy Chermak remembers. "We were not only running behind, we were running in the red. So Universal very understandably said, 'Why go further into the red with two more episodes when ABC has canceled it? What's the point?' That was when they pulled the plug on it."

No longer would trains roar past the INS window, shaking the office and putting a halt to conversations. As far as prime-time television was concerned, Carl Kolchak was hanging up his straw hat and sneakers. At this point, the production team had two more completed scripts, another well on the way to being finished and several others in various stages of development.

"There was over $75,000 in unproduced material," says Darren McGavin, who gave story ideas to writers and battles Universal over the direction the show should take. "There were unproduced scripts, story outlines, story ideas. There were about ten ideas in some form of development when we shut down."

If there had been a twenty-first episode, it probably would have been "Eve of Terror," a script taken to final draft by Stephen Lord and Michael Kozoll in early March. The two writers had collaborated on "Demon in Lace." Kozoll was one of the writers on "The Knightly Murders."

"Eve of Terror" opens in the audio control room of an acoustics laboratory. Behavioral researcher Myra Deckbar and technician Wayne Franks are studying the effects of high-frequency sound on guinea pigs. The sonic stimulation experiment goes tragically wrong when Myra is mistakenly trapped in the sound chamber. One hazardous frequency unleashes a murderous alter ego in the mild-mannered scientist. Her first victim is Wayne Franks. One might describe the unproduced episode as Dr. Deckbar and Ms. Hyde. How about Kolchak meets She-Hulk? While the influences might be obvious (they usually were in *Kolchak* episodes), the writers' motives were sensational.

"That was our statement on noise pollution," Kozoll said. "You could do that kind of thing on *The Night Stalker.* I don't think you saw much of that on television at that time."

The other completed script was "The Get of Belial," which Donn Mullally submitted in early January. Mullally was one of the six writers who had worked on "The Devil's Platform," and, like that episode, this one involved the prince of darkness.

In "The Get of Belial," Kolchak is covering a miners' strike at the Associated Anthracite Building in West Virginia. Glenn Maynard, the president of Associated, is considered the prince of darkness by picketing union miners. When Maynard is killed, the union is suspected. But the real culprit is Sonny Blackshear, possessed son of faith healer Sarah Blackshear. A beautiful child, Sonny was turned into a beast by the devil, "Old Belial." Belial offered Sarah a deal. She could have her beautiful child back if she would stop preaching and healing. She refused, and only her mother's love can temporarily bring out the good in Sonny. The climactic confrontation takes place in a coal mine. After nearly killing Kolchak, Sonny falls to his death in a deep shaft. In death, the beast is gone. There remains only the smooth features of Sarah Blackshear's beautiful boy. When Carl tries to get the story printed, he asks Tony if he's ready to accept a living devil. "I have to, Kolchak," the editor answers. "I hired you, didn't I?"

If "The Get of Belial" had been placed on the production schedule, story editors David Chase and Rudolph Borchert probably would have put it through a final-draft rewrite. Mullally's script was in five acts instead of the usual four. Some have speculated that the religious content might have made ABC nervous, but Chase says there were other down-to-earth reasons why "The Get of Belial" was moved back on the order of scripts.

"It was a good story," Chase says. "But, as I recall, most of it took place in West Virginia. That would have required expensive location shooting of some kind. We always faked Chicago by using the Universal backlot sets. That helped to keep costs down on an expensive show. We were always looking for ways to keep costs down."

To that end, Chase was writing a script that would be very cheap to shoot.

"I was working on what's called a bottle show," he recalls. "That's when you never have to leave the studio. You can do the whole thing on the lot. Everything is in the bottle. My idea was to have Carl Kolchak on assignment in Hollywood, and there's a monster hiding out on the old *Phantom of the Opera* set. Everything could have been done at Universal, which was the studio where Lon Chaney shot *The Phantom of the Opera*."

In interviews granted during the 1974-75 season, McGavin, who maintained a strong creative input, told reporters that the writers were working on stories involving Bigfoot and the Medusa of Greek mythology.

"You name a monster or legend from any culture," Chase says, "and we probably talked about using it. If there had been a second season, sooner or later, we'd have gotten around to Bigfoot."

"Bigfoot was the other idea Bob Gale and I pitched to them," Zemeckis recalls. "That was the one they rejected. I think we just took it to story. I don't there ever was a full script."

Like a Kolchak monster, other unproduced scripts and ideas jump up and surprise Chermak more than twenty years after the series left the air.

"I was working the other day with two producers at Showtime," Chermak says, "one of them said, 'You don't remember that we pitched you a script that would be used on the second season of *Night Stalker*.' I have to tell you, I didn't remember it."

Over last few years, Chermak has been reminded of a Russell Bates story titled "The Piasa Bird," which supposedly would have launched the second season, and "The Executioners," a script pitched by writer Max Hodge. Bates was the co-author (with David Wise) of "How Sharper Than a Serpent's Tooth," an October 1974 episode of the animated *Star Trek* series. A Native American writer, Bates had taken "The Piasa Bird" to the treatment stage. It would have dealt with a militant Native American leader who could summon an ancient bird creature.

Like Richard Matheson and William F. Nolan's *The Night Killers*, though, these were destined to be unproduced adventures of Carl Kolchak.

## SIZING THE SERIES

Want to start an argument? Ask a room full of *Star Trek* fans to compare the original NBC series with the syndicated *Next Generation*. You can bet your weight in dilithium crystals that there won't be much harmony on the old final frontier. But this is good-natured jousting. The general agreement is that both incarnations of Star Trek are pretty good shows.

Was The *Outer Limits* better than *The Twilight Zone*? Was *Taxi* better than *M*A*S*H*? Was *Barney Miller* better than both of them? Again, the argument is quality versus quality. The debate starts on a fairly high plane. You'll never find unanimity. There's always one person in the crowd who thinks that *Hill Street Blues* was a piece of junk, just as there's always one who thinks *My Mother the Car* was a cultural landmark (and, in a way, it was). Unanimity is impossible. Consensus, though, is typical.

Yet there is no consensus on *Kolchak: The Night Stalker*. Oh, sure, most everybody loves the original movie. You can't start much of a fight on that score. The series, however, can really divide a panel of experts. If our mythical room was filled with television critics, horror fans and media historians, and we had a pro and con side on *Kolchak: The Night Stalker*, guess what would happen? That room would very quickly divide into even teams. Let's convene a panel of experts and consider the complaints and commendations.

I suppose it should be mentioned prominently that leading the charge to the side of the room against the series would be Darren McGavin, Dan Curtis, Jeff Rice and Richard Matheson. Here, at least, you'll find unanimity. Each of them thought the series was a dreadful mistake, and their testimony can't be taken lightly.

"I'm surprised that people don't look at it and say, 'It should be better,' " McGavin argues. "I know there's an enormous affection for it, and it's wonderful that people feel that way. Fans say, 'Didn't you have fun doing the series?' And they're shocked when I say, 'No, it wasn't fun at all.' It's fun to watch. It wasn't fun to do. It's providential that they got made at all. We were turning in wet negatives. How can you talk about artistic judgment?"

All right, perhaps McGavin is transferring all of those production woes into his judgment on the series. How about Dan Curtis? How did he feel about the show?

"I wanted nothing to do with that," Curtis says. "You can't do that each week. It was a disaster. It was a terrible show. It deserved to be quickly off the air."

Matheson is slightly kinder, but only slightly: "They did come up with some interesting ones, I thought, but egocentric though it may sound, since Dan and I weren't involved in the series, I'll say that it missed two of the key building blocks."

And Rice, even though he created the series, wasn't able to mold it. "Well," he says, "it must be quite obvious by now that I don't look upon my series — my offspring, if you will — with the same sense of love and loyalty most true fans of *Kolchak: The Night Stalker* feel. Most of you who read this, I would guess, for the most part, loved and still love that show. Good. I offer no argument why you shouldn't. But, in all honesty, I think you were all cheated, in a sense, because my series was nowhere near to what it might have been, what I feel it could have been. Certainly, it was not what I wanted it to be."

Siding with these gentlemen are horror writer Stephen King, television historian Ric Meyers and veteran TV critic R.D. Heldenfels.

In his book-length treatise on horror, *Danse Macabre,* King (drawing on Berthe Roeger's analysis for *Fangoria*) gives high marks to Curtis, McGavin and the first *Night Stalker* film. But while calling *The Night Stalker* one of the best TV movies ever made, the author of *'Salem's Lot* and *The Shining* has almost nothing good to say about the series. The main problem, as King sees it, is one of believability. Okay, Kolchak found a vampire in Las Vegas. That was neat. All right, he found another monster in Seattle. That was a little tougher to swallow. In Chicago, however, he was bumping into something supernatural every week. For King, it became impossible to suspend disbelief. Why was this reporter stumbling over monsters at every turn?

"After a while, you're asking yourself, 'What is it about this guy that attracts the supernatural?' " says R.D. Heldenfels, former president of the Television Critics Association, author of *Television's Greatest Year: 1954* (Continuum, 1954) and the television critic at the *Akron Beacon Journal*. "You can't send him out after a monster every week without it becoming silly. Balancing comedy and horror is a very difficult thing to do, particularly on a weekly basis and a series budget. They set themselves an almost-impossible task. Another problem with believability was that he was the only real reporter in that newsroom. That always bothers me in a series, but my basic problem was that it was a series variation on *Billy the Kid vs. Dracula* — too strained and silly for the horror to work."

Similar complaints are voiced by Ric Meyers, the author of two insightful non-fiction books about television: *TV Detectives* and *Murder On the Air*. "I like the original movie," he explains. "I was less impressed with the sequel movie. I didn't think they needed the cookie-cutter aspect to the story. But the series was ludicrous from the get-go. The decision to make it monster-of-the-week was the big mistake. This was the horror version of *The A-Team*. And because the central problem was one of conception, they never solved that problem. The original movie was special and different and unusual. The series rarely came close. Look, you've got an actor as talented as Darren McGavin. Why ask him to do so little? They always asked him to play between the same two notes. They never gave him the whole scale. For what he had to work with, McGavin was terrific. But week by week, they took him to caricature. And that was the concept again. He reacted the same way every single time he found a monster. There was no sense of we've got to stop meeting like this."

McGavin believes the series would have worked if Kolchak had been sent after the real monsters of the world. Rice agrees: "I had originally envisioned a series which dealt primarily with the real and believable activities of an investigative reporter; a series set up in such a way that it would allow the occasional episode to deal with unexplained phenomena, but not to concentrate on it exclusively. That was the only logical way, it seemed to me, to handle the problem of having the same lead character appear every week without having him seem to be a certifiable nut case."

Rice also believes that the series should have explored the love-hate relationship between Carl Kolchak and Tony Vincenzo. This, he thinks, would have kept the characters away from caricature.

Vincenzo "is a man, not merely a symbol of the establishment," Rice warned before the series premiered. "At some point in his life he just might have had the news instincts Kolchak retains. So what happened? And why?

Why does he keep a man like Kolchak on his payroll when he knows it means nothing but trouble? Can it be because Kolchak, for all his foibles, represents a piece of Vincenzo that Vincenzo has lost and can't ever recover? On the other hand, Kolchak should not be presented as a total ingrate. Because, considering his checkered career record, who else but Vincenzo would employ him and put up with him?"

More sense of character and more character development is the prescription offered by Meyers. "Kolchak was an outcast and a loser," he says, "and it's easy to love a loser, an underdog. I think the show would have been more effective if the supernatural was happening inside someone else's life, then Kolchak comes in to help. It makes him more heroic. Everyone else can think he's a bum. He knows. He has the heart of a knight. They got close to that with the episode about the creature

**177**

that takes on the image of the person you trust the most. Kolchak starts out concerned with other people's problems in that one ("Horror in the Heights"). More of that would have been nice."

While he has his own suggestions to make, Heldenfels also raises a larger question.

"Maybe a continuing adversary, a Professor Moriarty figure, would have helped by providing a compelling villain for your hero," Heldenfels says. "That might have made it more feasible. But, then again, maybe nothing would have helped. We get *"V"* or *Something Is Out There* as a miniseries, and the ratings go through the roof. Then the network orders a series, and the audience won't come back for what's essentially the same thing every week. They'll show up on a one-time basis, but you can't get them back every week. *Kolchak* was not a well-made show, but, even if it had been, even if it had been the best horror show of all time, it probably still would have failed."

It's a valid point. Until Fox's *The X-Files* was around long enough for to build on its cult following, no hour-long fantasy, horror or science-fiction series had ever made the list of top fifteen shows for any season since 1950 (when A.C. Nielsen started counting). Not one. *Star Trek* never cracked the top thirty. Even during a season when CBS had seventeen of the top twenty-five series, *The Twilight Zone* couldn't make the top thirty. The only pre-*X-Files* fantasy drama to ever land in a season's top twenty was Jack Webb's *Project U.F.O.* (number nineteen for the 1977-78 season). Nothing else soared higher — *The Outer Limits, Lost in Space, The Time Tunnel, Flash Gordon, Captain Video, Land of the Giants, Voyage to the Bottom of the Sea, Thriller, Amazing Stories, Something Is Out There, "V", Tales of the Unexpected, Battlestar: Galactica, Buck Rogers in the 25th Century, Starman, Alien Nation, Manimal, Misfits of Science, Quantum Leap, The Flash, Dark Shadows, The Planet of the Apes.* You name it.

Fantasy, particularly literate fantasy, tends to attract a select audience. On a weekly basis, you don't get that massive rating that the networks demand. So, it's very likely that Heldenfels is correct. Good or bad, *Kolchak: The Night Stalker* had little chance of survival.

Bleak as that may sound, it doesn't put a dent in the enthusiasm of the show's defenders. Fred Clarke, the editor and publisher of Cinefantastique magazine, contends that *Kolchak: The Night Stalker* is one of the finest fantasy series ever to hit the airwaves. He, too, is in fine company. On his side of the room we find film historian Stuart M. Kaminsky and TV critics David Bianculli, John Carman and Tom Feran. In fact, in a poll of critics and mystery writers taken by John Javna and Max Allan Collins for their 1988 book, *The Best of Crime & Detective TV, Kolchak: The Night Stalker* was voted one of the five best shows featuring an amateur sleuth. Kolchak might not get any respect from police and city officials, but he sure gets it from critics and authors.

Kaminsky views the series from several impressive vantage points. A professor with many film books to his credit, he is the director of Florida State University's Motion Picture, Television and Recording Arts Conservatory. He also is the Edgar-winning author of not one, but two series of best-selling mystery books: the Holly-wood novels with Toby Peters (*High Midnight, Bullet for a Star, Never Cross a Vampire*) and the Russian adventures of Inspector Porfiry Rostnikov (*A Cold Red Sunrise, The Man Who Walked Like a Bear*).

"It was my favorite television series of all time," Kaminsky says. High praise, indeed, considering that his list of favorite shows include *Harry O, Hill Street Blues, City of Angels, Twin Peaks, The Prisoner, The Avengers* and *Barney Miller*. There's nothing wrong with this guy's tastes.

"The wit and originality of *The Night Stalker* series was, in my opinion, unmatched by anything in the genre that has come since," Kaminsky continues. "In one sense, *The Night Stalker* was wonderfully, nostalgically old fashioned. It was like a newspaper movie of the early '30s, filled with idealism and determination and, above all, wit. It managed to juggle humor with genuine horror, to keep me on the edge of both fear and laughter at the same moment. Many have tried to do this. Few have succeeded."

But the greatest attraction for Kaminsky was the character of Carl Kolchak — "the rumpled, enthusiastic fringe professional hero with no credibility who persevered in spite of the impossibility of the situation. Carl had a curiosity and determination that one seldom sees in any but the most two-dimensional characters. He was a pre-*Indiana Jones* without the benefit of good looks or professional respect."

Kaminsky also lavishes praise on the guest detectives (particularly John Dehner in "The Knightly Murders") and the running characters (Tony, Ron, Emily) – "the family that tolerated but never quite supported him."

In an essay for *Cinefantastique,* Kaminsky describes Kolchak as "the most unlikely heir to Dr. Van Helsing that one could imagine. . . He is not a spiritual figure or a doctor common to the destroyers of horror in the past, but a reporter, a representative of the non-mystical, who possesses no skills or knowledge beyond our own. He is not a superior or inferior being. He is, in many ways, a common man. His only drive is to get the story even if no one wants it, to uncover the truth. . . He may run screaming, but he always recovers, turns, and faces the creature, who always appears in the night world of horror, the world of dreams, not the world of daytime violence in police shows. . . Our hero is a pragmatist, a reporter, who accepts that horror exists, that it is violent and sudden, and that it is his and, possibly, our responsibility to face it."

Can this be the same series so abused by McGavin and Curtis? Can something so roundly criticized by its star and creator be worthy of such extravagant praise? Yes, say most television critics.

"At the time, I thought it was one of the few good things on television," says David Bianculli, TV critic of the *New York Daily News.* "It was about the only thing I actually looked forward to watching. There was a modern setting, but you had Darren McGavin as a reporter who hadn't evolved from the *Front Page* era. Then you had him battling legends that predated even the '20s Chicago sensibility. So, in each episode, you had three very different time zones at play with each other. They also had a nerd (Ron Updyke) before we had the word for a nerd. Until [Home Box Office's] *Tales from the Crypt* came along, it was the only show with a real comic-book feel to it. Lots of people have pointed out that plots bounced effectively between humor and horror, but remember that both are extremely difficult to do."

Another critic rising to the show's defense is John Carman of the *San Francisco Chronicle:* "It was something I looked forward to every week. It struck a chord, and not even as monster programming. With its lonely offices and almost film noir look, there was something about it that harkened back to early television. It was almost primitive, yet Darren McGavin was playing a character that was the opposite of a traditional TV hero. He had more courage and persistence than brains. I liked the character. He was interesting. And the show was fun. It had sort of an after-midnight appeal."

The monsters also hooked *Cleveland Plain Dealer* TV critic Tom Feran, but he, too, senses something grander in the series.

"The monsters are just an excuse for Carl Kolchak to be in constant conflict and constantly defending his credibility," Feran says. "The show was really about dealing with authority. I've never worked in a newsroom like most of the ones you see on television, but I have worked in plenty like the INS newsroom. Yes, the stretching of budget was often hilarious, but it was just as often ingenious. But, again, that was all just a backdrop. It was a perfect series for the time it was out. It was a Watergate series — imaginative, well-written, stylish. I think Thomas Pynchon should have written for *Kolchak*. You felt that the writers were having fun, and the viewers were supposed to be enjoying it, too."

So the weight of opinion rests on neither side. Instead, the opinions — strong and well-reasoned — are equally dispersed on the two sides of the debating hall. King sees bosh where Kaminsky sees brilliance.

Few TV series divide a room so neatly and quickly and effectively. Almost no one is left standing in the middle. . . no one. . . except, maybe, the author of this volume, and, well, he's taken several steps closer to the side with McGavin, Rice, Curtis, Matheson, Meyers and Heldenfels. I suppose it's most difficult for me to understand how someone who loves and appreciates the Night Stalker movie can be blind to the obvious faults of the *Night Stalker* series. I mean, we have a yardstick here, and, by my calculations at least, the episodes don't measure up.

Yes, the repetition of formula bothered me, too. And, yes, Carl and Tony should have been allowed to grow as characters. But, more often than not, I would view a Kolchak episode as a missed opportunity caused by sloppiness, fuzzy writing, over-stretched budget, lack of time or all of the above. A lot of this you chalk up to, "Sorry, I noticed." For instance, I noticed that the lycanthrope in "Werewolf" looks like an animated shag carpet that needs a distemper shot. I noticed in "The Ripper" that the writers failed to explain why the title monster is afraid of electricity or how his life was unnaturally prolonged. Did the murders have something to do with this longevity? I noticed that the "headless rider" in "Chopper" was obviously a stunt man with prop shoulders and the leather jacket pulled over those shoulders. I noticed that the reptilian creature in "The Sentry" seemed to be a papier-mâché refugee from a *Lost in Space* set. Horror makes such extreme demands on the suspension of disbelief that you have to play fair and get all the bases covered. Let's face it, *Kolchak* often fudged the horror elements.

Still (and here's where I can't join Rice and Curtis), if a failure, *Kolchak: The Night Stalker* was far from a total failure. First, you have Darren McGavin, who's always going to make the script stand up and dance. There is so much life (and Kaminsky would say life-affirming qualities) in his performance that it's impossible for any episode to be completely lifeless.

You also were assured of laughs, even when the horror was half-baked. In many ways, *Kolchak* worked better as a comedy than a horror show. Certainly David Chase and many of the writers felt more secure in humor than horror.

And, finally, at times, we were treated to glimpses of what the series tried to be. Sometimes these glimpses were just parts of an episode, like the suspenseful finale of "The Ripper." Sometimes the vision was sustained for an entire episode ("Horror in the Heights," "The Spanish Moss Murders" and, to a lesser extent, "The Knightly Murders"). Asked to name his favorite episodes, producer Cy Chermak gives high marks to "The Vampire," "Horror in the Heights" and, with qualifications, "Chopper." That's not a bad list. These were the few outings when the horror matched the humor. These were the rare occasions when the formula worked perfectly. These were the times when you can see the grander elements sensed by Kaminsky, Clarke, Bianculli, Carman and Feran.

If *Kolchak: The Night Stalker* only received a six-episode order (quite common these days) and only the six best episodes had been produced, there might be something close to a consensus. If those six episodes were, say, "Horror in the Heights," "The Spanish Moss Murders," "The Ripper," "The Vampire," "Chopper" and "The Knightly Murders," we might all be talking about a short-lived, unappreciated gem. *Kolchak* might have been the *Police Squad* of horror series. Yet they made twenty episodes, and too much goes wrong in too many of them for there to be consensus.

Well, you've got to think Carl Kolchak would prefer it that way. He's accustomed to people having strong opinions about him.

Kolchak being escorted to his ringside seat for "Legacy of Terror."

An unusually quiet moment in the reporter-editor relationship between Carl Kolchak and Tony Vincenzo.

# Part IV

# After ABC

## or, "When You Comin' Back, Carl Kolchak?"

*"Kolchak's desire is to make the public aware of the horror which lurks in their midst."*
— **Stuart M. Kaminsky**

*"Well, I for one am very interested to see what's going to happen next."*
— **Derek Jacobi as Franklyn Madson**
***Dead Again* (1991)**

### LATE NIGHT STALKER

It looked as if *Kolchak: The Night Stalker* would remain nothing more than a pleasant memory to its few devoted fans. Then ol' Carl was allowed to prowl the back alleys of television later than ever before. *Kolchak* reruns started showing up as part of the *CBS Late Movie* package in the late '70s.

True believers happily renewed acquaintances with Tony, Ron, Emily, Monique, Gordy and, most joyously of all, Carl. And a new generation flocked to the show. Remember, in the few years since *Kolchak* had left ABC, the horror boom had turned into a megaton explosion. Stephen King was up and selling. John Carpenter was up and directing. And *Kolchak* came back to claim his audience.

Although the four episodes edited into the syndicated TV movies *Crackle of Death* and *Demon and the Mummy* were not included in the CBS package, the *Late Movie* appearances proved so successful that *Kolchak* was brought back again and again during the next decade. The revival was on.

In *Danse Macabre* (1981), King dismissed the revival as the TV equivalent of a packed midnight-movie showing of *Reefer Madness*. It was a hip audience, King argued, wallowing in crap. It had nothing to do with viewers sensing any quality, originality or merit.

The opinions expressed by so many leading critics and fantasy experts at least partially deflate King's theory. Stuart Kaminsky, for example, clearly doesn't respond to the series on a hee-haw, ain't-that-awful, midnight-movie level. *Cinefantastique* founder Fred Clarke, who, by the way, also thinks the world of Stephen King's works, thinks the world of *Kolchak: The Night Stalker*.

Other reruns on the *CBS Late Movie* suffered greatly at the hands of editors cramming for commercials and allowing for double-features. The carefully crafted *Columbo* mysteries, for instance, were particularly difficult to watch. Key scenes or vital clues might be snipped out. *Kolchak: The Night Stalker* got off with comparatively few nicks and bruises (annoying as the cuts were). Some of the more graphic scenes might be missing (ABC did some pruning just for reruns at eight p.m.). A title might be changed. But, with running times of only an hour (compared to ninety minutes and two hours for *Columbo*), the damage was kept to a minimum.

New fans could discover the wonderfully weird and atmospheric music of Gil Mellé, Jerry Fielding and Luchi De Jesus. They could savor the sneaky jokes and clever satirical twists fashioned by David Chase, Michael Kozoll and the other writers. And most of all, they could smile and cheer at Darren McGavin's portrayal of Carl Kolchak.

## CABLE CARL

Carl Kolchak found a new television home in the '90s – cable's Sci-Fi Channel. Here, he was welcome. Here, he was appreciated. Here, he was surrounded by the likes of *Sightings*, Rod Serling's *Twilight Zone, Dark Shadows, Thriller, Night Gallery, Quantum Leap* and *Tales from the Darkside*.

The one disappointment to Kolchak fans was that the Sci-Fi Channel's package, like the *CBS Late Night* lineup, did not include the four "missing" episodes: "Fire Fall" (or "The Doppleganger"), "The Energy Eater" (or "Matchemonedo"), "Demon in Lace" and "Legacy of Terror" (or "Lord of the Smoking Mirror"). The cable channel did, however, offer occasional showings of the two Universal movies fashioned from these episodes: *Crackle of Death* and *Demon and the Mummy*.

Meanwhile, over on Fox, *The X-Files* was growing from a cult favorite to a mainstream hit. Agents Scully and Mulder were staring at you from the covers of almost every major entertainment and genre magazine: *TV Guide, Entertainment Weekly, Rolling Stone, People, Cinefanastique, Sci-Fi Universe, Starlog, Cinescape* and the Sci-Fi Channels' own *Sci-Fi Entertainment*. Whenever interviewed, the series' creator and executive producer would acknowledge *Kolchak: The Night Stalker* as the inspiration for his supernatural show.

"*The Night Stalker* wasn't appreciated when it was first on," Carter says. "My thought, when creating *The X-Files*, was to have a show that had that sensibility – that was scary and unlike anything on television."

Aware of their heritage, Carter and his writers gave us a senator named Richard Matheson and left the door open for McGavin to appear as a guest star. Indeed, McGavin was approached several times with offers to appear on *The X-Files*. One scenario had him reviving the Kolchak character. Another had him playing Senator Matheson. Yet another had him playing Mulder's father.

These hopes were dashed when, in late 1996, McGavin blasted *The X-Files* in an interview with the *New York Post*. Acknowledging the overtures from Carter, the actor accused the Fox series of ripping off what they had done on *Kolchak: The Night Stalker*. Why, McGavin asked the *Post* reporter, would he ever want to appear on such a humorless show? They were harsh words, and they indicated that McGavin wasn't paying particularly close attention to *The X-Files*. Kolchak may have been the inspiration for *The X-Files*, but these remain very different shows in tone and execution. In no universe can *The X-Files* be casually dismissed as merely a derviative rehash of *Kolchak: The Night Stalker*.

McGavin did agree, however, to tape some *Kolchak* interview material for the Sci-Fi Channel and to appear in a December 1997 episode of Carter's *Millenium*.

"Kolchak is the foundation for *The X-Files*," says Barry Schulman, the Sci-Fi Channel's vice president in charge of programming. "But, while Chris Carter has generously recognized this foundation, it must also be said that he has masterfully taken that concept and embellished it brilliantly. It's much more than *Kolchak. The X-Files* is a remarkable show."

The Sci-Fi Channel has played *Kolchak* in several time slots. In October 1996, Schulman took advantage of the *X-Files* connection by scheduling *Kolchak* at nine p.m. Fridays (the time slot just vacated by *The X-Files*).

"I'd like it to be a part of the Sci-Fi universe for a long time," Schulman says. "Obviously, you burn through the run pretty quickly when there are only sixteen episodes, so you have to drop it off the schedule for a while, then bring it back. But it's a small classic. And I think anytime the makers of a new classic, like *The X-Files*, give credit to a series twenty years old, that's significant. You don't hear Jerry Seinfeld giving credit to *My Mother, The Car*. There are shows in the history of television that are infinitely and instantly forgettable. *Kolchak* is an important show in the history of science-fiction television. It has a legacy."

## FROM COLUMBIA HOUSE TO YOUR HOUSE

Until October of 1996, Carl Kolchak's presence on home video had been minimal, confined basically to two tapes. Magnetic Video (a precursor of CBS Fox Video) released *The Night Stalker* in the mid-'80s. In 1987, MCA Home Video released *Two Tales of Terror* (a tape containing "The Ripper" and "The Vampire"). This tape was rereleased by MCA in 1995 with a closed-captioning option. In 1996, Fox rereleased *The Night Stalker* as part of its Twentieth Century-Fox Selection series. Fox also issued a laserdisc edition of *The Night Stalker*.

So that was it – *The Night Stalker*, "The Ripper" and "The Vampire." Only three of Carl's twenty-two investigations could be found in video stores. In October of 1996, however, the Columbia House Video Library began issuing all twenty series episodes on ten tapes — including the four "missing" shows not seen in syndication or on cable since the mid-'70s. Working with MCA Home Video, Columbia House packaged sparkling, uncut versions of the episodes.

The episodes were not issued in the order of airing, and, if that bothers you, blame the author of the book you're holding. He grouped the episodes and wrote the liner notes. With only twenty shows, it was decided to pair them up thematically. Therefore, "Bad Medicine" and "Energy Eater," the two Native American stories, are on the same tape. "U.F.O" (or "They Have Been, They Are, They Will Be. . . ") and "Mr. R.I.N.G.," the two episodes most likely to have influenced *The X-Files*, are on the same tape. "The Spanish Moss Murders" and "Demon in Lace," the two episodes with Keenan Wynn as Captain Joe Siska, are on the same tape. "Chopper" and "The Knightly Murders," the two episodes with vengeful ghosts wielding medieval weapons, are on the same tape. Hey, look, it made sense to me.

In its December 13, 1996, issue, *Entertainment Weekly* ran a positive review of the Columbia House release (" 'Night' Writer: 'X-Files' precursor 'Kolchak' haunts and pecks") with a color picture of McGavin as Kolchak. The videos, said critic Bruce Fretts, prove "how profound an influence" *The Night Stalker* was on *The X-Files*. "Students of the Carter oeuvre will spot parallels," the reviewer pointed out.

"The response was immediate and gratifying," says Gretchen Lindensmith, production coordinator for the Columbia House Video Library. "It definitely hit a nerve. We're only sorry that there are only twenty episodes."

Okay, that gives fans access to *The Night Stalker* and the twenty episodes. Two companies, Columbia House and Anchor Bay Entertainment, secured the rights to both *The Night Stalker* and *The Night Strangler* in late 1997. With spring 1998 releases scheduled by both companies, fans finally have access to the "complete" *Kolchak*.

## CARL BY THE BOOK

At this point, the author must jump from Kolchak chronicler to on-the-field participant in Carl's spotty history. It feels awkward to be both observer and player, but the reasons for this duality will soon be clear. I grant you, this jump may not be completely graceful, but it is necessary for a complete rundown on our hero's post-series career.

Carl Kolchak's rocky road back into print starts with the first edition of this book, *Night Stalking: A 20th Anniversary Kolchak Companion.* That was published in October 1991. While the author enjoyed the writing of that book, he was not satisfied with Image Publishing's design and distribution (or lack thereof). But Kolchak creator Jeff Rice was satisfied with what he considered the balanced account of his novel being turned into a hit TV movie. Rice was so pleased, he agreed to sign a five-year contract with Image founder Ed Gross for new Kolchak novels.

It was the start of an often-stormy four-year relationship between Rice and Gross. The initial five-year plan, however, was sound and ambitious. Gross would use Image's sister imprint, Cinemaker Press, to publish a mix of original novels and adaptations of the series episodes. Rice would have approval of the writers for books he did not wish to write himself. He also would have editorial control of the project. Publishing two or three books a year in the trade paperback size (six by nine), Cinemaker projected anywhere from ten to fifteen novels by the time the five-year contract was finished. Those of you still waiting know that it didn't quite work out this way.

The project was to start with a reprint of the first two novels, *The Night Stalker* and *The Night Strangler.* These would be followed by an original novel. Gross did not have the funds to make it worth Rice's while to write a new novel, so Gross asked him for a recommendation. Rice suggested the author of *Night Stalking.* I was flattered but not at all certain I could come up with a story worthy of Rice's character. Before agreeing to terms, I submitted five story ideas to Rice and Gross. Everyone agreed that the first idea was the most promising, so I set to work researching the book that would become *Grave Secrets.* Each of the books was to be published under the umbrella title of *The Kolchak Papers* (Rice's original title for *The Night Stalker*). In other words, the titles would be *The Kolchak Papers: The Night Stalker, The Kolchak Papers: Grave Secrets,* and so on and so on.

Unfortunately, we never got to "so on and so on." The reprint of *The Night Stalker* was published in 1993 with a foreword by Stuart M. Kaminsky and original artwork by Kevin Barnes and Sterling Clark, Jr. It was printed in paperback and hardcover, but Gross was having no luck finding a distributor who could place Kolchak books in bookstores.

Delays with artwork pushed *Grave Secrets,* the first original Kolchak novel in twenty years, ahead of *The Night Strangler.* It was published in late 1994 as a trade paperback with original artwork by veteran illustrator Ed Silas Smith. Bringing Kolchak into the '90s was tricky, but the trick was accomplished in concert with Jeff Rice. How to deal with the twenty years before the end of the series and new adventures? Simple, just act as if they didn't happen. We decided that the last episode of the series, "The Sentry," was the case that got Carl fired from the INS Bureau in Chicago. A little later, Tony took a job as an editor with the *Los Angeles Dispatch,* a scrappy little tabloid nicknamed "the Disgrace." Tony, of course, hires Carl, and, fast-forward, it's 1994. Carl is the same age. He talks the same. He acts the same.

During a trip to Los Angeles, Jeff Rice and I scouted locations for Carl's new home base. The old *Hollywood Citizen-News* building, a few blocks off Hollywood Boulevard, became the site for "the Disgrace." We checked out an unbelievably depressing hotel nearby and decided to check Carl in. "Dare we do this to him?" Kolchak's creator asked me as we stood in the shabby room. As we were leaving, Jeff Rice opened the minuscule closet and observed, "Hmm, just enough room for a straw hat and seersucker suit."

*Grave Secrets* opens with the mysterious death of land baron Glen Gilmore. The grave secret behind this killing is buried more than two-thousand miles away and more than 150 years in the past (heh-heh-heh). It would be immodest to quote from the reviews. All right, modesty is in short supply today. *Sci-Fi Universe* magazine called it "a wonderful book with memorable, offbeat characters and an imaginative plotline that twists and turns to an exciting finale." *Scarlet Street* magazine said it was "a welcome return of a time-honored favorite, with a startlingly original menace."

Needless to say, I was pleased. And I was even more pleased to learn that Jeff Rice was pleased. All in all, a very pleasing situation, right? It would have been if *Grave Secrets* had received anything that could be charitably called distribution. Back at Cinemaker, though, things were going from bad to train wreck.

Instead of *Night Strangler,* Gross announced an omnibus edition of both *The Night Stalker* and *The Night Strangler.* Meanwhile, writer Doug Murray had finished the second original Kolchak novel, *The Grand Inquisitor.* Neither the omnibus nor *The Grand Inquisitor* ever saw print, although Ed Silas Smith completed a striking omnibus cover showing Kolchak "haunted" by Janos Skorzeny and Dr. Richard Malcolm.

In 1996, about four years into his five-year-contract with Cinemaker, Rice pulled the plug. Fed up with the constant delays, broken promises and the lack of distribution, he declared the publisher in breach of contract and pulled back the rights to his characters.

"You tell the story in your own way," Rice said to me. "I find it incredibly frustrating to talk about the whole situation."

The sad story is this: After four years, Cinemaker published two Kolchak books, the reprint of *The Night Stalker* and *Grave Secrets.* Work on the omnibus and *The Grand Inquisitor* was completed, but neither book was published. Gross, later editor of *Cinescape* magazine and co-author of *Captains' Logs: The Unauthorized Complete Trek Voyages* (Little, Brown, 1995), accepts responsibility for the projects' failure. He admits he is "no businessman," and concedes that his ambition was greater than his resources.

The *Cinemaker* collapse has left Rice and Kolchak without a publisher. There have been overtures from a couple of major publishing houses, but nothing on terms creatively and financially acceptable to Rice, who emerged from the lawsuit settlement with firm control over the literary rights to Kolchak. He hopes that someday a publisher with ambition and resources will see the possibility in print adventures for Carl Kolchak.

## COMIC BOOK KOLCHAK

Well, we'll see. Topps Comics had been promising a series of *Kolchak* comic books for about four years. The company's biggest sucess has been its line of *X-Files* comic books, so a Kolchak connection would have made sense. Topps' other titles include *Dracula* (a tie-in with the Francis Ford Coppola movie), *Jurassic Park* (another tie-in) and *The Ray Bradbury Chronicles.* All in all, it seemed a proper home for Carl.

Cover art by Ed Silas Smith for the *Grave Secrets* novel.

Sterling Clark, Jr.'s striking cover art for the only authorized appearance of Kolchak in a comic book. Kolchak and Renegade teamed up for this one-time partnership.

Marvel Comics' cover of
"Night Gawker" spoof.

Jeff Rice signed a Topps contract in late 1992. He also wrote a comic-book script for *The Night Stalker*. Since then, both Marvel and DC Comics have expressed an interest in Kolchak.

But in the spring of 1997, Topps' new editor-in-chief, Len Brown, stated his intention to put Kolchak on a front burner. In May, however, Brown pulled the plug, telling Rice that his boss, Topps' publisher, had instituted a policy that prohibits the launching of "any new titles."

A frustrated Rice noted that "two 'factors' seem to have been at work for years both in regard to the publication of a series of novels and in regard to the publication of comic books: first, that publishers in either or both fields keep trying to acquire the rights for pennies and balk at paying Rice nearly anything at all, doing their best to keep Rice from doing any writing if possible." The second "factor" is Rice's fear that deals are fashioned with the intention of keeping Kolchak locked up and off the market.

Jumping into the fray in 1997 was Dave Campiti, owner of Glass House Graphics, a company that packages comic books for all of the major publishers, including DC and Marvel. A frustrated Rice asked Campiti to stop jumping in late 1997. So the only quasi-Kolchak comics published to date are: the 1974 Marvel spoof, *The Night Gawker*; Marvel's *Night Stalker*-inspired *Paul Butterworth–The Night Staker! (The Tomb of Dracula*, April 1976); and Carl's Rice-approved cameo appearance in Sterling Clark's *The Renegade No.1* (Ripoff Press/Magnecom, October 1993).

## REGARDING RICE

Since 1969, Jeff Rice has maintained residences in Hollywood and Las Vegas. The acting career never got going, but he continued to pursue a wide variety of interests. He wrote radio plays, short fiction and freelance articles on everything from submarines to filmmakers. He studied law for two years (1988-90) at Los Angeles City College, and, in 1990, was certified as a legal assistant/paralegal.

He has not been overlooked by the fantasy community. In 1975, at the Twenty-Eighth Annual West Coast Regional Science Fantasy Conference, he received the Westercon 28 Certificate of Award for Outstanding Achievement in Television for creation of the series *Kolchak: The Night Stalker*. In 1977, at Fantasy Film Fans International, he received the Starcon Fantasy Fiction Award for "Contributions to the Fantasy Genre in Literature and Television." In 1978, he was honored with the Millennia 9000 Science Fiction & Fantasy Conclave Citation of Merit for "creating fantasies in short stories, novels and screenplays and enriching the genre of speculative fiction." And in 1984, he was given a ShadowCon Citation of Merit "for contributions to the fantasy genre in literature and television."

Rice also has written a two-volume analysis of a twelve-issue combined copyright infringement and tort lawsuit. And he reorganized, revised and updated the law text *Civil Rights & Liberties: Principles of Interpretation* by A.L. Bonnicksen.

In 1992, he became the leader of an anti-drug, anti-gang watch-patrol group in Hollywood. About two years later, he became a member of one of the Los Angeles Police Department's Community Police Advisory Boards. For the LAPD and the board, he researched and created *Sentries*, a massive 1,102-page "directory and manual for neighborhood watch groups, covering everything from passive surveillance up to pro-active contact work, survival and use-of-force training, weapons, and the law. This was done during the period of 1994 and 1995."

"As for my personal life," Rice says, "well, I've had one, of sorts, and I keep it personal. I have a few friends; a somewhat larger number of correspondents; even more acquaintances; and a surprisingly large number of die-hard fans, some of a generation barely out of diapers when Kolchak was chasing down monsters. I had a wife. I have a son, James," who, as of this writing, is about to become a high school graduate.

In 1994, of course, Rice guided Kolchak back to print by serving as an advisor and editor on the novel *Grave Secrets*. In late 1996 and early 1997, he was contacted by Dan Curtis about the possibility of a big-screen remake of *The Night Stalker*. He remains dubious about all efforts to revive Kolchak, particularly when the proposals come from "experts" sure they know more about the character than Jeff Rice.

## FROM MARTIAN BLUES TO MURPHY BROWN

Happy to bid the long hours of *Kolchak* good-bye, Darren McGavin continued to jump between television and the big screen. In 1976, the year after *The Night Stalker* left the air, he starred in two TV movies (*Brink's: The Great Robbery* and *Law and Order*) and *No Deposit, No Return*, a theatrical film that continued his long association with Disney.

His other TV movies include *The Users* (1978), *Love for Rent* (1979), *Waikiki* (1980), *The Baron and the Kid* (1984), *My Wicked, Wicked Ways The Legend of Errol Flynn* (1985), *Inherit the Wind* (1988, as E.K. Hornbeck, the reporter based on H.L. Mencken) and *Perfect Harmony* (1991 for The Disney Channel).

The actor's association with fantasy adventure did not end with the last Kolchak episode. In 1980, McGavin was featured in NBC's miniseries version of *The Martian Chronicles*, Ray Bradbury's classic collection of Mars stories. The script was by Bradbury's chum Richard Matheson, yet the production was quite tedious and dull. Bradbury blamed the direction, not the script or the actors.

McGavin has appeared in two other miniseries (ABC's Ike and NBC's *Around the World in 80 Days*), as well as episodes of *Hotel, Highway to Heaven, Fantasy Island, Nero Wolfe, Magnum p.i., The Love Boat, The Hitchhiker, Tales from the Darkside* and *Tales from the Hollywood Hills.*

His greatest big-screen satisfaction was getting to play the Old Man in *A Christmas Story*, the acclaimed 1983 film based on several essays by humorist Jean Shepherd. The movie already has become a modern Yuletide classic.

"It will live," a justifiably proud McGavin says.

Other theatrical films include *The Natural* (1984), *Turk 182!* (1985), *Raw Deal* (1986), *From the Hip* (1987) and *Dead Heat* (1988).

McGavin made a sixth attempt to launch a series in 1983. The private-eye comedy *Small & Frye* (CBS) lasted only three months.

Television, though, was ready to provide another moment of triumph. McGavin was asked to play the title character's father on the CBS comedy *Murphy Brown*. The role, (appropriately enough) that of a veteran newspaper journalist, won him an Emmy.

The actor also enjoyed playing all of the characters for the Random House Audiobook series of Travis McGee novels by John MacDonald.

## ANOTHER CALL FOR CARL?

The notion of another *Night Stalker* movie is not so farfetched as you might think. The '80s was the decade of the reunion movie. Look at the characters lured back to prime time: Perry Mason, Andy Taylor, Lieutenant Columbo, Frank Cannon, Maxwell Smart, Marcus Welby, Jeannie the genie, the men from U.N.C.L.E., Jed Clampett, the Bionic Woman.

Take this trend and combine it with the fantasy-horror-science-fiction explosion of the '90s. *Star Trek: The Next Generation* took science-fiction to warp speed in syndication, paving the way for other *Trek* incarnations and *Babylon 5*. The *X-Files* became a hit on a network's prime-time schedule, spawning such imitators as *Millennium* and *Profiler. Jurassic Park* was the top film of 1993. *Independence Day* was the top film of 1996. *The Lost World*, the sequel to *Jurassic Park*, set box-office records for an opening weekend, and *Men In Black*, another *Kolchak* inspired movie became a runaway hit in July 1997. Such Stephen King miniseries as *It* and *The Stand* grabbed impressive ratings for ABC. The refurbished *Star War* trilogy set winter box office records in early 1997. Cable's Sci-Fi Channel offers a round-the-clock diet of fantasy, horror and science-fiction. King, Clive Barker, Anne Rice and Dean Koontz regularly hit the top spot on the best-seller lists. The time seems right for a Kolchak comeback.

And, in the early '90s, just about all of the principals had kicked around the idea, and all considered it a definite maybe. Dan Curtis mentioned it to Richard Matheson. Dan Curtis mentioned it to Darren McGavin. Dan Curtis mentioned it to ABC.

"Why not?" Matheson said at the time. "With so much interest in the old series, I think people would love to see another *Kolchak*."

"Sure, I'd do another one," McGavin said, "if the script was good. I'd do four movies-of-the-week if it could be worked out. I'm too old and fat to do it every week."

Then Curtis stopped mentioning and started working on the idea. By 1991, he had developed a new *Night Stalker* sequel for ABC, which still owned the dramatic rights to the character. The network and McGavin would have to okay the completed script, but Curtis believed he could get both to jump aboard for the ride.

Working from a concept outlined by Curtis, Steve Feke, a writer on NBC's prime-time revival of *Dark Shadows*, completed a *Kolchak* script that was shopped around in 1991. Titled *The Return of the Night Stalker*, the script failed to snare the interest of a studio or network.

"This, too, could be for laughs," Curtis said of the storyline. "Kolchak shows up twenty years later in New York City —down at his heels and out of luck. The Vincenzo character's son is the editor of a newspaper in New York, a Harvard Business School graduate and a very uptight guy. Kolchak comes wandering in still wearing the same seedy suit and terrible little hat. When this guy finally hires him, of course, a series of strange murders are taking place in New York. It turns out that the body of Janos Skorzeny was never cremated, so Kolchak has to go back to Las Vegas. It's the same thing. Nobody believes Kolchak. It's wild. It's funny."

Jeff Rice certainly believed there was more mileage in the characters: "There was so much more I wanted to say, through Kolchak and Vincenzo, and about their symbiotic relationship and their strange little 'family' at INS. . . so much more. But I never had the chance.

"But, who knows? Maybe. . . Someday. . . "

Someday was not 1991 for *Kolchak*. During the next four years, *Kolchak* turned up on the Sci-Fi Channel and *The Night Stalker* became known as the inspiration for *The X-Files*. Dan Curtis decided it was time to try again.

Instead of sequel, however, Curtis opted to try for a big-screen remake of *The Night Stalker*. Although still set in Las Vegas, the original story would be brought into the '90s. New actors would be used.

This last item will, of course, upset *Kolchak* fans who believe that Darren McGavin is the only actor who can properly fill that seersucker suit. No question, he was Carl Kolchak, just as Simon Oakland was Tony Vincenzo. Sadly, if McGavin had agreed to do *Return of the Night Stalker*, it would have lacked any further exploration of

Kolchak descendants: *The X-Files'* Agents Scully (Gillian Anderson) and Mulder (David Duchovny).

that symbitoic relationship Rice described. Oakland died on August 29, 1983, one day after his sixty-first birthday.

Whether or not another actor could play Kolchak is a matter for debate. But can you see any other actor playing Vincenzo to McGavin's Kolchak? Curtis and Feke wisely decided not to include the character in that sequel script. It wasn't even a consideration. That's how perfectly Oakland's Vincenzo fit McGavin's Kolchak.

Still, by November of 1995, when Curtis and Feke had completed a revised first draft for a big-screen remake, some tunes had changed. Sour relations had once again set in between Curtis and McGavin.

With the switch from a sequel to a remake, Curtis no longer wanted to use McGavin as Kolchak. He wanted a younger actor who could carry a big-screen project. And McGavin was saying, without qualification, "I won't work with Dan Curtis."

In December 1996, Curtis and Feke had a revised version of the remake — "based on the screenplay by Richard Matheson and the novel by Jeff Rice." On December 12, 1996, the following headline appeared on the front page of *The Hollywood Reporter*: " 'Night Stalker' on prowl in pic." The story reported that Curtis and Morgan Creek Productions had agreed to make the new *Night Stalker*. Curtis would direct.

"Very few TV movies from the late 1960s and early '70s hold up in the '90s," Morgan Creek chief executive James Robinson said. "The story has not aged at all. Everything that worked in the original film works today."

The article stated that Robinson would produce the remake, "and Gary Barber and Bill Todman Jr., who brought the project into the company, will executive produce."

Curtis told *The Hollywood Reporter* that "we should have made" the original *Night Stalker* as a feature. No casting was announced, although, at one point, Nick Nolte expressed interest in playing the part. In February of 1997, however, Morgan Creek Productions pulled out of the deal. That left Curtis looking for a new producing partner, which, as of May 1997, was precisely what he was doing.

Why does Carl Kolchak continue to seize our imagination and win our admiration? Maybe it's because, as Darren McGavin says, he's "a kind of folk hero" battling the forces of evil for us. Maybe it's because, as Stuart Kaminsky says, the character and concept are "filled with idealism and determination and, above all, wit." Or maybe it was Simon Oakland's Tony Vincenzo who gave us in one memorable sentence both the most apt description of Carl Kolchak and his reason for putting up with the often-troublesome employee. It's because, deep down, beneath his loathing for hassles, Tony, like Carl, believes that the public has the right to know. And Tony, like us, knows that, "Kolchak, you're one hell of a reporter."

# -30-

# R.I.P.

| | |
|---|---|
| Wally Cox (Titus Berry in *The Night Strangler*) | (1924-1973) |
| Ruth McDevitt (Emily Cowles in *Kolchak: The Night Stalker*) | (1895-1976) |
| Stanley Adams (Fred Hurley in *The Night Stalker* and Louie the Bartender in "The Devil's Platform") | (1915-1977) |
| Barry Atwater (Janos Skorzeny in *The Night Stalker*) | (1918-1978) |
| Charles McGraw (Chief Masterson in *The Night Stalker*) | (1914-1980) |
| Victor Jory (Charles Rolling Thunder in "Bad Medicine") | (1902-1982) |
| Hans Conried (Mendel Boggs in "The Knightly Murders") | (1917-1982) |
| Simon Oakland (Tony Vincenzo in the movies and series) | (1922-1983) |
| Carolyn Jones (Registrar in "Demon in Lace") | (1929-1983) |
| John Marley (Captain Molnar in "Primal Scream") | (1907-1984) |
| Margaret Hamilton (Professor Crabwell in *The Night Strangler*) | (1902-1985) |
| Kent Smith (District Attorney Paine in *The Night Stalker*) | (1907-1985) |
| Phil Silvers (Harry Starman in "Horror in the Heights") | (1912-1985) |
| Marvin Miller (Lecturer in "The Trevi Collection") | (1913-1985) |
| Murray Matheson (Lane Marriot in "Horror in the Heights") | (1912-1985) |
| Scott Brady (Captain Schubert in *The Night Strangler)* | (1924-1985) |
| J. Pat O'Malley (Cemetery Caretaker in "The Zombie") | (1901-1985) |
| George Savalas (Demosthenes) (Kaz the Cab Driver in "The Youth Killer") | (1927-1985) |
| Benny Rubin (Buck Fineman in "Horror in the Heights") | (1899-1986) |
| Keenan Wynn (Captain Joe Siska in "The Spanish Moss Murders" and "Demon in Lace" | (1916-1986) |
| Scatman Crothers (Uncle Filemon in "The Zombie") | (1910-1986) |
| Jackie Vernon (Coach Toomey in "Demon in Lace") | (1925-1987) |
| Ralph Meeker (Bernie Jenks in *The Night Stalker*) | (1920-1988) |
| John Carradine (Llewellyn Crossbinder in *The Night Strangler)* | (1906-1988) |
| Jeff Donnell (Ralph Danvers in "The Knightly Murders") | (1921-1988) |
| Jim Backus (Herb Bresson in "Chopper") | (1913-1989) |
| Ken Lynch (Captain Warren in "The Ripper") | (1908-1990) |
| John Hoyt (Dr. Lamar Beckwitch in "The Sentry") | (1904-1991) |
| John Dehner (Captain Vernon Rausch in "The Knightly Murders") | (1915-1992) |
| Fritz Feld (The Waiter in "U.F.O.") | (1900-1993) |
| Claude Akins (Sheriff Warren Butcher in *The Night Stalker*) | (1918-1994) |
| Sorrell Booke (Mr. Eddy in "Legacy of Terror") | (1930-1994) |
| Robert Emhardt (Coat of Arms Dealer in "The Knightly Murders") | (1916-1994) |
| Elisha Cook, Jr. (Mickey Crawford in *The Night Stalker*) | (1906-1995) |
| Svern Darden (Dr. Aaron Pollack in "The Spanish Moss Murders") | (1937-1995) |
| Mary Wickes (Dr. Bess Winestock in "U.F.O.") | (1916-1995) |
| Michael Fox (Frank Wesley in "The Energy Eater") | (1921-1996) |
| David Doyle (Cardinale in "Fire Fall") | (1929-1997) |
| Jesse White (Watchman in "Chopper") | (1919-1997) |

# BIBLIOGRAPHY

*The interviews listed in the Acknowledgments were the primary sources of information for this book, but several works about television, the horror field and mythology were of great value. I also found several books with chapters or passages about* The Night Stalker. *And there were some newspaper and magazine articles that filled in vital bits of information.*

## Books:

Aldiss, Brian W. *Trillion Year Spree: The History of Science Fiction.* New York: Atheneum, 1986.

Bianculli, David. *Dictionary of Teleliteracy: Television's 500 Biggest Hits, Misses, and Events.* New York: Continuum, 1996.

Brooks, Tim, and Earle Marsh. *The Complete Directory to Prime Time Network TV Shows: 1946—Present* (Fourth Edition). New York: Ballantine Books, 1988.

Burlingame, Jon. *TV's Biggest Hits: The Story of Television Themes from "Dragnet" to "Friends".* New York: Schirmer Books, 1996.

Butler, Ivan. *Horror in the Cinema.* New York: Warner Paperback Library, 1972.

Castleman, Harry, and Walter J. Podrazik. *Watching TV: Four Decades of American Television.* New York: McGraw-Hill Book-Company, 1982.

Cavendish, Richard (ed.) *Man, Myth & Magic* (24 volumes) New York: Marshall Cavendish Corporation, 1970.

Clarens, Carlos. *An Illustrated History of the Horror Film.* New York: Capricorn Books, 1967.

Collins, Max Allan, and John Javna. *The Best of Crime & Detective TV.* New York: Harmony Books, 1988.

Davis, Richard (ed.) *The Encyclopedia of Horror.* London: Octopus Books, 1981.

Deane, Hamilton, and John L. Balderston, *Dracula: The Vampire Play.* Garden City: Nelson Doubleday, Inc., 1971.

Douglas, Drake. *Horror!* Toronto: The Macmillian Company, 1966.

Fireman, Judy (ed.) *TV Book: The Ultimate Television Book.* New York: Workman Publishing Company, 1977.

Gerani, Gary, with Paul H. Schulman, *Fantastic Television.* New York: Harmony Books, 1977

Gerrold, David. *The World of Star Trek*, New York: Ballantine Books, 1973.

Gertner, Richard (ed.) *1984 International Television Almanac.* New York: Quigley Publishing Company, Inc., 1984.

Gifford, Denis. *A Pictorial History of Horror Movies.* London: Hamlyn Publishing, 1973.

Glut, Donald F. *True Vampires of History.* New York: HC Publishers, Inc., 1971.

Goldenson, Leonard H., with Marvin J. Wolf, *Beating the Odds.* New York: Charles Scribner's Sons, 1991.

Goldstein, Fred, and Stan Goldstein *Prime-Time Television: A Pictorial History from Milton Berle to "Falcon Crest".* New York: Crown Publishers, Inc., 1983.

Gross, Edward, and Mark A. Altman, *Captains' Logs: The Unauthorized Complete Trek Voyages.* Boston: Little, Brown and Company, 1995.

Grossman, Gary. *Superman: Serial to Cereal.* New York: Popular Library, 1977.

Halliwell, Leslie. *The Filmgoer's Companion* (Sixth Edition). New York: Avon Books, 1978.

Hutchinson, Tom, and Roy Pickard. *Horrors.* London: Chartwell Books, Inc., 1983.

Javna, John. *Cult TV.* New York: St. Martin's Press, 1985.

Katz, Ephraim. *The Film Encyclopedia* (Second Edition). New York: HarperPerennial, 1994.

King, Stephen. *Danse Macabre*, New York: Everest House, 1981.

King, Stephen. *Salem's Lot*. New York: Doubleday and Company, 1975.

Lowry, Brian. *The Truth is Out There: The Official Guide to The X-Files*. New York: Harper Prism, 1995.

Maltin, Leonard (ed.) *Movies and Video Guide* (1994 Edition) New York: New American Library, 1993.

Mank, Gregory William, *It's Alive!* San Diego: A.S. Barnes & Company, Inc. 1981.

Masters, Anthony. The Natural History of the Vampire. New York: Berkley Medallion, 1976.

McCarthy, John, and Brian Kelleher. *Alfred Hitchcock Presents: An Illustrated Guide to the Ten-Year Television Career of the Master of Suspense*. New York: St. Martin's Press, 1985.

McHargue, Georgess *Meet the Vampire*. New York: Dell Publishing, 1979.

McNally, Raymond T. *A Clutch of Vampires*. Greenwich, Connecticut: New York Graphic Society, 1974.

McNally, Raymond T., and Radu Florescu. *In Search of Dracula*. Greenwich, Connecticut: New York Graphic Society, 1972.

McNeil, Alex. *Total Television: A Comprehensive Guide to Programming from 1948 to the Present*. New York: Penguin Books, 1984.

Melton, J. Gordon. *The Vampire Book: The Encyclopedia of the Undead*. Detroit: Visible Ink Press, 1994.

Melton, J. Gordon. *Video Hound's Vampires on Video*. Detroit: Visible Ink Press, 1997.

Meyers, Ric. *Murder on the Air*. New York: The Mysterious Press, 1989.

Meyers, Richard. *TV Detectives*. San Diego: A.S. Barnes & Company, Inc., 1981.

Moore, Darrell. *The Best, Worst and Most Unusual Horror Films*. New York: Beekman House, 1983.

*Movies Made for Television: The Telefeature and the Mini-Series*. New York: Baseline, 1987.

Parish, James Robert, and Vincent Terrace. *The Complete Actors' Television Credits*, 1948-88 (Second Edition). Metuchen, New Jersey: The Scarecrow Press, Inc., 1989.

Pierson, Jim. *Dark Shadows Resurrected*. Los Angeles: Pomegranate Press, 1992.

Poe, Edgar Allan, *Complete Stories and Poems*. Garden City, New York: Doubleday & Company, Inc., 1966.

Polley, Jane. *American Folklore and Legend*. Pleasantville, New York: Reader's Digest Association, Inc., 1978.

Price, Vincent, and V.B. Price. *Monsters*. New York: Grosset & Dunlap, 1981.

Reiss, David S. *M*A*S*H: The Exclusive, Inside Story of T.V.'s Most Popular Show*. Indianapolis: Bobbs-Merrill Company, 1980.

Rice, Anne. *Interview With the Vampire*. New York: Alfred A. Knopf, 1976.

Rice, Jeff. *The Night Stalker*. New York: Pocket Books, 1973.

Rice, Jeff. *The Kolchak Papers: The Night Stalker*. Massapequa Park, New York: Cinemaker Press, 1993.

Rice, Jeff. *The Night Strangler*. New York: Pocket Books, 1974.

Scheuer, Steven H. (ed.). *The Television Annual: 1978-79*. New York: Collier Books, 1979.

Scott, Kathryn Leigh, and Jim Pierson (eds.). *Dark Shadows Alamanac: 30th Anniversary Tribute*. Los Angeles: Pomegranate Press, 1995.

Steinberg, Cobbett S. *TV Facts*. New York: Facts on File, Inc., 1980.

Stock, Rip. *Odd Couple Mania*. New York: Ballantine Books, 1983.

Strosser, Edward (ed.) *The Armchair Detective Book of Lists*. New York: The Armchair Detective, 1989.

Wedeck, Harry E. *Dictionary of the Occult*. New York: Philosophical Library, 1956.

White, Patrick J. *The Complete Mission: Impossible Dossier*. New York: Avon Books, 1991

Whitten, Leslie H. *The Alchemist*. New York: Avon Books, 1974.

Whitten, Leslie H. *Progeny of the Adder.* Garden City, New York: Doubleday & Company, Inc. 1965.

Wolf, Leonard (ed.). *The Annotated Dracula (including the complete 1897 text of Bram Stoker's Dracula)* New York: Ballantine Books, 1975.

Zicree, Marc Scott *The Twilight Zone Companion.* New York: Bantam Books, 1982.

## Magazines, newspapers and unpublished material:

"Bill Castle, McGavin Among Winners of Ann Radcliffe Awards," *Variety,* March 26, 1975, p. 1.

Burns, James, H. "TZ Interview: Richard Matheson." *Rod Serling's The Twilight Zone Magazine* (September 1981), pp. 43-54, (October 1981), pp. 14-21.

Crick, Robert Alan. "Kolchak: The Night Stalker." *Scarlet Street* (Fall 1994), pp. 80-96, a series overview accompanied by interviews conducted by Sean Farrell, Richard Valley and Jessie Lilley. Separate articles on Darren McGavin, Jack Grinnage, Carol Ann Susi and John Fiedler.

"Darren McGavin, U Sign Unique Long-Term Pact," *Variety,* April 11, 1974, p. 1

Flynn, John L. "The Kolchak Papers: Grave Secrets," *Sci-Fi Universe* (June 1995), p. 76.

Freeman, Don "Palance a Good Jekyll, Hyde," *The Sacramento Union* January 11, 1968, p. D2.

Fretts, Bruce. " 'Night' Writer: 'X-Files' precursor 'Kolchak' haunts and pecks,' " *Entertainment Weekly* (Dec. 13, 1996), p. 95.

Gross, Edward. "The X-Files: The Truth is Here. . . ," *Cinescape* (November 1994), pp. 34-45

Hill, Roger "Unshot." The Clipper Trade Ship (October 1979), pp. 18-24.

Honeycutt, Kirk. " 'Night Stalker' on prowl in pic," *The Hollywood Reporter*, December 13, 1996, pp. 1, 44.

"it couldn't happen here. . ." Volumes 1 (Fall 1996), 2 (Winter 1996) and 3(Spring 1997), quaterly Kolchak newsletter published by Mark Schultz.

Kaminsky, Stuart M. "Kolchak: The Night Stalker," *Cinefantastique* (Volume 4, Number 1), pp. 40-42.

Kennedy, Dana. "The X-Files Exposed," *Entertainment Weekly* (March 10, 1995), pp. 17-24

McDonnell, David. "Medialog: Kolchak & The Captains Nemo," *Starlog* (March 1997)

Mosby, Wade H. "As I See It," *The Milwaukee Journal*, February 16, 1975, TV section.

O'Connor, John J. "TV: 'Planet of the Apes,' 'Kodiak' and 'Chico and the Man' Bow," The New York Times, September 13, 1974, p. 73.

Rice, Jeff. *The Kolchak Story.* Private circulation, copyright 1984 by Jeff Rice.

Roegger, Berthe, "Kolchak: The Night Stalker," *Fangoria* (Issue #3), December 1979, six-page overview of the series.

Satian, Al, and Heather Johnson. "The Night Stalker Papers," *Monsters of the Movies* (June 1974), pp. 16-21.

Stevens, Kevin. "Uncovering The X-Files," *Sci-Fi Universe* (August 1995), pp. 20-28.

Sullivan, Drew. "Grave Secrets," *Scarlet Street* (Winter 1995), p. 97.

Thomas, Kevin. "Reporter on Trail of Vegas Vampire," *The Los Angeles Times*, January 11, 1972, Part IV.

Thompson, Howard. "TV: A.B.C.'s Yeasty 'Night Strangler.' " *The New York Times* (January 16, 1973), p, 79.

"U-TV's 'Stalker, Starring McGavin, To Be ABC Series," *Variety*, April 24, 1974, p. 1

Vitaris, Paula, "Pushing Horror's Enevelope: X-Files," *Cinefantastique* (October 1995), pp. 16-89, 30 articles about the series.

# Index

## A

ABC ... 4, 7, ix-x, 13, 16, 19-21, 23, 28-29, 32-34, 38, 40, 44, 46, 52, 55-58, 63, 65-66, 68, 70, 78, 80-84, 87-92, 97-100, 106-109, 113-114, 121, 133, 137, 139, 145, 160, 163, 165, 170-175, 183-184, 191-192, 199
ABC Circle Films ... 20, 87
Adams, Julie ... 152-153
Adams, Stanley ... 48, 62, 128, 140-141, 162, 196
Adventures of Superman, The ... 152
Aidman, Charles ... 92, 126-127
Akins, Claude ... 48, 57, 90, 196
Alchemist, The ... 69, 198
Alfred Hitchcock Hour, The ... 81, 171-172
Alfred Hitchcock Presents ... 44, 62, 113-114, 133, 135, 139, 147, 151, 198
Alien ... 141, 178
Alien Nation ... 178
All in the Family ... 113, 173
All the President's Men ... 14
Almost Grown ... 109
American Werewolf in London, An ... 137
Amory, Cleveland ... 110
Anderson, Richard ... 74, 76, 81, 87
Angier, John ... 100
Anselmo, Vince ... 61-62
Anthony, Lysette ... 94
Archerd, Army ... 133, 135
Archerd, Selma ... 133
Aresco, Joey ... 161
Around the World in 80 Days ... 16, 191
Astredo, Humbert Allen ... 34
Atwater, Barry ... 48, 57-60, 62, 172, 196
Avengers, The ... 55, 179
Avery, Margaret ... 171-172
Aykroyd, Dan ... 67

## B

Back to the Future ... 163
Backus, Jim ... 111, 152, 161-162, 196
"Bad Medicine" (Kolchak #8) ... 7, 144-145, 152, 158, 166, 185, 196
Baldwin, Bill ... 133
Ballinger, Bill S. ... 138-139, 151, 156, 158
Barker, Clive ... 31, 192
Barnes, Kevin ... 186
Barney Miller ... 133, 173, 176, 179
Baron, Allen ... 102, 121, 128, 135, 139-141
Barrett, Nancy ... 38
Bates, Russell ... 175
Baxley, Craig ... 152, 157, 165-166, 171
Baxley, Gary ... 126, 156
Baxley, Paul ... 157
Beal, Raymond ... 121, 126, 128, 133, 135, 144, 146, 150, 152, 156, 158, 161, 164-165, 167, 169, 171
Beaumont, Charles ... 30
Beckman, Henry ... 152, 156, 170
Beir, Fred ... 138
Belding, Richard ... 121
Bennett, Joan ... 33, 38
Bianculli, David ... 11, 66, 128, 178-179
Bid Time Return ... 31
Bieri, Ramon ... 144-145, 165-166
Bionic Woman, The ... 81
Birds, The ... 113
Bisoglio, Val ... 126
Black, Karen ... 92
Blatty, William Peter ... 88
Bloch, Robert ... x, 31, 57, 79, 114, 123, 151
Blue, Teddie ... 164
Bob Newhart Show, The ... 111, 114
Booke, Sorrell ... 165-166, 196
Boone, Randy ... 146

Borchert, Rudolph ... 121, 128, 148, 158-159, 169, 175
Born of Man and Woman ... 30-31
Bosley, Tom ... 139, 171
Bowers, Hoyt ... 56, 73
Bradbury, Ray ... 30-31, 187, 191
Brady, Scott ... 74, 196
Braeden, Eric ... 136-137
Brandon, Henry ... 159
Brian's Song ... 20-21, 63, 65, 71
Brooks, Mel ... 26, 67, 94, 137
Brown, Reb ... 170
Browne, Kathie
    See McGavin, Kathie Browne
Browne, Ronald W. ... 133, 135, 138, 140, 144, 146, 148, 150, 152, 156, 158, 161, 164-165, 167, 169, 171
Burlingame, Jon ... x, 64, 119
Burns, Jere ... 118
Burton, Tim ... 38

## C

Caffey, Michael T. ... 150, 152
Campanella, Frank ... 171
Campos, Victor ... 165
Carey, Michele ... 90
Carman, John ... 11, 178-179
Carradine, John ... 26, 74, 80, 84, 92, 196
Carroll, Francine ... 103
Carter, Chris ... x, 13-14, 132, 184
Cassidy, Ted ... 145
Castle, William ... 57, 62
Cat People ... 62
CBS ... 4, 16-17, 19-20, 30, 33, 37, 44, 56, 65, 71, 80-81, 84, 92, 109, 113-114, 127, 137, 145, 160, 167, 170-172, 178, 183-185, 191
CBS Late Movie ... 183
Chambers, Everett ... 29, 40, 52
Charny, Suzanne ... 133-134
Chase, David ... x, 101-102, 104-105, 108-109, 116, 121, 126, 133, 135, 140, 146, 156-157, 161, 163, 167, 175, 180, 184
Chermak, Cy ... ix-x, 14, 103, 105, 109, 116, 121, 134, 152, 162, 166, 173-174, 180
Chico and the Man ... 108, 127
CHiPs ... 106, 166
"Chopper" (Kolchak #15) ... 7, 109-110, 152, 160, 162-163, 170, 180-181, 185, 196
Clark, Sterling ... 186, 189-190
Clarke, Frederick S. ... x
Cobert, Robert ... x, 48, 70, 73, 119
Colen, Beatrice ... 121
Collins, Max Allan ... 178
Collins, Roberta ... 122
Colossus: The Forbin Project ... 137
Columbia House Video Library ... x, 16, 167, 185, 205, 207
Columbo ... x, 19, 29, 46, 81-82, 84, 90, 97, 103, 114, 119, 133, 135, 153, 168, 183-184, 191, 205
Connors, Chuck ... 71
Conried, Hans ... 168-169, 196
Cooper, Jeanne ... 140
Costello, Robert ... 34
Cox, Wally ... 74, 80, 84, 88, 113, 196
Crackle of Death ... 167, 183-184
Crime Photographer ... 44
Crosby, Cathy Lee ... 169-170
Cross, Ben ... 94
Crothers, Scatman ... 126-127, 152, 196
Curtis, Dan ... 4, 6, ix-x, 14, 22-23, 32-35, 37-38, 40, 44, 46-48, 55-58, 63-64, 66, 70-71, 73, 78-82, 87-95, 99, 176-177, 179, 191-192, 194
Cushing, Peter ... 67

# D

Daniels, William . . . x, 133, 135, 145
Danny Thomas Show, The . . . 169
Danse Macabre . . . 177, 183, 198
Dante, Joe . . . x, 38, 83, 162
Darden, Severn . . . 146-147
Dark Shadows . . . 5, x, 15, 32-34, 36-38, 40, 44, 57,
  63, 87, 90-91, 93-95, 160, 178, 184, 192, 198, 207
David, Thayer . . . 34, 38
Davis, Roger . . . 38
De Jesus, Luchi . . . 120, 148, 184
de Souza, Noel . . . 133
Dehner, John . . . 128, 168, 179, 196
"Demon in Lace" (Kolchak #16) . . . 7, 120, 139, 152,
  163, 165, 167, 184-185, 196
Demon and the Mummy . . . 167, 183-184
Dennis, John . . . 140
DiCenzo, George . . . 74, 87
Diller, Barry . . . 20, 40, 63, 89, 100
Donnell, Jeff . . . 168, 196
Donner, Richard . . . 141
Doran, Dan . . . x, 58, 80, 173
Doyle, David . . . 138-139, 196
Dracula . . . 5, 16, 19, 23, 26-27, 34, 49, 56, 67, 69,
  80-81, 92, 94, 151, 157, 172, 177, 187, 197-199
Duel . . . 31, 70
Dukes, David . . . 93
Dwyer, John M. . . . 121

# E

Easton, Robert . . . 152, 156
Eastwood, Clint . . . 21, 113, 120, 149
Edmonds, Louis . . . 38
Eisner, Michael . . . 20, 98
Elliott, Denholm . . . 38
Emhardt, Robert . . . 168, 196
Epstein, Allen . . . 28, 58, 70, 100
Estrada, Erik . . . 165-166
"Eve of Terror" . . . 174
Evening Shade . . . 97
Exorcist, The . . . 88

# F

F Troop . . . 133-134
Faison, Earl . . . 126, 128
Falk, Peter . . . 19, 21, 29, 46, 90, 97, 156
Fantasy Island . . . 135, 191
Fargas, Antonio . . . 126
Farr, Jamie . . . 152, 156, 158
Feke, Steve . . . 192
Feld, Fritz . . . 129, 132, 196
Feran, Tom . . . 11, 16, 178, 180
Fiedler, John . . . 79, 104, 114-115, 126, 129,
  169-170, 199
Fielding, Jerry . . . 120, 135, 138, 140, 144, 146, 148,
  152, 156, 158, 161, 164-165, 167, 169, 171, 184
"Fire Fall" (Kolchak #6) . . . 7, 137, 139, 153, 158,
  167, 184, 196
Foch, Nina . . . 158, 160
Fox, Michael . . . 13-15, 20, 29, 55, 71, 73, 80-82, 91,
  118, 137, 148, 178, 184-185, 196
Francy Productions . . . 4, ix, 103, 121
Franken, Steve . . . 161-162, 170
Frankenstein . . . 13, 26, 67, 80, 91-92, 97, 107, 151,
  157
Freed, Bert . . . 152-153
Freeman, Kathleen . . . 169-170
Frid, Jonathan . . . x, 33, 36, 38
Frommer, Ben . . . 126, 128
Front Page, The . . . 26-27, 32, 60, 74, 84

# G

Gale, Bob . . . 109, 161, 163, 175
Garner, James . . . 19, 90, 109
Gautier, Dick . . . 136-137, 152

# G (continued)

Get Smart . . . 61, 137, 160
Ghostley, Alice . . . 144-145, 152
Gilbert, Mickey . . . 122, 166
Glass, Ned . . . 146, 150-151
Goldenson, Leonard H. . . . 20
Gordon, Barry . . . 150-151
Grasshoff, Alex . . . 102, 116, 126, 128, 139, 144,
  148-149
Grave Secrets . . . 187
Gregg, Julie . . . 140
Gregg, Virginia . . . 146-147
Gregory, James . . . 129, 133, 169
Grinnage, Jack . . . 4, ix-x, 108, 111-112, 114, 118,
  121, 128, 133, 136, 138, 140, 144, 146, 148, 150,
  152, 156-158, 161, 164-165, 167-169, 199
Gross, Ed . . . 186

# H

Hall, Grayson . . . 34, 38
Hall, Sam . . . x, 37-38, 91
Hamilton, Margaret . . . 74, 80, 87, 196
Hammett, Dashiell . . . 108
Happy Days . . . 97-98, 135, 139
Harrington, Pat . . . 152, 156, 158
Hastings, Bob . . . 136-137, 152
Hecht, Ben . . . 69
Hell House . . . 31
Helter Skelter . . . 65, 87
Henesy, David . . . 33, 38
Hessler, Gordon . . . 146-147
Hickman, Dwayne . . . 169-170
Hill Street Blues . . . x, 109, 135, 174, 176, 179
Hitchcock, Alfred . . . 44, 61-62, 79, 81, 113-114,
  133, 135, 139, 147, 151, 171-172, 198
Hodge, Max . . . 175
Hope, Bob . . . 43, 67, 135
"Horror in the Heights" (Kolchak #11) . . . 7, 120,
  147, 150-152, 159, 168, 178, 180-181, 196
Hoyt, John . . . 171-172, 196
Huggins, Roy . . . 20
Hugo, Michael . . . 48, 57
Hunter, Ian McLellan . . . 38

# I

I Am Legend . . . 31
I Love Lucy . . . 133, 152
I Married Joan . . . 162
Incredible Shrinking Man, The . . . 31
Independence Day . . . 192
Interview With the Vampire . . . 26
Ironside . . . 61, 81, 103, 106, 135
Irving, Clifford . . . 21

# J

Jarlson, Alan . . . 24, 107
Jellinek, Herb . . . 82-83, 100
Jillson, Joyce . . . 148
Jones, Carolyn . . . 111, 164-165, 196
Jones, Henry . . . 130, 136-137, 162
Jones, Ike . . . 122, 140
Jory, Victor . . . 144-145, 196
Jourdan, Louis . . . 26, 92
Joyce, Jimmy . . . 133, 161

# K

Kaminsky, Stuart M. . . . 5, x, 17, 27, 178, 183, 186
Kaplan, Marvin . . . 145, 152
Karlen, John . . . x, 33-34, 38, 91
Karloff, Boris . . . 31, 62, 79, 107, 157
Kiel, Richard . . . 144-147, 149, 166
King, Stephen . . . 26, 31, 38, 177, 183, 192
Kojak . . . 108-109, 170
Kolchak Papers, The . . . 4, 16, 26-29, 32, 40, 44, 46,
  52, 55, 57, 63, 79, 88-89, 186, 198-199
Kolchak Story, The . . . x, 23-24, 27-28, 199

Kolchak: The Night Stalker . . . 199
Koontz, Dean R. . . . 31
Kopell, Bernie . . . 158, 160
Kozoll, Michael . . . x, 109, 163, 167, 173-174, 184

# L

Lacy, Jerry . . . x, 37-38
Langella, Frank . . . 26, 92
Lederer, Francis . . . 26
Lee, Christopher . . . 26, 38, 92
Leeds, Phil . . . 129
"Legacy of Terror" (Kolchak #17) . . . 7, 120, 145,
    165-167, 184, 196
Levinson, Richard . . . 119, 153
Levitt, Gene . . . 152
Lewis, Al . . . 74, 80, 87
Lewis, Harold . . . 60, 73
Link, William . . . 119, 153
Linville, Larry . . . 48, 56, 61, 68, 101, 161-162
Lithgow, John . . . 30
"Lord of the Smoking Mirror"
    See "Legacy of Terror"
Lord, Stephen . . . 163-164, 174
Lugosi, Bela . . . 23, 26, 34, 160
Lynch, Ken . . . 121, 123, 196
Lynley, Carol . . . 48, 51, 56, 58, 62

# M

M*A*S*H . . . 56, 65, 81, 135, 141, 158, 162, 176, 198
Magician, The . . . 101, 135
Magnum p.i. . . . 191
Make Room for Daddy . . . 169
Maltin, Leonard . . . 40, 57, 79, 83
Mantooth, Donald . . . 122, 146, 164
Marley, John . . . 156-158, 170, 196
Marquette, Desmond . . . 48, 63, 70
Marx, Groucho . . . 120
"Matchemonedo"
    See "The Energy Eater"
Matheson, Murray . . . 150-151, 196
Matheson, Richard . . . 6, ix-x, 22-23, 26, 28, 30-31,
    44, 48, 55, 58, 66, 70, 73, 78-80, 82, 88-89, 91, 99, 123,
    127, 176, 184, 191-192, 194, 199
McDevitt, Ruth . . . 104, 108, 113-115, 118, 122-123,
    136-137, 140-141, 144, 146, 148, 150, 152, 158, 161,
    164, 169, 196
McDougall, Don . . . 165, 169
McEveety, Vincent . . . 167, 169
McGavin, Darren . . . 2, 5-6, ix-x, 13-14, 16-17, 21-23,
    27, 32, 43, 45-48, 51, 53, 58, 67-68, 70-71, 74, 76-77,
    80, 83, 87, 97, 100, 103, 106, 111, 114, 119, 121, 126,
    128, 130, 133, 136, 138, 140-141, 144, 146, 148, 150,
    152, 156, 158, 160-161, 164-165, 167, 169, 171,
    173-174, 176-177, 179-180, 184, 191-192, 194, 199
McGavin, Kathie Browne . . . 47, 80, 82, 108
McGraw, Charles . . . 48, 62, 196
Meeker, Ralph . . . 48, 68, 196
Mellé, Gil . . . 101-102, 119-121, 126, 128, 133, 146,
    148, 164-165, 169, 184
Meyers, Ric . . . x, 177
Mickey Spillane's Mike Hammer . . . 44, 57, 114
Miller, Marvin . . . 158, 160, 196
Mission: Impossible . . . 44, 58, 71, 84, 92, 101, 147,
    169, 198
Mitchum, John . . . 148
Moxey, John Llewellyn . . . x, 40, 44, 46, 48, 54-55, 70,
    80, 101
"Mr. R.I.N.G." (Kolchak #12) . . . 7, 139, 152, 156-157,
    166, 170, 185
Mullally, Donn . . . 140, 174
Murphy Brown . . . 7, 118, 191
Murray, Jan . . . 133, 152

# N

Napier, Charles . . . 57
NBC . . . 16, 19-21, 30, 33, 44, 57-58, 65, 79, 81, 90-91,
    93-94, 101, 103, 108, 111, 113-114, 118-119, 127, 135,
    141, 145, 149, 152-153, 172, 176, 191-192
Neale, L. Ford . . . 144, 152, 171
Night Gallery . . . 57, 99, 119, 184
Night Killers, The . . . 90, 97, 176
Night Stalker, The . . . 4-6, ix-x, 13-21, 23-24, 27,
    30-33, 37, 40, 43, 46-48, 51, 56-58, 60, 62-71, 78,
    80-84, 88-92, 95, 97-111, 113-114, 116, 118-121, 123,
    127-128, 132, 139, 141, 147, 152, 156, 163, 167, 169,
    171-172, 174, 176-181, 183-187, 190-192, 196,
    198-199, 205, 207
Night Strangler, The . . . 4, 6, 14, 16, 24, 56, 70, 73-74,
    76, 79-84, 87-92, 99, 123, 128, 185-187, 196, 198
Nolan, William F. . . . 30, 89-90, 92, 176
Nolte, Nick . . . 194
Norliss Tapes, The . . . 90-91, 94
Nosferatu . . . 26, 67, 92

# O

O'Connor, John J. . . . 21, 110
O'Malley, J. Pat . . . 126, 128, 196
Oakland, Simon . . . 48, 56, 61, 71, 73-74, 77, 80, 83,
    98-99, 104, 108, 111, 113, 118, 121, 126, 128, 132-133,
    136, 138, 140-141, 144, 146-148, 150, 152, 156-158,
    161, 163-165, 167-169, 171, 192, 194, 196
Omega Man, The . . . 31
Outer Limits, The . . . 178
Outsider, The . . . 21, 43-44, 111

# P

Palance, Jack . . . 26, 38, 79, 81
Parker, Lara . . . x, 34, 40, 158, 160
Perry Mason . . . 61, 81, 84, 90, 191
Pflug, Jo Ann . . . 74, 81, 92
Phantom of the Opera, The . . . 133, 175
Planet of the Apes, The . . . 178
Playdon, Paul . . . 101-103, 109, 118, 121, 135
Poe, Edgar Allan . . . 17, 19, 31, 48
Predator . . . 132
Prescription: Murder . . . 153
Presley, Elvis . . . 111, 113
Price, Frank . . . 104, 173
Price, Vincent . . . 30-31, 62
"Primal Scream" (Kolchak #13) . . . 7, 152, 156, 167,
    170, 196
Prisoner, The . . . 21, 179
Progeny of the Adder . . . 68-69, 199
Psycho . . . x, 55, 61, 75, 79

# Q

Questor Tapes, The . . . 119

# R

Rhodes, Jordan . . . 48
Rhue, Madlyn . . . 138-139
Rice, Anne . . . 26, 89, 192
Rice, Jeff . . . 4, 6, ix-x, 13-14, 16-17, 22-23, 25, 27,
    31-32, 40, 43, 48, 55, 66, 68, 70, 73, 80, 83, 88-89, 99,
    104, 107, 110, 121, 176, 186-187, 190-192, 194, 199
Riverboat . . . 44
Robbie, Seymour . . . 171
Rodan, Robert . . . 34
Roddenberry, Gene . . . 70, 81, 119
Rubin, Benny . . . 150, 152, 196

# S

Samuel Goldwyn Studios . . . 48
Sangster, Jimmy . . . 150-151
Schulman, Barry . . . x, 184
Sci-Fi Channel . . . 4, x, 16, 95, 167, 174, 184-185, 192

Scott, Kathryn Leigh . . . 4, ix, 34, 38
Seitz, Christopher H. . . . 48, 73
Selby, David . . . x, 34, 40, 91
Serling, Rod . . . 16-17, 30, 38, 55, 57, 114, 119, 127, 147, 151, 184, 199
Seymour, Jane . . . 31, 92-93
Shatner, William . . . 30
Sheinberg, Sid . . . 98, 100, 104
Shelley, Mary . . . 26, 91, 97, 107
Shrinking Man, The . . . 31
Silver, Johnny . . . 146
Silverman, Fred . . . 93, 172
Silvers, Phil . . . 150, 152, 169, 196
Singer, Robert . . . x, 40, 48, 56, 58, 73, 80
Skerritt, Tom . . . x, 140-141
Smith, Dick . . . 38
Smith, Ed Silas . . . 186-188
Smith, Kent . . . 48, 62, 196
Smith, William . . . 148-149
Sofaer, Abraham . . . 150-151
Somewhere in Time . . . 31
Spielberg, Steven . . . 31, 70, 172
Springsteen, Bruce . . . 38
Spy Who Loved Me, The . . . 145
Star Trek . . . 16, 31, 58, 62, 69, 79, 106, 110, 114, 123, 151, 165, 171-172, 175-176, 178, 192, 197
Star Trek: The Next Generation . . . 192
Starger, Martin . . . 20, 98, 100, 173
Stoddard, Brandon . . . x, 20
Stoker, Bram . . . 5, 19, 26, 60, 69, 92, 199
Storch, Larry . . . 133-134, 152
Strange Case of Dr. Jekyll and Mr. Hyde, The . . . 38, 91
Supertrain . . . 93, 172
Susi, Carol Ann . . . 4, ix-x, 104, 113-114, 117, 126, 128, 132, 138-139, 170, 199

## T

Talbot, Nita . . . 136-137
Tales from the Crypt . . . 163, 179
Tarantino, Quentin . . . 38
Tatelman, Harry . . . x, 167
"The Devil's Platform" (Kolchak #7) . . . 7, 109, 128, 139, 141, 174, 196
"The Doppleganger"
    See "Fire Fall" (Kolchak #6)
"The Energy Eater" (Kolchak #10) . . . 7, 120, 148-149, 166-167, 184, 196
"The Get of Belial" . . . 174-175
"The Humanoids"
    See "Primal Scream"
"The Knightly Murders" (Kolchak #18) . . . 7, 128, 167, 170, 174, 179-181, 185, 196
"The Rakshasa"
    See "Horror in the Heights"
"The Ripper" (Kolchak #1) . . . 6, 102, 109-111, 120-124, 139, 166, 180-181, 185, 196
"The Sentry" (Kolchak #20) . . . 7, 110-111, 113, 128, 139, 166, 170-172, 174, 180, 186, 196
"The Spanish Moss Murders" (Kolchak #9) . . . 7, 120, 146, 151, 157, 159, 166, 168, 180-181, 185, 196
"The Trevi Collection" (Kolchak #14) . . . 7, 139, 158, 160, 196
"The Vampire" (Kolchak #4) . . . 7, 16, 110, 120, 133-134, 139, 145, 152, 168, 180-181, 185
"The Werewolf" (Kolchak #5) . . . 7, 113, 120, 130, 135, 139, 152
"The Youth Killer" (Kolchak #19) . . . 7, 109, 120, 169-170, 196
"The Zombie" (Kolchak #2) . . . 6, 102, 108, 111, 120, 126, 128, 152, 168, 196

"They Have Been, They Are, They Will Be..."
    See "U.F.O.")
Thin Man, The . . . 108
Thinnes, Roy . . . 90, 94, 119
Thriller . . . 79, 178, 184
Time Killer
    See The Night Strangler
Tobias, George . . . 74, 88
Trilogy of Terror . . . 92-95
Trilogy of Terror II . . . 94-95
TV Guide . . . 44, 80, 110
Twain, Mark . . . 5, 75, 205
20th Century-Fox . . . 73, 81-82, 185
Twilight Zone, The . . . 16, 30-31, 57, 61-62, 111, 114, 123, 127-128, 133, 137, 145, 147, 151, 168, 172, 174, 176, 178, 199
Twilight Zone: The Movie . . . 30, 127
Twin Peaks . . . 66, 84, 179

## U

"U.F.O." (Kolchak #3) . . . 7, 109, 118, 120, 128, 132, 139, 152-153, 178, 196
U.S. Steel Hour . . . 43
Universal City Studios . . . 4, ix, 121
Used Cars . . . 163

## V

Van Patten, Dick . . . 129, 152, 169
Vernon, Jackie . . . 152, 164-165, 196
Vigran, Herb . . . 150, 152
Virginian, The . . . 44, 61, 103

## W

Wallace, Art . . . 37
War and Remembrance . . . 91, 93-95
Waters, Chuck . . . 126, 157-158
Wayne, Nina . . . 74
Webb, Jack . . . 69, 97, 178
Weis, Don . . . 105, 128, 133, 135, 138-139, 158, 164-165
Whale, James . . . 67
When Every Day Was the Fourth of July . . . 93
White, Jesse . . . 152, 161-162, 196
Whitelaw, Billie . . . 38
Whitten, Leslie H. . . . 68
Who Framed Roger Rabbit . . . 163
Wickes, Mary . . . 129, 133, 196
Williams, Trevor . . . 48, 55, 70, 73, 83
Winds of War, The . . . 91, 93-95
Winfrey, Lee . . . 110
Wise, Robert . . . 61
Wizard of Oz, The . . . 80
Wouk, Herman . . . 91
Wynn, Keenan . . . 30, 146-147, 164-165, 185, 196

## X

X-Files, The . . . 13-15, 29, 106, 132, 153, 178, 184-185, 192-193, 198-199

## Y

Young and the Restless, The . . . 137

## Z

Zemeckis, Robert . . . x, 161-162
Ziker, Dick . . . 60, 62, 73

**MARK DAWIDZIAK** is the critic-at-large in the entertainment department of the *Akron Beacon Journal*. A journalism graduate of George Washington University, he has worked as a theater, film and television critic for almost twenty years. His nonfiction books include *The Barter Theatre Story: Love Made Visible* (1982), *The Columbo Phile: A Casebook* (1989) and *Mark My Words: Mark Twain On Writing* (1996). He is also the author of *Grave Secrets* (1994), the first Kolchak novel in about twenty years. And he has written the liner notes for the Columbia House Video Library Collector's Edition of *Kolchak: The Night Stalker*. His play *To Preserve, Protect and Defend* (1982), a two-act drama about Abraham Lincoln and Theodore Roosevelt, has been produced on both sides of the Mason-Dixon line. He has been a regular contributor to such magazines as *Commonwealth, TV Guide, Cinefantastique, Scarlet Street, Sci-Fi Universe* and *Mystery Scene*. He lives with his wife, Sara, and their daughter, Rebecca Claire, in northeastern Ohio.

# Books by Pomegranate Press, Ltd.

The *Night Stalker* Companion
The *Dark Shadows* Almanac
*Dark Shadows* Music Book
*Dark Shadows* The Comic Strip Book
Shadows On The Wall
*Dark Shadows* Program Guide
*Dark Shadows* Resurrected
The *Dark Shadows* Companion
The *Dark Shadows* Companion Audio Book
My Scrapbook Memories of *Dark Shadows*
*This is Jim Rockford...*The Rockford Files
Maverick: *Legend of the West*
The *Fugitive* Recaptured
The *Fugitive* Recaptured Audio Tape
Word of Mouth: A Guide To Voice-Over Excellence
Word of Mouth Audio Tape
Lobby Cards: The Classic Films
Lobby Cards: The Classic Comedies
Hollywood Goes On Location
Following the Comedy Trail
Michael Landon: *Life, Love & Laughter*
Hollywood At Your Feet: The Chinese Theatre
Hollywood's Chinese Theatre
Rupert Hughes:A Hollywood Legend
The Logical Lexicon Of Useless English
Coya Come Home
Barnabas and Josette with Music Box: 30th Anniversary Poster
Barnabas in Graveyard: Comic Strip Poster

To receive a free current catalog and order form, please
send a large, stamped, self addressed envelope to:
**Pomegranate Press, Ltd.**
**Post Office Box 17217**
**Beverly Hills, CA 90209-3217**


For more information on **Dark Shadows,** write to:
**Dark Shadows**
**Post Office Box 92**
**Maplewood, NJ 07040**

**Night Stalker** Videos are available from: **Columbia House Video Library**
*Kolchak: The Night Stalker* The Collectors Edition. 10 volumes total.
First volume is $4.95 with your subscription. Subsequent volumes are $19.95.
**Columbia House customer service, telephone toll free: 1-800-457-0866**

All 1,225 original episodes of *Dark Shadows* are available exclusively on
**MPI Home Video**. For more information, write or call customer service:
**MPI Home Video, 16101 South 108th Avenue, Orland Park, IL 60462**
**Toll free telephone: 1-800-323-0442**